Contents

Aesthetics, Community Character, and the Law

CHRISTOPHER J. DUERKSEN
R. MATTHEW GOEBEL

As Americans, we treasure natural beauty and the distinctive character of our communities. We know this from ordinary conversation, from polling data, and from our nation's long and distinguished tradition of protecting beautiful places as public forests, parks, private gardens, and estates.

Yet, the American landscape is suffering "death by a thousand cuts." The billboard industry constructs 5,000 to 15,000 new billboards each year on federal highways and many more on state roads and city streets. Developers clear-cut thousands of acres of trees to make way for new development. Cellular communications operators erect huge towers without regard to the visual impact on local neighborhoods or even our national parks. Franchise operators and "big box" retail developers threaten to locate elsewhere unless communities permit their cookie-cutter buildings. State highway departments too often build and rebuild roads without regard to their impact on the land. Day by day, by a thousand cuts, we are losing our cherished scenic heritage.

But something more powerful is also at work: a thousand efforts in a thousand communities building a national movement for scenic conservation. In city halls and county seats, citizens are demanding new, smarter approaches to community growth. But all too often, neither they nor their elected officials are aware of successful models elsewhere to protect scenic character by banning the construction of new billboards, enacting tree and landscaping ordinances, protecting viewsheds, writing tough legislation governing cellular towers, requiring franchise operators to work within local design guidelines, saving historic buildings, and adopting new statewide standards for road design.

Aesthetics, Community Character and the Law shows how to write laws that protect a special sense of place. Scenic America is proud to have helped make this publication possible. Every day we work with citizens who need the information on aesthetics and community character that they will find here.

We wish to extend special thanks to Julian Price of Asheville, North Carolina, for generously underwriting the publication, and to the Turner Foundation for additional support of this project. Tony Wood of the Ittleson Foundation and Dale McKeel of Scenic North Carolina reviewed the drafts and provided valuable comments based on their own experience. Scenic America vice presidents Ray Foote and Frank Vespe contributed much valuable knowledge and material from our files; our citizen members contributed their wisdom and experience from the front lines of civic action.

We are especially grateful to authors Chris Duerksen, a member of Scenic America's Board, and Matt Goebel, both of Clarion Associates, for sharing their knowledge and insights from the outstanding work they do nationwide advising communities about how to create better places to live and work. *Aesthetics, Community Character and the Law* makes one thing clear: Change is inevitable; ugliness is not.

Meg Maguire
President, Scenic America

Chapter 1

Introduction

Growth is inevitable and desirable, but destruction of community character is not. The question is not whether your part of the world is going to change. The question is how.

EDWARD T. MCMAHON, THE CONSERVATION FUND

HOW WE DEVELOP AND MANAGE THE LAND AROUND US CAN DRAMATICALLY AFFECT THE QUALITY OF OUR LIVES. Recognizing this basic fact, planners for decades have been questioning the environmental and economic consequences of development: Will a new subdivision contaminate the groundwater? What tax revenues will a proposed new shopping center generate? Throughout most of the history of the planning profession, planners have considered the quality-of-life impacts of new development primarily by relying on such technical inquiries.

Happily, the situation has changed. Planners today focus not just on the essential, but sometimes dry, details of fiscal analyses and environmental impact reports when considering new development. They also recognize that the *aesthetic* aspects of development can play a significant role in the lives of our communities. Increasingly, the key issues revolve around appearance: color, height, setbacks, landscaping, signage, and the like. Should homes be built on ridgelines and hillsides? How do we protect community gateways? How do we control cell towers? Are there more sensitive ways to design roads and highways? And, overall, how do we ensure that new development fits in appropriately with surrounding buildings and the neighborhood, and protects what is special about the places in which we live? In other words, how do we define and protect that elusive thing known as "community character"?

In 1986, when the first edition of this report was written, planners were just beginning to appreciate the variety of tools available to regulate aesthetics and protect community character. Design review, for instance, which for years had been applied solely in the context of historic preservation, increasingly was being applied to new development. Communities were just learning how to map and regulate development in viewsheds in order to protect significant scenic vistas and view corridors.

Today, efforts to define and protect aesthetic resources and community character make up one of the most interesting, exciting, and rapidly developing areas of land-use planning—indeed, there has been a veritable explosion of activity as planners employ increasingly creative and complex tools to identify and protect aesthetic resources.

Examples abound across the country. Fifteen years ago, there were hardly any significant tree-protection ordinances in the country; today, there are hundreds, and most communities rewriting their land development regulations at least consider adopting some tree and vegetation protection standards. The booming New Urbanism movement has brought planners and developers together in many places to improve quality of life by regulating the aesthetics of new development—through narrower streets, uniform setback requirements, front porches, and public gathering areas. From Kentlands, Maryland, to Celebration, Florida, New Urbanist, or "neotraditional," developments are reminding homeowners of the special aesthetic qualities that have helped traditional urban neighborhoods endure.

Many western states now are taking a once unheard of position by questioning whether houses should be allowed along ridgelines and steep slopes, asking themselves, Do we really want this type of development in our communities? And cities as diverse as Dallas, Texas, Lincoln, Nebraska, and Cambridge, Massachusetts, have begun protecting "conservation areas"—concentrations of unique resources that do not qualify as full-fledged historic districts but which nevertheless have important cultural, visual, or other significance.

Planners and local officials are employing more aggressive and creative strategies to identify and protect what is special about their communities. Carrboro, North Carolina, for instance, voted in 1998 to ban all new drive-through businesses in the downtown—in part, an effort to cut down on noise, traffic, and air pollution, but also an attempt to protect the town's quaint, village-like aesthetic character from the rapidly encroaching crowds of the Research Triangle. Elsewhere, planners are confronting the aesthetic implications of aging suburbs, an issue common across the country. Lakewood, Colorado, for example, is fighting to remove so-called "fence canyons" that mar the key gateways to their city. These "canyons" are actually suburban streets lined on either side with run-down privacy fences and no grass or trees, but lots of concrete. Planners are working to replace the old fences and revise zoning and subdivision regulations to ensure that new developments are more sensitively designed.

Many communities are striving to ensure that their aesthetic regulatory efforts are incorporated into, and consistent with, broader community goals. The highly successful revitalization of Denver's Lower Downtown area, or "LoDo," is an excellent example of how a community can forge a linkage between aesthetic objectives and other key goals—in that case, economic development and downtown revitalization. In Augusta, Georgia, protection of community character is at the heart of a complex partnership of planners, the business community, local governments, and non-profit conservation organizations that have joined together to revitalize the historic canal running through the center city, one of the oldest functioning canal systems in the country.

In sum, today's planners are using myriad tools and techniques to identify and protect what is special about their communities—through historic preservation ordinances, improved sign controls, computerized viewshed protection regulations, tree-planting and landscaping requirements, cell tower controls, and the like. As the level of activity in the field has increased dramatically, so has the number of court cases challenging aesthetic-based regulation. For the most part, courts have continued to be very supportive of such regulations, so long as they are grounded in sufficient enabling authority and are based on clear, objective standards. Legislatures, too, have become more sympathetic to such regulations. The Utah legislature, for instance, recently amended state law to add "aesthetics" as a new, and specifically permissible, public purpose for police-power regulations.

This report is an extensively updated and revised edition of Planning Advisory Service Report No. 399, *Aesthetics and Land-Use Controls: Beyond Ecology and Economics*, published in 1986. Like that report, this manual is intended to help land-use planners and citizens understand the law of aesthetics and the legal tools available to help their communities maintain their special features and sense of place.

109

The principal topics covered in the 1986 report included design review, view protection, tree protection, and sign controls. Those same topics are covered in separate chapters in this new edition, with major updates based on recent developments in the law and in planning practice. The chapter on sign controls, for instance, now addresses the important distinction between commercial and noncommercial speech in much greater detail, and discusses the implications of recent major court cases in this area, including several from the U.S. Supreme Court that have more clearly defined the scope of First Amendment protections afforded signs. The view protection chapter covers the increasing use of computers to model view corridors, and the chapter on tree and vegetation protection now includes a much more thorough discussion of how to draft an effective tree conservation ordinance.

Also, there is an entirely new chapter on one of the hottest planning topics of the last few years—the regulation of cell towers, satellite dishes, and other telecommunications facilities. Special emphasis is placed on understanding the complex federal law in this area and how local communities may regulate the aesthetics of cell towers without running afoul of the Telecommunications Act of 1996.

For all topics, the report follows the same basic structure: First is an introduction to important legal concepts and rules, including summaries of important cases from around the country where the laws have been tested and applied by local communities. Second are lessons for planning practice, including means by which local governments may regulate aesthetics, and recent developments in the field. The remainder of this introductory chapter provides some historical background on the evolving law of aesthetic regulation.

HISTORICAL PERSPECTIVE/BACKGROUND

The desire to protect community aesthetics has a long history in America. In the 1800s, for instance, there was concern about the preservation of privately owned, nationally significant buildings like Mount Vernon. At that time, such problems were usually solved by private citizens purchasing a threatened structure; regulations were unheard of. In fact, it was not clear in those early days whether governments even had the authority to buy or condemn land for aesthetic purposes. Thus, one of the earliest legal disputes in this area concerned the propriety of the federal government taking land for a national battlefield memorial at Gettysburg. In *United States v. Gettysburg Electric Railway Co.* (160 U.S. 668 (1896)), the Supreme Court held that the condemnation of land served a valid "public purpose"; namely, protection of important historical associations. However, the Court did not consider whether government might achieve a similar result by regulation, or justify its actions on aesthetic grounds alone without relying on references to historical events. Those two questions would come to the fore in the next period of the law of aesthetics.

As America became more urban, and as new architectural and building techniques allowed the construction of ever more massive structures, cities and towns increasingly showed concern about retaining their character. Drawing on European precedents, particularly from Germany, local governments began experimenting with zoning and land-use controls. Some of the pioneer cases involved height restrictions. As early as 1888, a New York court approved an 80-foot height limitation on residential structures. In 1904, the city of Baltimore adopted a 70-foot maximum height regulation to maintain the character of its neighborhoods and commercial areas. The same year, the city of Boston (which had grown sensitive to the need for preservation when, in the late 1800s, many historic buildings were destroyed) enacted similar legislation that prescribed a lower height for buildings constructed in residential areas than for those in commercial districts.

The Baltimore regulation was upheld in 1908 by Maryland's highest court on the grounds that it was designed to lessen fire hazards, in addition to advancing aesthetic goals (*Cochran v. Preston*, 70 A.113 (Md. 1908)). The Boston ordinance was challenged in a case that eventually made its way to the U.S. Supreme Court (*Welch v. Swasey*, 214 U.S. 91 (1909)). The Court upheld the restrictions on the grounds that they were reasonably related to the public welfare as a means of fire prevention. Yet, while upholding the regulation, the Court sidestepped the issue of whether government could regulate on the basis of aesthetics alone.

At about that time, cities also were beginning to regulate billboards. In one early case, a court upheld local sign regulations on the grounds that billboards could be a haven for trash, illicit sex acts, and other indiscreet behavior. Another court approved such controls on the grounds that unsafe billboards might topple and kill passersby.

Thus, while courts of this era were generally sympathetic to aesthetic regulations, such as sign controls and height restrictions, they generally justified their approvals based on fire protection, safety, and economics. Aesthetics were considered to be a matter of luxury and taste; courts generally struck down laws based solely on aesthetic considerations.

This approach to aesthetic regulation—the so-called "aesthetics-plus" doctrine—was dominant into the 1950s, although it had begun to erode a bit earlier when a handful of cities adopted historic preservation laws. Charleston, New Orleans, and San Antonio were among the first communities to place restrictions on the demolition of historic structures. The courts were sympathetic to efforts to protect these special places, but still invoked other reasons for upholding local ordinances, such as the importance of historic areas to the tourist-based economies of these cities.

Aesthetics finally began to stand on its own two feet in the 1950s with a U.S. Supreme Court decision (*Berman v. Parker*, 348 U.S. 26 (1954)). Language in this case (which involved, ironically, the condemnation of old buildings for urban renewal purposes) gave strong support for government action based solely on aesthetic considerations.

> The concept of the public welfare is broad and inclusive. . . . The values it represents are spiritual as well as physical, aesthetic as well as monetary. It is within the power of the legislature to determine that the community should be beautiful as well as healthy, spacious as well as clean, well-balanced as well as carefully patrolled. (*Berman v. Parker*, at 33)

Relying on this language, courts began upholding billboard controls, preservation regulations, and height restrictions on aesthetic grounds alone. By 1978, things had evolved so quickly that the U.S. Supreme Court, in a case upholding the validity of local landmark protection laws, could say:

> . . . [W]e emphasize what is not in dispute. . . . This court has recognized, in a number of settings, that states and cities may enact land-use regulations or controls to enhance the quality of life by preserving the character and the desirable aesthetic features of a city. . . . (*Penn Central Transportation Co. v. New York City*, 438 U.S. 104 (1978) at 129)

Today, no trend is more clearly defined in planning law than that of courts upholding regulations whose primary basis is aesthetics. Only a few die-hard states do not permit local governments to adopt aesthetic-based police power regulations. While local governments must still proceed carefully in enacting and implementing aesthetic-based laws (just as they must with any land-use regulation), particularly where they might impinge on forms of communication protected by the First Amendment's guarantee of freedom of speech (as in sign ordinances), they generally have great leeway in acting to protect community aesthetics, as this report attempts to show.

Since the mid-1980s, the trend toward judicial acceptance of aesthetic-based land-use regulations has continued, and decisions upholding such regulations are now commonplace. Two recent developments are worth noting, however. One is the increasing frustration by courts with vague and/or absent review standards and criteria; several examples appear throughout this report. Second, note that the federal government occasionally does preempt local design and aesthetic regulation. The most recent, and complex, example is the Telecommunications Act of 1996, discussed in detail in Chapter 6.

Chapter 2

Design Review

These standards and guidelines are a response to dissatisfaction with corporate chain marketing strategy dictating design that is indifferent to local identity and interests. The main goal is to encourage development that contributes to Fort Collins as a unique place by reflecting its physical character and adding to it in appropriate ways.

FORT COLLINS, COLORADO, CITY COUNCIL

DESIGN REVIEW OF PROJECTS, A COMMON FEATURE OF LAND-USE CONTROL SYSTEMS IN ENGLAND AND EUROPE, HAS BECOME WIDESPREAD IN THE UNITED STATES AS PUBLIC DISSATISFACTION WITH THE SIZE AND STYLE OF NEW AND EVER-LARGER BUILDINGS INTENSIFIES. Initially spurred by a favorable U.S. Supreme Court decision upholding New York City's preservation law in *Penn Central v. New York City*, 438 U.S. 104 (1978), thousands of communities have enacted local preservation ordinances that place strong controls on new construction in historic areas.

And, while historic preservation continues to be the foundation for design review, courts are increasingly comfortable with design review in a much broader context. A growing number of local governments are imposing design review on new buildings and their environs in nonhistoric and suburban settings. Communities both small and large are serving notice that they do not adhere to the dogma "form follows function," and are demanding a greater say in the way buildings are designed and fit in with their neighbors.

This new generation of design review programs is characterized by increasingly sophisticated regulations that make extensive use of graphics and tables to summarize detailed information and illustrate complex concepts like "community character " and "harmonious devvelopment." Such visual aids increase the likelihood of even-handed, consistent interpretations of the regulations and decrease the likelihood of court challenges. Jurisdictions also are incorporating design review into all phases of their land-use management systems, from controls on demolition of existing structures to review of site plans and final plans for new construction. The concern over design of new projects poses some difficult challenges for planners and lawyers charged with the task of drafting and administering design review regulations. Because good project and building design is, at least in part, an inherently subjective undertaking, regulators are confronted with the uneasy task of balancing community demands with project economics and creativity. Careful drafting of review standards and flexibility in administration can help smooth the process somewhat, although the inherent tension in this process cannot be solved by legal means alone.

This chapter includes three main sections. The first section discusses design review in historic areas, including the key legal issues of review standards and takings. The second section addresses design review in nonhistoric areas, including additional legal considerations and important recent developments. The third section presents general advice and guidance for communities interesting in creating and implementing a design review program.

DESIGN REVIEW IN HISTORIC AREAS

Although the first historic preservation ordinance was adopted by the city of Charleston in 1931, just a few years after the Supreme Court approved of zoning controls in the *Euclid* case, only a handful of cities followed suit over the next several decades. By 1960, there were fewer than 50 such ordinances, confined mostly to cities that relied heavily on historic buildings as tourist attractions. However, urban renewal and highway building in the 1960s spurred growing concern over demolition of historic buildings and prompted the adoption of stronger ordinances in many localities. When the Supreme Court placed its stamp of approval on local preservation ordinances in the *Penn Central* case, the die was cast, and today, communities across the country are exercising strong controls, not only over historic buildings but also over the design of new construction in historic areas.[1]

Perhaps the most visible, and often most controversial, power exercised by local preservation commissions is the review of applications for demolition or alteration of landmarks or for new construction in historic areas (often referred to collectively as applications for certificates of appropriateness). An application to demolish a landmark often will engender heated arguments, bringing commissions and their planning advisers face-to-face with the difficult task of juggling and balancing preservation goals with economic and political pressures. Dealing with alteration proposals—often less controversial than demolitions, but far more frequent—is no less difficult. The challenge here is to encourage upgrading and continued maintenance of existing landmarks and to guide the process of change so that it is sympathetic to the existing character of the historic area. In all but a few historic areas, freezing things in time would be neither feasible nor desirable.

Setting standards for reviewing such applications is a tricky task. Preservationists are concerned that a demolition "not have an adverse effect on the fabric of the district" or that new construction not be "incongruous," but rather that it should be "in harmony" with the "character," "significant features," or "atmosphere" of the area. Each of these terms is subjective and needs to be defined and limited in some fashion to give applicants reasonable notice of what is expected of them and to allow courts to judge the validity of the local decision.

The process of setting standards to govern this review and establishing sound administrative procedures to apply them is crucial, not only from a legal standpoint but also as a way for preservationists to evaluate where

Because good project and building design is, at least in part, an inherently subjective undertaking, regulators are confronted with the uneasy task of balancing community demands with project economics and creativity.

The challenge here is to encourage upgrading and continued maintenance of existing landmarks and to guide the process of change so that it is sympathetic to the existing character of the historic area. In all but a few historic areas, freezing things in time would be neither feasible nor desirable.

Scenic America

Scenic America

Whether it is Pennsylvania Avenue in Washington (upper left), a public building in Blakely, Georgia (above), or the distinctive fence treatment of a New Orleans building (left), local historic character can be identified and protected if standards are articulated well and applicants for new construction or change or given good notice of what is required of them.

their preservation program is leading. What kind of development, if any, do they really want in the local historic area? How do they intend to evaluate proposed changes? What is the most efficient and fairest way to administer review standards? These key questions are discussed below, with emphasis placed on the points in the process at which planners should pay close attention to standards and procedures.

Review Standards

While preservation controls raise a host of legal issues,[2] one of the most important involves the standards to be used by an agency in reviewing an application for new construction in a historic district. Generally, the failure of an agency to establish in advance coherent written standards and regulations to be applied in all cases amounts to a denial of due process. Although preservation standards often are based on taste, and are thus subjective to a certain degree (for example, some ordinances prohibit new construction in a historic area if it is "incongruous" with existing structures), sufficient standards can be articulated so as to pass judicial muster and give permit applicants some advance notice of what is required of them.

In practice, courts have shown great deference to local review bodies in this regard, as witnessed by the language of the Supreme Court in the *Penn Central* case. In rejecting the notion that regulation of landmarks is inevitably arbitrary because it is a matter of taste, the Court observed:

> There is no basis whatsoever for a conclusion that courts will have any greater difficulty in identifying arbitrary or discriminatory action in the context of landmark regulation than in the context of zoning or any other context. (at 133)

In his treatise on land-use planning law, Professor Norman Williams lists various considerations that might be used by a local commission in determining whether a proposed demolition or change is compatible with the landmark or district:

- The height of a building, its bulk, and the nature of its roof line
- The proportions between the height of a building and its width (i.e., is the appearance predominantly horizontal or predominantly vertical?)
- The nature of the open spaces around buildings, including the extent of setbacks, the existence of any side yards (with an occasional view to the rear) and their size, and the continuity of such spaces along the street
- The existence of trees and other landscaping, and the extent of paving
- The nature of the openings in the facade, primarily doors and windows—their location, size, and proportions
- The type of roof: flat, gabled, hip, gambrel, mansard, etc.
- The nature of projections from the buildings, particularly porches
- The nature of the architectural details, and, in a broader sense, the predominant architectural style
- The nature of the materials
- Color
- Texture
- The details of ornamentation
- Signs[3]

New townhouses (inset) mix perfectly with the established residences in this Washington, D.C., neighborhood. Height, proportion, the nature of architectural details–all of these features and more are the elements that commissions must look at to make sure that new development does not mar a neighborhood's historic character.

Meg Maguire

Not all these considerations will necessarily be relevant to every land-mark or district, but the list does suggest ways in which broad review standards may be narrowed.

Setting review standards in historic areas with a predominant style. Promulgating adequate review standards is relatively simple in historic areas that have a distinctive style or character. No one would object strenuously if a landmarks commission rejected a proposal to add a redwood railing around a second floor porch in the Vieux Carre district in New Orleans; everyone knows that iron railings are de rigueur. In places like New Orleans, Old Santa Fe, Old Town Alexandria, and Nantucket, the problem virtually solves itself. Thus, in a number of challenges to preservation restrictions, judges had little trouble upholding the action of the local review body because of the district's distinctive style. The legal rationale for those decisions is best explained in an early preservation case, *Town of Deering v. Tibbetts*, 105 N.H. 481,202 A.2d 232 (1964):

> While determination of what is compatible with the atmosphere of the town may on first impression be thought to be a matter of arbitrary and subjective judgment, under consideration it proves not to be. . . . [T]he language "takes clear meaning from the observable character of the district to which it applies." (at 232)

Similar reasoning was employed to uphold a very broad review standard in Raleigh, North Carolina, even though the local district encompassed several architectural styles (*A-S-P Associates v. City of Raleigh*, 258 S.E.2d 444 (1979)). The Raleigh preservation ordinance required the local landmarks commission to prevent activity that "would be incongruous with the historic aspects of the Historic District." The owner of a vacant lot within the city's Oakwood Historic District claimed this "incongruity" standard was so vague that it amounted to an unconstitutional delegation of legislative authority by the city council to the historic district commission. The Supreme Court of North Carolina, in a well-reasoned decision, found that the incongruity standard sufficiently limited the commission's discretion.

The general policy and standard of incongruity, adopted by both the General Assembly and the Raleigh City Council, in this instance is best denominated as "a contextual standard." A contextual standard is one that derives its meaning from the objectively determinable, interrelated conditions and characteristics of the subject to which the standard is to be applied. In this instance, the standard of "incongruity" must derive its meaning, if any, from the total physical environment of the historic district; the conditions and characteristics of the historic district's physical environment must be sufficiently distinctive and identifiable to provide reasonable guidance to the historic district commission in applying the incongruity standard.

> Although the neighborhood encompassed by the Historic District is to a considerable extent an architectural melange, the heterogeneity of architectural style is not such as to render the standard of incongruity meaningless. The predominant architectural style found in the area is Victorian, the characteristics of which are readily identifiable. . . . It is therefore sufficient that a general, yet meaningful contextual standard has been set forth to limit the discretion of the Historic District Commission. Strikingly similar standards for administration of historic district ordinances have long been approved by courts of other jurisdictions.[4]

Setting review standards in historic areas without a predominant style. The application of permit review standards to landmarks or districts that do not exhibit a single, distinctive style has been more troublesome to

A contextual standard is one that derives its meaning from the objectively determinable, interrelated conditions and characteristics of the subject to which the standard is to be applied.

some legal commentators, but, as the cases that follow demonstrate, even when a district lacks a predominant style, courts have almost universally upheld the local commission's decision. In some instances in which an ordinance contained relatively vague review standards, the court attached great importance to other criteria in the local law or regulations that narrowed commission discretion. In others, courts have looked to background reports and surveys that were incorporated by reference into the law. Courts also have relied on procedural protections to uphold broad standards. In still other instances, courts have held that appointing people with special expertise to a commission helps limit what might otherwise have been excessive discretion.

1. *Narrowing broad review standards with specific criteria.* The typical preservation ordinance sets forth broad review standards for demolition or development permits—often directing the commission to "maintain the character of the district"—and then recites criteria relating to, for example, height, texture of materials, and architectural style to further define that broad standard. Courts have uniformly approved the broad review standard in such cases. A case from the historic small town of Georgetown, Colorado, is an excellent example (*South of Second Associates v. Georgetown, Colo.*, 580 P.2d 807 (Colo. 1978)).In this case, the plaintiff developer alleged, among other things, that the standard the local commission was to apply in reviewing an application to construct new townhouses—what effect the proposed construction might have upon "the general historical and/or architectural character of the structure or area"—was unconstitutionally vague. The Colorado Supreme Court disagreed. It noted that the phrase "historical and/or architectural significance" was defined in the ordinance, and, more importantly, the ordinance set forth "six specific criteria that focus the attention of the commission and of potential applicants for certificates of appropriateness on objective and discernible factors" (at 810).[5]

The court attached particular relevance to one criterion that directed the commission to consider the "architectural style, arrangement, texture, and materials used on existing and proposed structures, and their relation to other structures in the area," reasoning that "these objective and easily discernible factors give substance to the ordinance's historical and/or architectural character" language. The court cited several decisions from other jurisdictions that upheld similar standards and concluded that the Georgetown ordinance "contains sufficient standards to advise ordinary and reasonable men as to the type of construction permitted, permits reasonable application by the commission, and limits the commission's discretionary powers" (see also *Faulkner v. Town of Chestertown*, 428 A2d 879 (Md. 1981)).

If a local ordinance does not contain such narrowing criteria, the preservation commission would be well-advised to adopt them by way of regulation or informal review guidelines (assuming the commission has power to do so).

2. *Standards found in background documents.* An excellent example of a court approving a local action based on criteria found in documents outside the preservation ordinance involves the city of New Orleans (*Maher v. City of New Orleans*, 516 F2d 1051 (5th Cir. 1975)). In this case, the court upheld the New Orleans preservation ordinance, even though the city admitted it had not articulated any review standards.

> Other fertile sources are readily available to promote a reasoned exercise of the professional and scholarly judgment of the commission. It may be difficult to capture the atmosphere of a region through a set of regulations. However, it would seem that old city plans and historic

Ron Ruhoff

documents, as well as photographs and contemporary writings, may provide an abundant and accurate compilation of data to guide the commission. And, as the district court observed, "In this case, the meaning of a mandate to preserve the character of the Vieux Carre takes clear meaning from the observable character of the district to which it applies."

Aside from such contemporary indicia of the nature and appearance of the French Quarter at earlier times, the commission has the advantage at present of a recent impartial architectural and historical study of the structures in the area. The Vieux Carre Survey Advisory Committee conducted its analysis under a grant to Tulane University from the Edward G. Schneider Foundation. Building by building, the committee assessed the merit of each structure with respect to several factors. For example, regarding the Maher cottage at issue here, the Louisiana Supreme Court noted that the survey committee "was of the opinion that this cottage was worthy of preservation as part of the overall scene. " While the Schneider survey in no way binds the commission, it does furnish an independent and objective judgment respecting the edifices in the area. The existence of the survey and other historical source material assist in mooring the commission's discretion firmly to the legislative purpose. (at 1063)

The historic mountain town of Georgetown, Colorado, survived a challenge to its preservation ordinance. Because the ordinance set forth six specific criteria for the local commission to follow in making decisions, the state Supreme Court found that the ordinance's standards were not unconstitutionally vague, as had been charged.

3. *Procedural safeguards.* Although procedural safeguards may not prevent challenges to review standards, the fact that there are such protections or that a landmarks commission, because of the expertise of individual members, is uniquely qualified to determine whether a demolition or new development might damage the character of a historic area has heavily and favorably influenced a number of courts. In at least two instances, procedural protections have received approving judicial reviews. In the

Raleigh case, the court thought that such protections helped to ensure against arbitrary action.

> The procedural safeguards provided will serve as an additional check on potential abuse of the Historic District Commission's discretion. Provisions for appeal to the Board of Adjustment from an adverse decision of the Historic District Commission will afford an affected property owner the opportunity to offer expert evidence, cross examine witnesses, inspect documents, and offer rebuttal evidence. Similar protection is afforded to a property owner by the right to appeal from a decision of the Board of Adjustment to the Supreme Court of Wake County. (at 455)

The *Maher* decision from New Orleans contains parallel language.

> The elaborate decision-making and appeal process set forth in the ordinance creates another structural check on any potential for arbitrariness that might exist. Decisions of the Commission may be reviewed ultimately by the City Council itself. Indeed, that is the procedure that was followed in the present case. (at 1062-63)

The existence of comprehensive background studies, the obvious character of most historic areas, and the application of standards by a uniquely qualified body all serve to distinguish historic preservation cases from those involving architectural review boards and aesthetic controls in less distinct areas. To a large extent, these differences help to explain why courts look so favorably on historic preservation controls, but sometimes view other design controls with a dubious eye.

The court also observed that the Vieux Carre ordinance "curbed the possibility for abuse . . . by specifying the composition of that body and its manner of selection."

Similarly, in a footnote to its decision interpreting the Georgetown, Colorado, preservation ordinance, the Colorado Supreme Court acknowledged the importance of a commission's expertise as a safeguard against arbitrary action.

> Although the composition of the commission is a matter exclusively within the municipality's legislative discretion, we note that the membership requirements under Ordinance No. 205 ensured that applications for certificates of appropriateness would be considered by a commission partially composed of persons familiar with architectural styles and zoning provisions in general. Such factors, while not important in the context of the present proceeding, may weigh heavily in a Rule 106 action concerned with an alleged arbitrary enforcement of an otherwise valid ordinance. (at 808-9, n.1)

The existence of comprehensive background studies, the obvious character of most historic areas, and the application of standards by a uniquely qualified body all serve to distinguish historic preservation cases from those involving architectural review boards and aesthetic controls in less distinct areas. To a large extent, these differences help to explain why courts look so favorably on historic preservation controls, but sometimes view other design controls with a dubious eye. Contrast the historic preservation cases just discussed with an aesthetic regulation case from New Jersey (*Morristown Road Associates v. Bernardsville*, 103 N.J. Super. 58, 394 A.2d 157 (1978)). In this case, the court held that review standards such as "displeasing" and "harmonious" as applied to new construction in a nonhistoric neighborhood were unconstitutionally vague. Several courts have specifically recognized that cases like *Morristown* are not applicable to preservation disputes:

> While most aesthetic ordinances are concerned with good taste and beauty . . . a historic district zoning ordinance . . . is not primarily concerned with whether the subject of regulation is beautiful or tasteful, but rather with preserving it as it is, representative of what it was, for such educational, cultural, or economic values as it may have. Cases dealing with purely aesthetic regulations are distinguishable from

those dealing with preservation of a historic area of a historical style of architecture.[6]

Design review outside of historic areas is discussed in the second part of this chapter.

Takings

Another important legal issue associated with design review in historic districts is the "taking" issue. As is discussed in more detail in Chapter 4, Tree and Vegetation Protection, the taking issue refers to the Fifth Amendment to the U.S. Constitution, which states, in part, that: ". . . nor shall private property be taken for public use without just compensation." The Fifth Amendment is a restriction on the power of the federal government to appropriate private property for its own use, also made applicable to state and local governments by the Fourteenth Amendment. A physical invasion of property by the government (e.g., to build a new post office) is the clearest example of a taking. Yet, a regulation also might so severely impact the value of property that its enforcement is considered a taking.

Generally, regulatory takings issues are decided on an *ad hoc* basis, with the court considering a variety of factors when making its decision, including: the nature of the economic impact, whether the regulation promotes valid police power objectives, the character of the government action, whether the regulation denies an owner all reasonable use of his or her property, and whether the regulation severely impacts the owner's distinct, investment-backed expectations. In the context of historic preservation, the takings inquiry is whether a design review regulation may be so onerous as to constitute a taking.[7] For example, do prohibitions on demolition or alteration, or restrictions on new development, completely limit future development opportunities or deprive the landowner of all reasonable use of his or her land? It is extremely difficult for the landowner to establish a taking under this test, as a sampling of cases illustrates.

Perhaps the most famous historic preservation case to litigate the takings issue was *Penn Central v. New York City*, mentioned above. In that case, Penn Central proposed building a 50-story skyscraper using air rights atop New York City's famous Grand Central Terminal, which had just been designated a historic landmark by the local preservation commission. Pursuant to that designation, any proposed construction or demolition involving a landmark required a "certificate of appropriateness" from the city. The city turned down Penn Central's application for a certificate, deciding that a skyscraper sitting atop the terminal would so affect and change the exterior architecture of the landmark as to be inappropriate. The company appealed, arguing that the denial of the permit kept the company from using its air rights and thus was burdensome enough to constitute a taking. While the lower court agreed and held for the company, the higher courts, including the U.S. Supreme Court, reversed and upheld the denial of the permit. The bottom line in the case, according to the Supreme Court, was the fact that the property had not lost all reasonable economic value—it could still be used as a train station.

Penn Central demonstrates the difficulties a landowner faces in establishing a taking claim: Regardless of the harsh economic and practical effects of a design control regulation—which the courts have made clear are treated no differently than any other land-use controls—it is very difficult to demonstrate that a regulation deprives a landowner of *all reasonable economic value* in his property.

5th Amendment

Generally, regulatory takings issues are decided on an ad hoc basis, with the court considering a variety of factors when making its decision, including: the nature of the economic impact, whether the regulation promotes valid police power objectives, the character of the government action, whether the regulation denies an owner all reasonable use of his or her property, and whether the regulation severely impacts the owner's distinct, investment-backed expectations.

The *Maher* case, mentioned above, also included an alleged taking claim.[8] In that case, a property owner wished to demolish a small bungalow in the historic Vieux Carre district in New Orleans and replace it with an apartment building. The local preservation ordinance forbade the demolition, and the owner sued, claiming, in part, that the ordinance deprived the property of all economic value. The U.S. Fifth Circuit Court held that the ordinance did not constitute a taking:

> Nor did Maher demonstrate to the satisfaction of the district court that . . . the ordinance so diminished the property value as to leave Maher, in effect, nothing. In particular, Maher did not show that the sale of the property was impracticable, that commercial rental could not provide a reasonable rate of return, or that other potential use of the property was foreclosed. (at 1066)[9]

Because of the substantial legal and practical difficulties faced by property owners in establishing that a regulatory taking has occurred, the taking issue is not as serious a legal concern in the design review context as the setting of adequate review standards. Nevertheless, planners and local officials should keep the takings issue in mind when drafting and enforcing design review programs in historic areas, always considering whether the regulations they draft may someday go too far and subject them to a court challenge.

No longer content to regulate traditional zoning aspects of development such as bulk, setbacks, and the like, communities throughout the country, both small and large, are demanding a greater say about height, architectural styles, building orientation, and many other aesthetic aspects of all new projects.

DESIGN REVIEW OUTSIDE HISTORIC AREAS

The increasing dissatisfaction with the appearance of new buildings and their relationship to surrounding structures and neighborhoods is manifest in the growing number of design review ordinances applicable *outside* historic districts. No longer content to regulate traditional zoning aspects of development such as bulk, setbacks, and the like, communities throughout the country, both small and large, are demanding a greater say about height, architectural styles, building orientation, and many other aesthetic aspects of all new projects.

Initially, this concern over better design was most prevalent in exclusive suburban communities, such as Santa Barbara, California, and Fox Point, Wisconsin, that capture a distinctive architectural style or atmosphere. One of the earliest ordinances was passed by West Palm Beach, Florida, in the mid-1940s, followed by a similar ordinance in Santa Barbara in 1949. Court review of such regulations soon followed.

The West Palm Beach ordinance was struck down in 1947 on the grounds that it bore no relationship to the promotion of public goals (a later decision in Florida, however, would make clear that aesthetic considerations alone *are* a proper basis for police power regulations). But, with the Supreme Court's pronouncements in favor of aesthetic regulation in the celebrated *Berman v. Parker* case in 1954, state courts began to uphold design review ordinances. Thus, a 1946 law enacted by the village of Fox Point, Wisconsin, near Milwaukee, that required new construction "not to be so at variance with" the exterior appearance of existing structures so as to depreciate property values, was upheld by the Wisconsin Supreme Court in 1955 (see discussion below). *Berman* was cited as controlling precedent in that decision.

By the 1970s, many communities that exhibited a variety of architectural styles and characters got into the act. So-called "appearance codes" proliferated, and today a multitude of design review-related efforts are in place in jurisdictions both large and small across the country. While the bulk of these efforts have been initiated by the public sector, the private sector also has been deeply involved in this movement in some important ways. For instance, many homeowners associations, which are established to oversee the maintenance and upkeep of private residential communities, exercise broad powers over any architectural changes to structures owned by their members (Mallett 1998). In addition, developers of corporate franchises, such as drug stores, fast-food restaurants, and gas stations, are recognizing that more demure building design and better site plans often translate into better neighborhood relations, and thus increased business.

Design review outside historic areas poses many of the same legal and practical challenges as protecting historic structures. However, experience demonstrates that careful planning and legal draftsmanship, coupled with a strong commitment to common-sense implementation and consistent administration, can do much to make design review work.

Legal Aspects

Design review programs outside historic areas tend not to raise takings issue questions because they are generally geared not toward stopping a project or greatly reducing its size, but more toward ensuring compatibility with surrounding structures and controlling details such as building appearance or pedestrian flow. Rarely will conditions imposed to achieve design goals create an absolute economic deprivation.

Instead, assuming a locality has been granted sufficient power by state statute, home rule, or other authority to regulate design of projects outside historic areas, the key legal issues revolve around the standards and procedures used for design review, and whether they are consistent with due process. The common-sense test used by courts to evaluate contested provisions in such cases is simply whether the standard or review criterion is sufficiently clear such that a person of ordinary intelligence can understand what it means.

The old design review provisions (recently redrafted) from Henderson, Nevada, for example, would have been a prime candidate for a court challenge on these grounds. The regulations noted that an application could fail architectural review if the planning director finds: ". . . the building alteration or addition so unsightly, undesirable, or obnoxious in appearance or function as to result in substantial depreciation of value of adjacent properties, . . . [or] to substantially deter adjacent property owners from maintaining their property." Given the tremendous subjectivity granted the planning director by this standard, the person of ordinary intelligence could be expected to have difficulty understanding what alterations or additions *would* be acceptable.

Generally, design review cases from nonhistoric areas that have reached the courts fall into two categories: those in which the local standards require compatibility of new projects with existing development, and those that require distinctiveness, aimed at preventing monotonous, "cookie-cutter" development. In some instances, local ordinances include both types of requirements (see, for example, *Old Farm Road, Inc. v. Town of New Castle*, 259 N.E.2d 217 (N.Y. 1970)).

One of the earliest aesthetic regulation cases involved a compatibility ordinance enacted by Fox Point, Wisconsin, an upper-income Milwaukee suburb (*Gates ex rel. Saveland Park Holding Co. v. Wieland*, 69 N.W.2d 217 (Wisc. 1955), cert. denied 350 U.S. 841 (1955)). The ordinance established a board that could not issue building permits unless:

> . . . the exterior architectural appeal and functional plan of the proposed structure will, when erected, not be so at variance with either the exterior architectural appeal and functional plan of the structures already constructed . . . in the immediate neighborhood or the character of the applicable [zoning] district . . . so as to cause a substantial depreciation of property value in the neighborhood.

Developers of corporate franchises, such as drug stores, fast-food restaurants, and gas stations, are recognizing that more demure building design and better site plans often translate into better neighborhood relations, and thus increased business.

Generally, design review cases from nonhistoric areas that have reached the courts fall into two categories: those in which the local standards require compatibility of new projects with existing development, and those that require distinctiveness, aimed at preventing monotonous, "cookie-cutter" development.

The trial court invalidated the ordinance on several grounds, including the vagueness of the standards prescribed to guide board review. However, the Wisconsin Supreme Court reversed, holding that the ordinance was a valid exercise of the police power and that the standards were adequate. It noted that courts had encountered little difficulty in assessing the impact of public improvements on private property for purposes of special assessments, and that to determine the impact of a new structure on adjoining ones would involve a similar calculus.

The second category of ordinances, those prohibiting excessive similarity of design, was the subject of scrutiny in a 1985 case involving a Pacifica, California, ordinance that precluded developments that would be detrimental to the "general welfare" and would be "monotonous" in design (*Novi v. City of Pacifica*, 215 Cal.Rptr. 439 (Cal. App. 1985)). The city denied development permits for eight condominium buildings on the grounds that the anti-monotony provisions were not met. In denying the permits, however, it specifically suggested that, if the project's density was reduced to achieve "at-random building placement, reduction in grading and use of retaining walls, avoidance of the linear monotony and massive bulky appearance, and the achievement of a small-scale village atmosphere characteristic of Pacifica," approval might be granted.

Rejecting the developer's claim that the anti-monotony standard was unconstitutionally vague, the court attached particular importance to the way it was applied in practice.

> The challenged ordinances were not applied to Novi in a vague manner. Indeed, vagueness was never a problem here. . . . [The developers] demonstrably understood what was required. . . . [The developers] deliberately chose to litigate rather than mitigate.[10]

A 1984 Ohio case dealt with an ordinance with both similarity and anti-monotony provisions (*Village of Hudson v. Albrecht, Inc.*, 458 N.E.2d 852 (Ohio 1984)). The city had created an architectural and historic board of review and directed it to "take cognizance of the development of adjacent, contiguous, and neighboring buildings and properties for the purpose of achieving safe, harmonious, and integrated development of related properties." In addition, the regulations stated that proposed structures should not violate certain look-alike provisions. Under these rules, the board could not approve an application if more than two specified building features were similar, including roof style; roof pitch; exterior materials; location of major design features or attached structures, such as porches and garages; and location of entry doors, windows, shutters, and the like.

Based on this general standard, the board took steps to stop the expansion of a shopping center that was proceeding without its permission. The property owner defended by arguing that the restrictions were unconstitutionally vague.

While two dissenting justices agreed with the owner, stating that the ordinance was based on "vague standards that are beyond any real definition or interpretation," the majority disagreed, citing the existence of other standards in the ordinance that defined "harmonious" as well as requiring that the project be integrated with vehicular and pedestrian traffic patterns. Specifically, the ordinance directed the board to take into account design, use of materials, finished grade lines, dimensions, and orientation and location of all main and accessory buildings in determining if the "harmonious" standard was met.

Contrast a 1993 case from Issaquah, Washington, which perfectly illustrates a successful challenge made by a landowner confronted with a set of vague review standards (*Anderson v. Issaquah*, 851 P.2d 744 (Wash. App. 1993)). Wanting to build a large commercial building on land zoned for general commercial use, Anderson, the developer, sought the necessary approval of the Issaquah Development Commission (IDC), the agency responsible for enforcing the city's building design standards. Unfortunately, these standards contained numerous vague terms and concepts (e.g., developments were to be "harmonious" and "interesting") and failed to provide meaningful guidance to the developer or to the public officials responsible for enforcing the provisions.[11]

As originally proposed, the commercial structure was to be built in a "modern" style with an unbroken "warehouse" appearance in the rear; large, retail-style, glass windows on the facade; off-white stucco facing; and a blue metal roof. The property was located on a major boulevard in a "natural transition area" between old downtown Issaquah and an area of new, village-style construction.

During their first review of the project, IDC commissioners commented upon several aspects of the design they found displeasing, including the color scheme, the blankness of the rear wall, and the fact that the relatively plain facade "did not fit with the concept of the surrounding area." One commissioner observed that he did not think the building was compatible with the "image of Issaquah." The commissioners continued the hearing to provide the landowner an opportunity to modify his design.

At the next meeting, the landowner presented modified plans that included a new building color and modified roof materials. Still unsatisfied, the commissioners struggled to provide more specific feedback. One suggested the landowner "drive up and down Gilman [Boulevard] and look at both good and bad examples of what has been done. . . ." Another member requested a review of the shade of blue to be used, noting that: "Tahoe blue may be too dark." The commissioners again continued the hearing to a later date to allow further modifications from the applicant.

At the third IDC meeting, the landowner presented plans that responded to the commissioners' concerns and featured new architectural detailing to break up the facade, additional landscaping, and enhanced rear-wall trim. Still unsatisfied, one commissioner presented a written statement of his "general observations" of the area's architectural character (e.g., "I see heavy use of brick, wood, and tile. I see minimal use of stucco. I see colors that are mostly earthtones, avoiding extreme contrasts."). Another commissioner noted, "There is a certain feeling you get when you drive along Gilman Boulevard, and this building does not give you this same feeling."

After nine months of meetings and investing more than $250,000, the understandably frustrated landowner volunteered to make one final modification to the building's facing, but would make no further changes. The IDC chose to deny the application, expressing concern that the proposed building—even with the agreed-upon modifications—would relate poorly to the surrounding neighborhood. The city council and trial court both upheld the denial.

On appeal, however, the Washington Court of Appeals found the local design code to be unconstitutionally vague:

> . . . [T]here is nothing in the code from which an applicant can determine whether his project is going to be seen by the Development Commission as "interesting" versus "monotonous" and as "harmonious" with valley and the mountains. Neither is it clear from the code just what else, besides the valley and the mountains, a particular project is supposed to be harmonious with. . . .

In attempting to interpret and apply this code, the commissioners charged with that task were left only with their own individual, subjective "feelings" about the "image of Issaquah" and as to whether this project was "compatible" or "interesting."

The point we make here is that neither Anderson [the developer] nor the commissioners may constitutionally be required or allowed to guess at the meaning of the code's building design requirements by driving up and down . . . looking at "good and bad" examples of what has been done with other buildings, recently or in the past. This is the very epitome of discretionary, arbitrary enforcement of the law. (at 76)

The *Issaquah* case underscores the main point to remember regarding standards for design review: Standards must be sufficiently clear so as to give effective and meaningful guidance to applicants as to what is being required in terms of design without them having to guess, and to the public officials responsible for enforcing the standards.[12] Otherwise, the regulations will be challenged frequently and may have a difficult time withstanding judicial review.

Recent Developments

As discussed, a rapidly growing number of communities are paying attention to design review in areas outside historic districts, spurred by growing citizen concern and supported by favorable court decisions. This section discusses some of the more important recent developments in the field, including the use of new tools and approaches to ensure compatibility of new construction with its surrounding architectural and environmental context, such as conservation districts.

We also consider the use of design review to combat traditionally problematic development types, such as big-box retail stores and corporate franchises.

Conservation districts. Conservation districts, geared to preserving the character of existing neighborhoods, are being considered or have been adopted in a growing number of jurisdictions across the United States as one alternative to more stringent historic district regulations. Many conservation districts have been implemented for areas that fall short of meeting the criteria for a local, state, or national historic designation, but which nevertheless have important cultural, visual, or other significance. Some are intended as step-down, buffer, or transition areas immediately surrounding a protected historic district. Others are directed at preserving the residential character of a neighborhood, maintaining a unique community center, or emphasizing an important cultural element of a community.

Design flexibility is an important attribute of conservation districts as compared to historic districts. Whereas the primary purpose of a historic district is to protect the historic integrity of an area (usually by preventing demolition and requiring appropriate renovation or highly compatible new construction), conservation districts can, depending on how they are drafted, be much more flexible and can allow design elements that might accent or complement a particular neighborhood feature as long as the general character of the area remains intact. Conservation districts also can easily accommodate the protection of more than one style or era within the district.

Conservation districts generally are an effective means of protecting neighborhood character. They can be specifically tailored to the needs of a discrete area, greatly reducing the potential for problems associated with vague design standards applicable to large areas. Moreover, conservation district regulations are typically less stringent than historic district regula-

---

The Issaquah case underscores the main point to remember regarding standards for design review: Standards must be sufficiently clear so as to give effective and meaningful guidance to applicants as to what is being required in terms of design without them having to guess, and to the public officials responsible for enforcing the standards.

Conservation districts generally are an effective means of protecting neighborhood character. They can be specifically tailored to the needs of a discrete area, greatly reducing the potential for problems associated with vague design standards applicable to large areas.

tions, thus reducing political opposition to their adoption and enforcement. Design guidelines in conservation districts generally are not overly detailed and are developed on the basis of specific neighborhood concerns and features, such as building height, setbacks, bulk, and landscaping.

Conservation districts have been established for many different purposes, and the criteria for the definition of an area typically reflect both the visual elements that need to be protected and the community issues giving rise to the need for protection. The diversity and flexibility of conservation districts also is apparent in the types of activities that are regulated and the way they are administered. The experiences of two cities illustrates some of the successes and problems that have been encountered.

Dallas, Texas, has seen an upsurge in concern about the impact of new projects outside historic areas. As a result, the city has enacted a "conservation district" ordinance that allows citizens to petition for special design and other controls in areas that do not qualify as historic districts. Designation can be initiated only by a majority of landowners in an area and can be granted only if the area contains "significant architectural or cultural attributes" and has a "distinctive atmosphere or character that can be conserved by protecting those attributes." Once the designation process is initiated, the city planning department prepares a conceptual plan for the proposed district that identifies important features and assets worthy of protection. If the city council approves the plan, an ordinance is drafted that may institute special controls on building heights, setbacks, landscaping, and signs, and that may include ". . . additional regulations the city council considers necessary to conserve the distinctive atmosphere or character of the area."

Several separate districts show the variety of regulated activity. The strictest controls apply to an area containing English Tudor cottages built in the 1930s, with Prairie and ranch-style, noncontextual infill structures built in the 1950s. The character of the infill structures may be preserved and remodeled, but if the style is changed, it must conform to the existing Tudor style. Regulations also include paint color restrictions and significant landscaping controls. Resident participation is extremely high, and the city receives many calls from neighbors about what other neighbors are doing.

Another conservation district in Dallas was established in an English Tudor area to maintain building setbacks that became unenforceable under revised zoning codes. The district protects the existing 60-foot building setback and prohibits fences in front yards. Large porches may be enclosed only with glass or screens, not walls. A third area has less restrictive guidelines and consists of smaller craftsman and Prairie-style houses. Visible elements are subject to review by city staff. Although this district is supported by neighborhood residents, it is typical for small violations to occur without the complaint of other residents.

The enforcement of regulations for all conservation districts in Dallas is by staff review only. Initially, an appeal could be brought before the planning commission, zoning board of adjustments, or the city council. After a problem arose with this approach, however, review was limited to the zoning board of adjustment on the basis of its quasi-judicial authority to determine whether the ordinance was correctly interpreted by the planning director.

In Massachusetts, there is no specific enabling authority for conservation districts, and the requirements for historic preservation status are very restrictive. However, under home rule authority, many municipalities have enacted conservation districts and related ordinances. Because there is a definite awareness of the significant historic architecture in the Cam-

Conservation districts have been established for many different purposes, and the criteria for the definition of an area typically reflect both the visual elements that need to be protected and the community issues giving rise to the need for protection. The diversity and flexibility of conservation districts also is apparent in the types of activities that are regulated and the way they are administered.

bridge area, there is also a high interest in preserving historically or architecturally significant community features that do not meet rigid historic preservation standards.

Compared to the administration of conservation districts in other states, the administration of the Cambridge districts is very structured and complex. There are two levels of review: Mandatory review applies to new structures over 750 square feet, and advisory review applies to all other remodeling and construction. The reviews are conducted by commissions that are administered under the state historic commission management umbrella. The commissions are made up of residents in the district, with one state historic commission seat.

The majority of reviews conducted are in the advisory, nonbinding category. These cases typically consist of remodeling projects, including decks, dormers, and bay window expansions. Some in the private sector generally see this level of review as an unnecessary safeguard and consider the requirement a waste of time. The city sees the process as an educational opportunity and as a means of allowing the public an opportunity to participate and comment.

Even with this structured administrative framework, the two main districts that have been established in Cambridge are functionally very different. The Half-Crown district is comprised of 75 residential buildings on very small lots near Harvard Square, a major commercial area with significant historical features. The principal interest of the property owners is to protect the residential area from outside influences, particularly office and commercial uses. The property owners are so involved in the district that it is almost self-governing. The group reportedly has a definite "us versus them" approach, which sometimes includes the city in the "them" category.

The second district is the Mid-Cambridge district and includes about 2,000 buildings. Beginning in the 1950s, large houses were being demolished to make way for "modern" seven- to eight-story apartment buildings. In response, the city amended the zoning code in the 1970s to encourage small-scale, townhouse/condominium development and attached single-family additions. This led to problems associated with the resulting high densities, including reduced parking and the loss of yards, open space, and large trees. While this trend slowed during the late 1980s because of the national economy, the conservation district now helps to monitor growth and preserve the neighborhood character. In addition, the area was downzoned as the result of "recasting" the townhouse ordinance.

Because many jurisdictions have conservation districts that have been in place for several years, those drafting new ordinances can now draw on a variety of useful models from around the country. These existing models can be evaluated and used as the basis for developing new ordinances without "reinventing the wheel." Recently adopted programs include Lincoln, Nebraska; Orlando, Florida; and Portland, Oregon, in addition to the examples mentioned above.

Design standards for large retail establishments. The meteoric rise of large-scale retail stores such as Wal-Mart has been one of the headline planning stories of the 1990s. Commonly called "big-box" retailers, these enterprises typically occupy more than 50,000 square feet and derive their profits from high sales volumes. While such stores vary widely in size and market niche, they tend to share common design features, including: large, rectangular, single-story buildings with standardized, often blank facades; reliance on auto-borne shoppers who are accommodated by acres of parking; and no-frills site development that often eschews community or pedestrian amenities such as trees or sidewalks.

While [big box] stores vary widely in size and market niche, they tend to share common design features, including: large, rectangular, single-story buildings with standardized, often blank facades; reliance on auto-borne shoppers who are accommodated by acres of parking; and no-frills site development that often eschews community or pedestrian amenities such as trees or sidewalks.

Such stores depend on high visibility from major public streets. In turn, their design determines much of the character and attractiveness of major streetscapes in the city. The marketing interests of many corporations, even with strong image-making design by professional designers, can be detrimental to a community's sense of place when they result in massive individual developments that do not contribute to or integrate with their surroundings in a positive way.

An increasing number of communities are worried about the aesthetic blight of big-box retailers (in addition to the economic impact on existing downtown merchants and the sprawl-inducing effects of such development). In response, they are enacting standards and guidelines to control the aesthetics of such establishments. One example is Fort Collins, Colorado, which has adopted some of the most comprehensive guidelines and standards in the country to shape the appearance and impact of big-box retailers. In adopting its new standards, the Fort Collins City Council noted:

> These standards and guidelines are a response to dissatisfaction with corporate chain marketing strategy dictating design that is indifferent to local identity and interests. The main goal is to encourage development that contributes to Fort Collins as a unique place by reflecting its physical character and adding to it in appropriate ways.

Before adopting its big-box standards, Fort Collins already had detailed regulations in place dealing with signage and landscaping, the typical means by which communities attempt to soften the visual impact of retail superstores. Yet Fort Collins was interested in moving beyond such traditional approaches, and at the time was fortunate enough to have a strong economy and a creative staff and local elected offi-

Clarion Associates

Big-box retail developments are typically characterized by large, rectangular, single-story buildings with standardized blank facades, enormous parking lots, and the lack of amenities like trees and sidewalks.

Clarion Associates

In contrast to the typical big-box, both this Wal-Mart and K-Mart show how variation in color, roof line, materials, and signage can make such development fit better with a community's aesthetics and the building's natural setting.

Meg Maguire

cials who could afford to resist the temptation of large tax revenues the superstores might generate. The city decided to focus on requiring a basic level of architectural variety, compatible scale, pedestrian and bicycle access, and mitigation of negative impacts.

The resulting regulations apply to new "large" retail establishments (i.e., any one or a collection of retail establishments in a single building, occupying more than 25,000 gross square feet of lot area, or an addition to an existing large retail establishment that would increase the gross square feet of floor area by 50 percent). They include both "standards," which are mandatory, and "guidelines," which are not mandatory but are provided in order to educate planners, design consultants, developers and local staff about the design objectives. The standards are not intended to limit creativity; rather, the city hopes they will serve as a useful tool for design professionals to engage in site-specific design in context. The standards and guidelines address the following issues.

Architectural Character. To prevent blank, windowless, faceless facades, the standards:

- forbid uninterrupted length of any facade in excess of 100 feet (by requiring recesses, projections, windows, awnings, and arcades);

- require that smaller retail stores that are part of a larger principal building have display windows and separate outside entrances;

- direct the use of a repeating pattern of change in color, texture, and material modules;

- dictate variations in roof lines; and

- require that each principal building have a clearly defined, highly visible customer entrance with distinguishing features such as canopies or porticos.

Color and Materials. To ensure higher-quality development, the standards:

- require predominant exterior materials to be of high quality, such as brick, wood, sandstone, or other native stone;

- require facade colors to be of "low reflectance, subtle, neutral, or earth tone colors," and prohibit the use of high-intensity or metallic colors; and

- prohibit the use of neon tubing as an accent material.

Relationship to Surrounding Community. To ensure that superstores are compatible with surrounding streets and commercial and residential development, the standards require:

- all facades visible from adjoining properties and/or public streets to contribute to the pleasing scale of features of the building and encourage community integration by featuring characteristics similar to a front facade;

- all sides of a principal building that directly face abutting public streets to include at least one customer entrance;

- minimum setbacks for any building facades of 35 feet, within which a six-foot earth berm planted with evergreen trees must be included if the facade faces adjacent residential uses;

- loading docks, trash collection, and other outdoor storage and activity areas to be incorporated into the overall design of the building and the landscaping, so that the visual and acoustic impacts are fully contained; and

- the provision of community and public spaces such as water features, clock towers, or patio seating areas.

> *Fort Collins*

> The standards are not intended to limit creativity; rather, the city hopes they will serve as a useful tool for design professionals to engage in site-specific design in context.

Bob Blanchard

Fort Collins, Colorado, moved beyond traditional signage and landscaping regulations to incorporate big-box standards that address architectural variety, compatible scale, pedestrian and bicycle access, and mitigation of negative impacts. The results are evident in this series of photos of big-box and power center development in Fort Collins.

Pedestrian Flows. To encourage pedestrian accessibility, the standards require:

- sidewalks of at least eight feet in width along all sides that abut public streets;

- sidewalks along the full length of any facade featuring a customer entrance and any facade abutting a public parking area;

- internal pedestrian walkways to provide weather protection features such as awnings within 30 feet of all customer entrances; and

- internal pedestrian walkways must be distinguished from driving surfaces through the use of special paving materials.

Parking Lots. To prevent huge expanses of asphalt separating the superstores from streets, the standards encourage structures to be located closer to streets and to break parking areas up into modules separated by landscaping and other features. No more than 50 percent of the off-street parking area for the entire property shall be located between the front facade and the primary abutting public street.

The Fort Collins standards provide a strong model for other communities concerned about mitigating the aesthetic impacts of large-scale retailers on the local landscape. Other jurisdictions should be careful, however, to tailor new standards to their own local political and economic contexts.[13]

Design standards for corporate franchises. Big boxes aren't the only retail outlets being subjected to an increasingly stringent and sophisticated generation of design review programs. Local governments are realizing that smaller-sized businesses may just as quickly erode community character if not properly integrated with their natural and architectural surroundings. Design review can ensure that drug stores, roadside motels, gas stations, and the like are designed so as to respect community character. Such design review efforts have been particularly successful with corporate franchises, especially gas stations and fast-food restaurants, since many of these are controlled by national chains that are beginning to understand how sensitive design can make good business sense. Fleming (1994) discusses the evolution of today's standardized franchise designs and explains how communities can use design review to require corporate franchises to respect community character.

Fleming notes that both gas stations and chain restaurants cater to, and rely heavily on, the automobile, and their most prominent design features are attributable to the car. Since the bulk of their customers arrive by road, corporate marketing departments demand instant recognition from passing motorists. As a result, gas stations feature tall, colorful, well-illuminated signs displaying the corporate logo, often visible from miles away. Chain restaurants rely on oversized architectural details (e.g., golden arches), bright colors, and huge banners advertising the current sale or promotional gimmick. Not only do these stores cater to the automobile, but they also encourage further sprawl by continuing to require more land and higher parking-lot-to-building ratios, and by marketing aggressively to new suburban development. Rehabilitation of older facilities is unusual for both gas stations and fast-food chains, since both find it more cost-effective to invest in new construction.

The need for speed and convenience also influences franchise design, resulting in site plans that emphasize efficiency over respect for community character. Gas stations feature additional pumps to reduce wait times, pay-at-the-pump stations to allow fill-ups without ever entering the store, and broad, brightly lit canopies covering large service plazas to shelter customers from the weather. Anxious to accommodate rushed

---

Big boxes aren't the only retail outlets being subjected to an increasingly stringent and sophisticated generation of design review programs. Local governments are realizing that smaller-sized businesses may just as quickly erode community character if not properly integrated with their natural and architectural surroundings.

Fleming notes that both gas stations and chain restaurants cater to, and rely heavily on, the automobile, and their most prominent design features are attributable to the car.

The need for speed and convenience also influences franchise design, resulting in site plans that emphasize efficiency over respect for community character.

motorists, stations emphasize self-service and incorporate convenience stores selling quick snacks for the road. Fast-food chains configure sites to allow ample parking and easy auto access to and from the drive-through window. The cumulative effects of such design features are structures and sites that disregard their surrounding community context in favor of the bottom line, allowing marketing concerns to trump aesthetic compatibility.

Fortunately, many such chain stores are locally owned, and independent franchise owners have significant say over such important design issues as decor and landscaping. Some independent owners have learned that compatibility with the surrounding neighborhood makes good business sense. In Asheville, North Carolina, for example, one new chain gas station in the Biltmore Station neighborhood has been designed so sensitively that it almost looks like an annex to the adjacent, historic church. The station's owner notes that his profits are much higher than they would be if his station looked like any of the surrounding cookie-cutter chain outlets (Clark 1996).

Not wanting to rely exclusively on enlightened franchisees, however, local governments are using design review to require higher-quality development from the franchises. They are requiring the same types of features, discussed above, that are being applied to big-box retailers: sensitive landscaping, smaller signs, appropriate lighting, setbacks uniform with existing development, muted colors, and architectural styles and materials consistent with local traditions. Also, recognizing that drive-through windows are major sources of revenue for fast-food restaurants, local governments are conditioning approval of such windows (if allowed by the underlying zoning restrictions) on the in-

Marty Roupe

Marya Morris

Sensitivity in design can make corporate franchises good neighbors and makes good business sense. Here, two McDonald's, one in Hilton Head, South Carolina (above), and the other in Sedona, Arizona (left), reflect the colors, textures, and materials that are typical for their respective areas.

corporation of design features that mitigate congestion and traffic-related impacts, such as sidewalks and landscaping. (See Fleming (1994) for an excellent visual essay on franchise design alternatives.)

Opportunities for design review are increasing as corporate franchises move into new areas, such as downtowns, to take advantage of marketing opportunities away from their traditional strongholds, the suburban neighborhoods and interstate highways. Adjusting to these new locations often means tailoring their facilities in sensitive ways, perhaps by adding underground parking or reconfiguring floor plans to fit narrow historic buildings. The major food-service corporations (e.g., McDonald's, Burger King) have shown a willingness to adapt to unusual spaces if it makes good economic sense: Being a good neighbor can promote a healthy corporate image, which translates into increased sales.

> The major food-service corporations (e.g., McDonald's, Burger King) have shown a willingness to adapt to unusual spaces if it makes good economic sense: Being a good neighbor can promote a healthy corporate image, which translates into increased sales.

Many communities are enjoying significant progress in their efforts to increase the quality of franchise design. The design guidelines for Albemarle County, Virginia, for example, feature a McDonald's restaurant as a model to be emulated, "an example of architecture compatible with historically significant local buildings" (Albermarle County Department of Zoning).

If necessary, however, local officials are going to court to enforce their design review programs, as was illustrated in a 1991 case from Holden, Massachusetts.[14] In that case, a local government refused a request from the Mobil Corporation to install a large, 19-foot canopy, similar to those the company installs on most of its stations, on a gas station in a historic district. A Massachusetts Superior Court upheld the denial, agreeing that the canopy would be incompatible with the surrounding architecture. In its opinion, the court underscored the importance of the local preservation commission's role in preserving the local architectural and cultural heritage.

Communities attempting to regulate the design of corporate franchises should be clear in their guidelines about the exact type of design they want. Extensive illustrations and definitions should be used to explain difficult concepts like "community character" to franchise owners and their architects. Local planners should be ready and willing to negotiate on design issues. They should educate themselves as to the economic needs of a franchise so they can suggest economically feasible alternatives to standard design templates. They should be able to cite examples from similar communities showing how changes mandated by design review required minimal investment (as a percentage of total project cost) and were recouped many times over in good will and customer loyalty. Finally, communities should be firm and strong-willed in enforcing their design review programs, if necessary defending their systems in court. As Ed McMahon, director of the Conservation Fund's American Greenways Program, has noted, "If you accept the lowest common denominator in development, you'll get it every time. If you insist on something better, you'll get that almost every time" (Clark 1996).

> Neotraditional neighborhoods attempt to recapture the sense of community found in successful neighborhoods that have endured for half a century or more by replicating the design elements of those neighborhoods and by fostering pedestrian-friendly environments that discourage reliance on the automobile.

New applications for neotraditional design standards. Neotraditional development, also known as New Urbanist development or traditional neighborhood development (TND), has enjoyed such booming growth and popularity over the last few years that, today, most every planner is familiar with its basic tenets. Neotraditional neighborhoods attempt to recapture the sense of community found in successful neighborhoods that have endured for half a century or more by replicating the design elements of those neighborhoods and by fostering pedestrian-friendly environments that discourage reliance on the automobile.

Many of the most sensitively designed neotraditional developments, such as Southern Village in Chapel Hill, North Carolina, are making extremely positive aesthetic contributions to the communities in which they are built. Typical design features of these developments include: front porches to encourage interaction with neighbors; garages that face alleys, rather than front streets, to de-emphasize the importance of the automobile; and narrow streets to discourage fast traffic in residential areas. Neotraditional developments also feature a mix of land uses to minimize the amount of driving time between home and work and other services, and a variety of housing types to encourage a diverse community, rather than one segregated by income or other socioeconomic factors. Above all, new development is encouraged to merge seamlessly with the surrounding built and natural environment, rather than ignoring the context in which it is built.

What is unusual is the increasing number of design review programs that are applying neotraditional design principles in new and unconventional ways. Local jurisdictions are learning that the principles of New Urbanism may just as easily be applied to a storage warehouse as they can to a residential subdivision. A good example of this trend is Hudson, Ohio, a

Whether it is called New Urbanist development or neotraditional development, neighborhoods built according to these design principles deemphasize the automobile and enhance the "human." Southern Village in Chapel Hill, North Carolina, is just such a development.

Clarion Associates

fast-growing suburb of Cleveland, which recently adopted design standards for industrial development that incorporate many neotraditional principles. Rather than allowing new industrial development to consist of bland, blank-walled warehouses isolated in an industrial park, as happens in so many communities, the Hudson requirements attempt to ensure that industrial development is compatible to the greatest extent possible with its natural and aesthetic surroundings.

Specifically, the Hudson zoning ordinance requires that all industrial development be consistent with community standards for architectural design. Structures should have elements that are interrelated and ordered.

The size and proportion of windows and wall openings should be related to one another and to the spaces between them within the overall facade. A group of structures should be designed as a single architectural entity, rather than as a collection of unrelated facades. Architectural character and detailing is required for all sides of structures in the public view. Efforts must be made to reduce the overall visual impact of large structures by using berming, landscaping, or architectural solutions to give the illusion of an apparently smaller mass. Building siting and orientation must take into account the relationship of new buildings to the street, parking areas, and other buildings, and must minimize disturbance of vegetation, wetlands, woodlands, riparian corridors, and other natural features. Landscaping and screening requirements provide an opportunity to create and preserve an identity for the specific site, while also relating the site to the community as a whole.

IMPLEMENTING AND ADMINISTERING DESIGN REVIEW

As the law relating to design review both inside and outside historic areas becomes more settled, efficient and effective administration of design review ordinances is becoming increasingly important. Because local planners often are responsible for acting as staff to local review bodies, they are in a position to help improve the administrative and procedural aspects of design review. Below are some general guidelines that communities should keep in mind when drafting and implementing design review regulations (Shirvani 1981; Erickson 1986). As design review becomes more commonplace, local governments will need to take all possible steps to anticipate criticism that design review procedures are overly burdensome and that the entire process is inherently subjective.[15]

1. *Employ community-based efforts to identify what is special, unique, or worthy of conserving in an area.* As noted above, design review programs in historic areas that feature consistent building styles usually feature the common architectural heritage as a reference point. Because newer neighborhoods do not always have a distinctive architectural style, however, it is particularly important that such areas attempt to reach a consensus on what matters to citizens in the way of design elements. Invariably, as experience is showing, review that goes beyond a primary focus on building design is most effective.

Recent advances in computer technology have made the difficult process of defining a community "vision" much simpler and less expensive. Computerized visual simulations are being used heavily in a variety of contexts to assist planners and elected officials in determining what proposed land-use activities will look like if approved. The Minnesota Department of Transportation, for instance, uses computerized visual simulations to help people understand how roads will look using different design options (e.g., different widths, various shoulder treatments, with bike trails versus without bike trails). Other communities are using visual simulations to determine what proposed subdivisions will look like, to show the effect of burying utility wires, and the benefits of tree conservation, among other things.[16]

One particular type of simulation, known as a Visual Preference Survey, is a trademarked technique that allows members of a community to jointly determine what type of development they find most acceptable.[17] A visual simulation generally consists of a series of slides featuring different types of physical environments shown to a group of people who then rate the images they see on a sliding scale, usually "+10" (best) to "-10" (worst). Each participant provides a personal rating for each image; thus, the same image might receive a "+10" from one person who responds very positively, and a "-4" from another person who responds somewhat negatively. Average scores for each image summarize the types of development most acceptable to all participants.

In communities in which such techniques have been used, such as Metuchen, New Jersey, the results have been dramatic, with some images rating almost 100 percent positive and others rating almost 100 percent negative. The survey in Metuchen thus confirmed that some types of development were very acceptable to a large number of local residents, while others were not.

Across various communities that have used such a process, images typically scoring very high include pristine natural areas, established neighborhoods, and new development designed according to neotraditional principles (e.g., narrow streets, mixed uses, pedestrian-friendly features). Images that tend to score negatively include parking lots, large-scale roads, industrial facilities, and deteriorating urban centers. Traditional suburban development tends to score poorly when presented alongside neotraditional development.

Advocates of the process note that the technique can be a powerful tool for bringing together disparate interests in the pursuit of a "common vision," which in turn can lay the political groundwork for support of what can often be a contentious regulatory process. Critics of the process, however, note that such slide presentations can be prohibitively expensive in many small- and mid-scale planning projects.

2. Ensure administration by a well-qualified board supported by adequate staff and resources, especially if detailed design review is to take place. As noted, several court decisions make clear that the application of review standards by an expert board will go a long way towards supporting the reasonableness of the regulatory process. Including architects and other design professionals on such a board comforts the judiciary when claims are made that review standards are vague and the process subjective.

Of equal importance, the review board must have resources available to establish and administer design standards. A background study and adequate continuing staff support are essential to effective and equitable design review. Communities should seek professional assistance either in-house or through consulting firms to ensure that the review board gets competent advice and that design restrictions are followed in practice.

3. Supplement written design standards with visual aids and guidebooks to make clear what the community desires, thus reducing uncertainty for prospective developers. An increasing number of communities are publishing illustrated design books and are undertaking educational efforts in the development community to help reduce delays when applications are submitted. Visual design guides might graphically illustrate, for example, what constitutes a "compatible" or "harmonious" design. Computerized visual simulation tools also can be, as noted above, excellent tools to clarify desired aspects of new construction to potential developers.[18]

4. Do not concentrate solely or even primarily on detailed building design review. Commissions and preservationists are slowly learning the importance of concentrating their efforts and attention on major cases and avoiding extended review of minor items, such as spacing of pickets in a fence, design of wrought iron gates, and similar issues that have led to heated political controversy in the past. Experience shows that government design regulations are most effective in dealing with issues like building height,

DESIGN REVIEW GUIDELINES

1. Employ community-based efforts to identify what is special, unique, or worthy of conserving in an area.

2. Ensure administration by a well-qualified board supported by adequate staff and resources, especially if detailed design review is to take place.

3. Supplement written design standards with visual aids and guidebooks to make clear what the community desires, thus reducing uncertainty for prospective developers.

4. Do not concentrate solely or even primarily on detailed building design review.

5. Carefully integrate design review with other planning goals for the area.

6. Keep records.

7. Draft efficient procedural requirements.

8. Be sure sufficient political will exists to enforce and maintain a design review program.

pedestrian pathways, street furniture, landscaping, and other more straightforward aspects of site design, rather than with the architecture of a specific building. Unless the community desires buildings of a distinct architectural style, it may well be advisable to set general parameters and leave the actual building design in the hands of the developer's architect.

5. *Carefully integrate design review with other planning goals for the area.* While design review of a specific site can do much to protect the character of an area, the relationship of a project to the overall development in a district is of equal importance. An up-to-date local comprehensive plan is perhaps the best source for determining preferred development principles and patterns for a community.

6. *Keep records.* Now that many local ordinances have real "teeth," local commissions must improve their record keeping, particularly minutes and transcripts from hearings dealing with projects that are controversial and may end up in litigation. The development of an institutional record ensures the consistent interpretation of regulations—and the fair treatment of applicants—over time.

7. *Draft efficient procedural requirements.* The most effective design review programs are characterized by streamlined administrative procedures that not only comply with the law, but also reduce time and resource requirements for local staff and applicants. Some examples of ways to make procedural requirements more efficient include the following:

- Preparing a succinct summary sheet of local preservation requirements that can be handed out to applicants by building officials.

- Holding preapplication meetings. Misunderstandings can be avoided if the project proponent is given a chance to meet informally with staff and commission members prior to submitting a formal application.

- Imposing time limits. Many local governments are placing limits on the time a local commission has to consider a project once a completed application is submitted. These time limits usually range from 30 to 60 days.

- Allowing generic approvals of preapproved sign designs. Some commissions have published booklets that contain five or six preapproved sign designs for a special area, such as a historic district. If the applicant adopts one of these preapproved signs, the normal review process can be waived.

8. *Be sure sufficient political will exists to enforce and maintain a design review program.* The tale of the design guidelines for the Three Rivers Parkway in Allegheny County, Pennsylvania, sounds a cautionary note for other communities concerning the political will needed to ensure long-term acceptance and enforcement of design review programs. The parkway connects the new Pittsburgh airport to the downtown and serves as a major gateway into the City of Pittsburgh. Along its route lies a dramatic series of hills and beautiful river valleys, some of which had been obscured by insensitive past development. Pittsburgh, a number of other municipalities, and the county all have land bordering the parkway.

In 1992, seeking to create a distinctive new visual identity for this important entry corridor into Pittsburgh and to ensure quality development and protect the natural environment, Allegheny County commis-

An up-to-date local comprehensive plan is perhaps the best source for determining preferred development principles and patterns for a community.

The development of an institutional record ensures the consistent interpretation of regulations—and the fair treatment of applicants—over time.

The most effective design review programs are characterized by streamlined administrative procedures that not only comply with the law, but also reduce time and resource requirements for local staff and applicants

sioned a "workbook for implementation" that sought to turn the parkway into an attractive, sensitively designed thoroughfare that could serve as a major economic asset and complement the new airport. The workbook included tough new design standards and guidelines in a variety of areas, including: uniform sign regulations, including controls on new billboards and off-premises signs; buffers, setbacks, and landscaping standards, including tree protection provisions; standards to restore and protect unique and environmentally sensitive areas; and building and site design guidelines intended to ensure compatibility with existing development.

Effective implementation of the workbook required adoption of the design review program by all affected jurisdictions in order to protect as much land along the parkway as possible. Counties in Pennsylvania have only limited land-use regulatory authority. Signing up the municipalities to the popular plan did not prove to be difficult, and, within 18 months, seven jurisdictions had adopted the design standards and guidelines. The popular plan even won a national award for its stringent, farsighted, regional approach to design review. Soon the entire planning effort was threatened, however, when Wal-Mart applied for a permit to build a new mega-store alongside the parkway in North Fayette Township. The proposed big-box development would consume almost an entire stream valley and would have required dozens of variances from the new design guidelines, tree protection regulations, and sensitive lands preservation standards. Local officials hesitated, wondering whether to uphold the design guidelines, deny the variances, and miss out on an opportunity to substantially increase the local tax base; or grant the variances, allow the development, and effectively gut the new plan not only for themselves but for all the communities along the parkway. Local citizens, furious with the proposed development, threatened a lawsuit if the variances were granted and the design standards were not enforced.

In the end, North Fayette Township repealed the design guidelines altogether, choosing short-term economic development over long-term aesthetic enhancement of the Three Rivers Parkway. The repeal effectively ruined the chances for uninterrupted implementation of the design standards along the entire parkway. Soon several other jurisdictions followed suit, allowing large, poorly sited and designed commercial development to mar the parkway.

The lesson? Be sure sufficient political will exists not only to adopt a design review program, but also to enforce standards even when tempted with big projects. Just as important, review standards should be no more stringent than the community is willing to enforce. If standards are too tough, the political pressure may be too great to grant variances or repeal the standards altogether, especially when faced with the difficult choice of economic development versus aesthetic compatibility.

> Be sure sufficient political will exists not only to adopt a design review program, but also to enforce standards even when tempted with big projects. Just as important, review standards should be no more stringent than the community is willing to enforce.

Notes

1. The best local design guidelines for historic areas will address design review issues in the larger context of communitywide needs and preferences, which ideally will be articulated in a comprehensive plan or similar document. For a good example, see the 1995 Historic District Conservation Guidelines prepared for the Over-the-Rhine Historic District in Cincinnati, published by the local planning department. Although prepared specifically for the historic district, the guidelines contain "development principles" applicable to the entire community (e.g., "The development, preservation, and maintenance of housing should be encouraged for persons of all income levels.").

2. For a discussion of these issues, see Christopher J. Duerksen, "Historic Preservation Law," in *The Law of Zoning and Planning*, 4th ed., edited by Arden Rathkopf, (New York: Clark Boardman, Co., Limited, 1975), Release 63, 1997; Christopher J. Duerksen, ed., *A Handbook of Historic Preservation Law* (Washington, D.C.: The Conservation Foundation, 1983); Richard J. Roddewig, *Preparing a Historic Preservation Ordinance*, Planning Advisory Service Report No. 374 (Chicago: American Planning Association, 1983).

3. Norman Williams, *American Land Planning Law*, 3.31 Sec. A.07. A good discussion of preservation criteria can be found in Weiming Lu, "Preservation Criteria: Defining and Protecting Design Relationships," in *Old and New Architecture: Design Relationships* (Washington, D.C.: Preservation Press, 1980), 180. As Lu notes, some local ordinances use sketches to illustrate standards. These sketches are typically contained in documents incorporated by reference into the ordinance.

4. A number of other courts are in agreement with this reasoning. See *City of Santa Fe v. Gamble-Skogmo, Inc.,* 389 P 2d 13 (N.M. 1964); *Maher v. City of New Orleans,* 516 F.2d 1051 (5th Cir. 1975); *Groch v. City of Berkeley,* 173 Cal. Rptr. 534 (1981).

5. The six criteria to be considered were:

> (1) the effect of the proposed change on the general historic and/or architectural character of the structure or area; (2) the architectural style, arrangement, texture, and materials used on existing and proposed structures, and their relation to other structures in the area; (3) the effects of the proposed work in creating, changing, destroying, or affecting otherwise the exterior architectural features of the structure upon which such work is done; (4) the effects of the proposed work upon the protection, enhancement, perpetuation, and use of the structure or area; (5) the use to which the structure or area will be put; and (6) the condition of existing improvements and whether or not they are a hazard to public health or safety.

6. *A-S-P Associates v. City of Raleigh,* 258 S.E.2d 444, 450 (N.C. 1979). Quoting Arden Rathkopf, *The Law of Zoning and Planning,* 4th ed. (New York: Clark Boardman, Co., Ltd., 1975), Sec. 15.01, p. 15-4. See also *City of Santa Fe v. Gamble-Skogmo, Inc.,* 381 P.2d 13,17 (N.M. 1964).

7. See David Bonderman, "Federal Constitutional Issues," in Christopher J. Duerksen, ed., *A Handbook of Historic Preservation Law* (Washington, D.C.: The Conservation Foundation, 1983), 350-68. Also see Christopher J. Duerksen and Richard J. Roddewig, *Takings Law in Plain English* (Washington, D.C.: American Resources Information Network, 1994).

8. 516 F.2d 1051 (5th Cir. 1975), *rehearing denied,* 521 F.2d 815 (1975), *cert. denied,* 426 U.S. 905 (1976).

9. For other cases illustrating the difficulty of a property owner establishing a taking as a result of a preservation ordinance, see *William C. Haas & Co. v. City and County of San Francisco,* 605 F.2d 1117 (9th Cir. 1979) (95 percent reduction in value held not a taking); and *South Terminal Corp. v. Environmental Protection Agency,* 504 F.2d 646 (1st cir. 1974) (forced 40 percent vacancy of parking lots held not a taking).

10. Other cases upholding design review ordinances include *Reid v. Architectural Review Board,* 192 N.E.2d 74 (Ohio 1963); *State ex rel. Stoyanoff v. Berkely,* 458 S.W.2d 305 (Mo. 1970).

11. Excerpts from the challenged design provisions of the Issaquah Municipal Code:

> 16.16.060(B). Relationship of building and site to adjoining area:
>
> Buildings and structures shall be made compatible with adjacent buildings of conflicting architectural styles by such means as screens and site breaks, or other suitable methods and materials. . . . Harmony in texture, lines, and masses shall be encouraged. . . .
>
> . . .

16.060(D). Building design:

Evaluation of a project shall be based on quality of its design and relationship to the natural setting of the valley and surrounding mountains.

Building components, such as windows, doors, eaves, and parapets, shall have appropriate proportions and relationship to each other, expressing themselves as a part of the overall design.

Colors shall be harmonious, with bright or brilliant colors used only for minimal accent.

Exterior lighting shall be part of the architectural concept. Fixtures, standards, and all exposed accessories shall be harmonious with the building design.

Monotony of design in single or multiple building projects shall be avoided. Efforts should be made to create an interesting project by use of complimentary details, functional orientation of buildings, parking and access provisions, and relating the development to the site. In multiple building projects, variable siting of individual buildings, heights of buildings, or other methods shall be used to prevent a monotonous design.

12. The importance of including more precise review criteria to narrow broad review standards also was illustrated by the contrasting result in the *Morristown* case noted above. Other cases striking down design review provisions include *Hankins v. Borough of Rockleigh*, 150 A.2d 63 (N.J. App. 1959) (regulations invalid in light of active physical development of locality); *R.S.T. Builders v. Village of Bolingbrook*, 489 N.E.2d 1151 (Ill.App. 1986) (regulations invalid due to vagueness and failure of ordinance to prescribe adequate standards to control review commission's actions); and *Waterfront Estates Dev., Inc. v. City of Palos Hills*, 597 N.E.2d 641 (Ill.App. 1992).

13. For more information on drafting and implementing big-box retail standards and the Fort Collins case study, see Christopher J. Duerksen, "Site Planning for Large-Scale Retail Stores," *PAS Memo*, April 1996. Also see Constance Beaumont, *How Superstore Sprawl Can Harm Communities and What Citizens Can Do About It* (Washington, D.C.: National Trust for Historic Preservation, 1994).

14. *Mobil Oil Corp. v. Holden Historic District Commission*, Superior Court Civil Action No. 91-01434, December 9, 1992. See the detailed discussion of this case in Fleming (1994, 16).

15. For more detailed information on creating and administering an effective design review program, see Mark L. Hinshaw, *Design Review*, Planning Advisory Service Report No. 454. (Chicago: American Planning Association, 1995).

16. Through Scenic America, you can obtain a videotape, *Looking at Change Before It Occurs* (1993), which describes various types of two- and three-dimensional visual simulations.

17. For more information on Visual Preference Surveys, see James Constantine, "Design by Democracy," *Land Development*, Spring-Summer 1992, 11.

18. See Appendix A, "Visual Simulation Tools," in *Tree Conservation Ordinances: Land-Use Regulations Go Green* by Christopher J. Duerksen, Planning Advisory Service Report No. 446 (Chicago: American Planning Association, 1993).

Chapter 3

View Protection

Communities are relying on a combination of tools—including height and use restrictions, sign controls, and landscaping regulations— to protect scenic views and scenic roadways. They are finding that comprehensive view protection programs, while more difficult to craft and implement, can achieve far more impressive results than isolated attempts to address individual eyesores.

COMPREHENSIVE PROGRAMS AIMED AT PROTECTING AND ENHANCING COMMUNITY AESTHETICS DO NOT RELY SOLELY ON TOOLS THAT IN- FLUENCE ARCHITECTURAL CHARACTER, LIKE HISTORIC PRESERVATION ORDINANCES AND DESIGN REVIEW REGULATIONS. They also make use of special techniques to protect panoramic vistas, view corridors, and scenic roads. Such features contribute to an area's unique sense of place and image, which, in turn, boost the overall quality of life and help attract new businesses.

Some view protection efforts concentrate on preserving sight lines to important public buildings, like the Texas state capitol in Austin. In other places, such as Denver, Colorado, mountain views have spurred special regulations to limit building heights. Still other communities and regions focus on creating and protecting scenic roadways and entryways to cities and towns. The federal government has instituted a very popular national scenic byways program, and many states have adopted special legislation to create their own scenic roadways. Many cities, including New Orleans and Houston, are sprucing up the entryways into their communities—the "welcome mat" areas where initial impressions are made, and where jumbles of signs, parking lots, overhead wires, and the other accouterments of urban development can detract from attractive views.

These view protection efforts can stir up surprisingly heated passions. An example is the so-called "view wars" occurring in and around Seattle. As more and more people move to desirable hillside neighborhoods in that picturesque area, conflicts are increasing as new homeowners try to force their neighbors to trim or remove trees to open up valuable mountain views. Landowners reluctant to engage in "tree-topping" are finding their trees chopped down under cover of night, girdled with chainsaws, or drilled and injected with poison. Many tree owners have been taken to court and forced to"top off" their trees to open up views for neighbors up the hillside. Washington communities are turning to view protection ordinances to try to resolve the conflicts.

The concern over view protection is not a new one, and regulatory efforts to protect scenic views date back at least to the late 1800s. One early case from 1896 involved a challenge to a Massachusetts ordinance that protected views of a state capitol building *(Parker v. Commonwealth,* 59 N.E 634 (Mass. 1896)). In the 1930s, a scenic roadway movement swept the country and resulted in the creation of the Blue Ridge Parkway and Skyline Drive, among others (both managed today by the National Park Service).

> Today, the concern over view protection is being rediscovered and reawakened with a vengeance. Polls show that protection of viewsheds, view corridors, and scenic roadways enjoys widespread political support.

Today, the concern over view protection is being rediscovered and reawakened with a vengeance. Polls show that protection of viewsheds, view corridors, and scenic roadways enjoys widespread political support. In a recent survey conducted for a comprehensive planning process in Chaffee County, Colorado, for instance, local officials learned that almost three-quarters of respondents favored the imposition of design standards to protect scenic views along the county's main highway (Clarion Associates et al. 1998). In Virginia, statewide interest has prompted the state legislature to initiate a comprehensive study and inventory of the state's scenic resources.[1]

Communities are relying on a combination of tools—including height and use restrictions, sign controls, and landscaping regulations—to protect scenic views and scenic roadways. They are finding that comprehensive view protection programs, while more difficult to craft and implement, can achieve far more impressive results than isolated attempts to address individual eyesores.

This chapter looks first at some of the key legal issues involved in view protection, followed by a discussion of the major types of view protection programs. The chapter concludes with a look at recent developments in the field, including the development of new methodologies to identify and evaluate scenic resources and the incorporation of view protection into rural preservation efforts.

LEGAL ASPECTS

In most jurisdictions, localities have the authority, under the "general welfare" prong of their police power, to impose restrictions that protect scenic views and maintain a high standard of design along certain roadways.[2] Although height controls were the primary protective tool used in the past *(Welch v. Swasey,* 79 N.E. 745 (1907), aff'd. 214 U.S. 91 (1909)), communities today are relying on a wider range of complementary tools, including setback requirements, design review, sign controls, landscaping restrictions, and various tools linked to environmental protection. For instance, as discussed below, some hillside protection laws not only prevent development on steep slopes that might cause erosion and other damage to natural areas, but also protect special views.

Efforts to protect the views of certain important structures, like state capitols, and to maintain the ambience of their environs have been upheld by some courts for almost 100 years. Boston, in particular, was a leader in this area, attempting to protect its beloved Copley Square from being overshadowed by surrounding buildings. The Massachusetts high court and the U.S. Supreme Court have upheld Boston's efforts. The Massachusetts court agreed that the erection of high buildings might exclude sunshine, light, and air to the detriment of the public health. Similarly, the court upheld a 70-foot height restriction on buildings located within 100 feet of any park or parkway (*Levanthal v. Buehler*, 191 N.E. 2d 128 (N.Y. 1963)). Only a few noteworthy court cases have challenged view protection ordinances, and generally these have met with little success.[3]

Cincinnati employs the Environmental Quality-Hillside District, a zoning overlay, to protect the natural features and views of the Ohio River valley.

Cincinnati Hillside Trust

One issue arising with increasing frequency is whether a landowner has any legal recourse when new construction blocks the view from his or her home. Although the ultimate answer will always depend on the particular laws in place in the jurisdiction, the answer generally is that the unfortunate landowner whose view is blocked is out of luck.

A 1996 case from Cincinnati offers a good example (*Cash v. Cincinnati Board of Zoning Appeals*, 690 N.E.2d 593 (Ohio App. 1 Dist. 1996)). A landowner, Neil Bortz, sought to build a house on a steep hillside lot on the side of Mt. Adams, next door to a historic church that is a major local landmark. The house would be located in the Environmental Quality-Hillside District, an overlay zoning district intended to ensure that hillside development is compatible with sensitive natural features, such as steep slopes. An additional stated purpose of the district is "to preserve the prominent view from the top or from the slopes of the hillside, and the natural contours thereof." The zoning code required buildings in the overlay zone, among other things, to "be planned and designed to respect views from other public buildings and from public viewing placed within the district." New development in the overlay district required approval by a hearing examiner, who was to approve applications if they conform "with all applicable laws and ordinances, and [are] in the public interest." Also, "failure . . . to conform with any single factor shall not necessarily be a sufficient basis for denial. The application which maximizes the public interest and private benefits shall be approved."

Bortz planned to build a three-story residence on the site that would enjoy spectacular views of the city and the Ohio River valley. Although the house would be situated substantially below street grade, it still required area and height variances from zoning code requirements. A similar three-story house for the site had been approved and granted these variances in 1986, but it had never been built, and the approval had expired. Bortz planned to build his new house on the same footprint of the house that had won earlier approval. Following negotiations with neighbors, during which the building plans were redesigned several times, the hearing examiner approved Bortz's plan, despite some remaining neighborhood opposition.

The new Bortz house would block the views of an adjacent landowner, Albert Cash, who had enjoyed river views while the Bortz property sat vacant. When the Bortz house won approval, Cash protested the hearing examiner's decision. The approval, Cash claimed, was illegal because it failed to protect Cash's property values, in that his property was substantially devalued by the loss of the river views.

The local Board of Appeals disagreed with Cash, as did the county court and the Ohio appellate court, which noted that the hearing examiner acted within the boundaries of the discretion provided to him by the Cincinnati zoning code. The court found that the examiner's decision was "well-considered" and properly balanced the public interest, the interests of adjoining landowners, and the interests of Bortz. The court specifically noted that the house would not block substantial public views, such as those of and from the nearby church. The court was impressed by the use of computer simulations that demonstrated the look of the new residence from various places in Mt. Adams and the valley below, which allowed the hearing examiner to see the potential impairment of views. Unfortunately for Cash, the court noted that:

> . . . He is only one landowner, and the elimination of his view is only one factor to be considered. No prescriptive right to the use of light and air over the property of an adjoining landowner can be acquired. . . . There is no private right to a view without an express easement, and the Cincinnati Zoning Code does not confer one. . . . Further, Cash was aware that someone else owned the lot next to his and the possibility always existed that the owner would build a structure there which might interfere with his view. . . . Consequently, we find his arguments unpersuasive. (at 596–597)

Another frequently litigated issue is whether view protection regulations may be so stringent as to deny all reasonable use of a parcel and thereby effect a taking. In 1986, the Colorado Supreme Court rejected a takings challenge to Denver's mountain view ordinance (*Landmark Land Company, Inc. et al. v. City and County of Denver*, 728 P.2d 1281 (Colo. 1986) (en banc), appeal dismissed, 483 U.S. 1001 (1987)). Enacted in 1968, the mountain view ordinance restricts buildings near Southmoor Park to a height of 42 feet, with an additional two feet allowed for each 100 feet the building was located from the reference point in the park. The plaintiffs wanted to construct a 21-story office building, which the current zoning would have allowed notwithstanding the limits in the mountain view ordinance. However, neighbors opposed the project and, in 1982, persuaded the city council to apply the challenged restrictions over objections of the plaintiffs and the planning board. Despite a finding that the restrictions caused a substantial diminution in value, the court held there was no taking because the properties were still extremely valuable. Moreover, the trial court judge, after visiting several parks protected by the law, rejected out-of-hand the contention that the ordinance did not serve a valid police power objective.

Generally, scenic protection measures will not be so onerous as to deny all reasonable economic use of a property. However, an Arizona case demonstrates that, in extreme circumstances, they may be so strict as to effect a taking (*Corrigan v. City of Scottsdale*, 720 P.2d 528 (Ariz. App. 1985), aff'd in part, rev'd in part, 720 P.2d 513 (Ariz. 1986)). In the *Corrigan* case, the City of Scottsdale had enacted a hillside protection ordinance that severely restricted development in the McDowell Mountains, a unique geographic area of hilly and mountainous terrain. The hillside ordinance established two areas: a conservation zone within which land was set aside solely for open space due to development limitations such as steep slopes, rockfalls or landslides, and soil erosion; and a development area in which land could be developed subject to certain limits. Development rights could be transferred from the conservation zone to alleviate potential hardship. Under the ordinance, 80 percent of the plaintiff's land was in the conservation area.

Finding that the city was actually attempting to establish a public mountain preserve without paying for it, the Arizona Court of Appeals struck down the ordinance as a taking and also held that only money, not density credits, could amount to "just compensation." Moreover, the court held that, under Arizona law,

> Public interest in aesthetics, standing alone, is often too vague to offset substantial injury to a landowner in a rezoning case. . . . The evidence does not support nor did the trial judge find that a deplorable condition exists or would exist without the Hillside ordinance.

This decision was upheld on appeal to the Arizona Supreme Court, which also ruled that damages were payable for a temporary taking while the offending regulations were in place.

While the *Corrigan* decision is limited in applicability to Arizona and has come under severe criticism from legal observers and planners, it nevertheless stands as a sober warning to local governments to proceed carefully when regulating development to protect scenic views, especially when restrictions effectively prohibit the use of large tracts of land.

Because of the rapidly growing number of telecommunications facilities being erected throughout the country, providers of such services increasingly may challenge local view protection regulations in cases where such regulations restrict the location of new towers. In the few cases to have examined this emerging issue thus far, the power of local governments to regulate aesthetics, including view protection, has been upheld by courts as not inconsistent with the federal Telecommunications Act of 1996 (which generally restricts local zoning authority in order to encourage competition in the telecommunications industry). For example, in a recent Colorado case, a federal district court upheld a local government's refusal to issue a special use permit for a telecommunications tower, on the basis that the tower would violate local zoning regulations designed to protect views of the Rocky Mountains (*Sprint Spectrum v. Board of County Commissioners of Jefferson County*, 59 F. Supp. 2d 1101 (D. Colo. 1999)). See Chapter 7 for more information on the complex relationship between federal telecommunications requirements and local zoning.

Generally, scenic protection measures will not be so onerous as to deny all reasonable economic use of a property.

While the Corrigan decision is limited in applicability to Arizona and has come under severe criticism from legal observers and planners, it nevertheless stands as a sober warning to local governments to proceed carefully when regulating development to protect scenic views, especially when restrictions effectively prohibit the use of large tracts of land.

There are two common types of viewshed ordinances. The first allows new development subject to some type of design review. . . . A stricter type of viewshed ordinance sharply curtails the types of new development allowed in viewsheds in order to preserve the scenic areas in a relatively undisturbed state. These ordinances require sensitive siting or screening of any buildings allowed in the viewshed. Should they restrict all reasonable uses of land, these ordinances will have takings implications.

TYPES OF VIEW PROTECTION

Local view protection programs may be characterized in a variety of ways, depending upon their emphasis (i.e., the particular type of views and/or scenic resources afforded protection). One program, for example, might emphasize protecting views of a major river valley running through a community, while another may focus on protecting views of a locally prominent building. Some jurisdictions employ a multifaceted approach that emphasizes protecting more than one type of scenic resource.

For ease of classification, this section divides view protection programs into four categories: (1) viewshed protection; (2) view corridor protection; (3) programs linking view and environmental protection efforts; and (4) scenic roadway protection.

Preserving Viewsheds

Perhaps the most common category of view protection ordinance focuses on preserving viewsheds—those grand, scenic vistas, visible from many vantage points, that encompass a multitude of elements, both natural and man-made, and that give communities their special identity.

There are two common types of viewshed ordinances. The first allows new development subject to some type of design review. For example, some jurisdictions have enacted ordinances that protect views of important local waterways by imposing height controls on new commercial buildings. One of these cities, Pittsburgh, has regulations that restrict heights of new buildings in two areas that flank the Monongahela River. The restrictions, geared to protect views of the city's riverfront, require staggering the height of buildings according to their distance from the river. Similarly, Park City, Utah, has adopted height and building design controls, including regulations on the color of roofs and building materials, to ensure that development on the hills around the city does not mar the scenery.

A stricter type of viewshed ordinance sharply curtails the types of new development allowed in viewsheds in order to preserve the scenic areas in a relatively undisturbed state. These ordinances require sensitive siting or screening of any buildings allowed in the viewshed. Should they restrict all reasonable uses of land, these ordinances will have takings implications. The ordinance invalidated in Arizona's *Corrigan* case, discussed above, was an example of such an ordinance. To deflect potential takings claims, viewshed protection ordinances often allow for, or encourage, mechanisms to transfer development out of protected areas, including cluster development and transfer of development rights.

Preserving View Corridors

A second category of view protection focuses on protecting view corridors—those openings in the urban fabric that allow either quick glimpses or more extended views of important constructed resources (e.g., state capitols and historic buildings) or natural features (e.g., public parks, mountains). View corridor regulations can vary widely in form. They can be simple and straightforward, as is the case with ordinances that attempt to prevent shadows from falling onto important view corridors and public places. San Francisco, for instance, has adopted height controls on commercial buildings designed to prevent shadows on public plazas and parks at certain prescribed times. Denver, also, regulates the height of buildings on its Sixteenth Street outdoor mall to ensure maximum sunlight reaches sidewalks for pedestrians at lunchtime ("Sunny". . ., *Denver Post* 1994).

View corridor regulations also may be more complex, as is the case with Denver and Austin programs that rely on mathematical formulas to calcu-

View corridor regulations can vary widely in form. They can be simple and straightforward, as is the case with ordinances that attempt to prevent shadows from falling onto important view corridors and public places. . . . View corridor regulations also may be more complex, as is the case with Denver and Austin programs that rely on mathematical formulas to calculate allowable building heights.

Denver's mountain view ordinance helps protect the panoramic view of the mountains from parks and public places. Here is a view of the Rockies from Cheeseman Park.

Since 1984, views of the state capitol building in Austin, Texas, have been protected by a view protection ordinance, which employs a sophisticated formula for determining allowable building heights.

Clarion Associates

late allowable building heights. Denver's mountain-view ordinance (which withstood the trial court challenge discussed above and was upheld on appeal) is a well-known example of this type of regulation. The Rocky Mountains have provided a stunning backdrop for Denver since the city's founding. To ensure that views of the mountains continue to exist from public places, the city enacted the mountain view ordinance to protect panoramic mountain views from parks and public places.

The city invokes both aesthetic and economic reasons to support the ordinance. The basic approach in Denver is to create a series of overlay zones with special restrictions tailored to each of the city's major parks. Thus, in Cranmer Park, no structure can be higher than 5,434 feet above sea level (the approximate height of the city) plus one foot for each 100 feet the structure lies from a reference point within the park. In practice, apartment buildings 300 feet from the reference point and at the same base elevation could be a maximum 30 feet high. In the Capitol/Civic Center district, the ordinance creates five zones, each with its own specific height limit, designed to protect the view of the Rocky Mountains from the state capitol and the view of the capitol itself.

The capitol view ordinance in Austin, Texas, is another oft-cited example of a view corridor protection scheme. Designed to protect views of the state capitol building from various vantage points around town, the Austin ordinance is similar in concept to the Denver mountain-view ordinance. What distinguishes it from other efforts, however, is the amount of study and analysis that preceded its adoption. Furthermore, the ordinance contains a much more complex formula for determining acceptable building heights.

Adopted in August 1984, the ordinance was introduced to serve aesthetic, educational, civic, and economic goals by protecting and preserving public views of the state capitol from selected points in the city such as parks, bridges, and major roads. The study that preceded adoption of the ordinance looked at the historical significance of the state capitol building (which is a facsimile of the U.S. Capitol, only a few feet larger) and Austin's skyline. It paid particular attention to the policies of the city's comprehensive plan, which placed emphasis on maintaining the unique character of the community. Sixty important view corridors were identified and broken down into four categories (stationary parks; thresholds along entryways to the city; sustained views; and dramatic glimpses). The study analyzed each view from the specific point identified (e.g., was the dome obscured?) and land uses within the corridor. The overall economic impact of the proposal was analyzed along with the economic impact within each corridor. All of this background work helped establish a strong framework for the ordinance and defused opposition to it as opponents realized that adverse impacts were not as great as expected.

$$\tan \theta = \frac{a}{b} = \frac{a'}{b'}$$

$$\tan \theta \times b' = a'$$

$$a' - e = h$$

VP = Viewpoint
RS = Review Site
a = 653' − VP elevation
b = Distance, VP to capitol
c = Sightline to capitol
e = RS elevation − VP elevation
a' = VP elevation to sightline at RS
b' = Distance, VP to RS
h = Allowable height

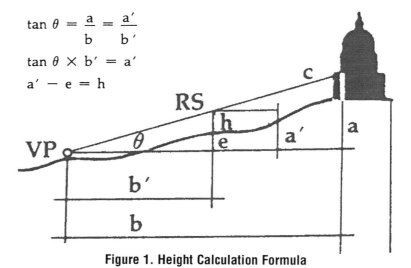

Figure 1. Height Calculation Formula

The final formula adopted (see Figure 1) establishes height allowances in each corridor defined by sightline elevations from the viewpoints to the base of the capitol dome. A grandfather clause governed projects already in the site plan review process. Local officials have been very pleased with the ordinance and have increased the number of designated corridors from the initial nine designated in 1984 to 26 as of 1998.

Linking View Protection and Environmental Protection

A third type of view protection program attempts to coordinate the protection of scenic resources with environmental protection efforts. Many communities are attempting to integrate relatively recent interests in regulating aesthetics with longstanding concerns for natural resource protection. One example is the increasing number of local tree and vegetation conservation ordinances, discussed in detail in the following chapter. Such ordinances not only conserve important aesthetic resources—the greenery that contributes so much to community character—but also fulfill important environmental objectives by preventing soil erosion and enhancing air quality. Other view protection efforts may work in tandem with efforts to protect wetlands, floodplains, aquifers, watersheds, and shorelines (for additional examples, see Bobrowski (1995)).

Regulating Hillside Development. Perhaps the best examples of a regulatory approach that focuses both on aesthetic and environmental protection are hillside development ordinances, which are becoming increasingly popular, especially in mountain states. A 1993 survey found that 234 such ordinances had been adopted in 22 states, with the majority in California (Olshansky 1996). The ordinances usually have at least two major objectives: the protection of views and the protection of natural features associated with sensitive hillside ecosystems. Many hillside development ordinances also have a host of other goals, including fire prevention, the preservation of wildlife habitat, and the provision of adequate roadways to ensure quick access for public safety vehicles. Yet, the most common area of emphasis is the protection of scenic resources. Indeed, the survey found that 75 percent of all the examined ordinances listed "aesthetics" as a major purpose.

In PAS Report 466, *Hillside Development*, author Robert Olshansky outlines the history of efforts to regulate hillside development and shows how the modern, multiple-objective ordinance actually represents the integration of different types of regulations that have matured over several decades. Olshansky notes that efforts to regulate hillside development began in earnest with grading ordinances in the Los Angeles area in the 1950s. Administered by local engineering departments, these ordinances were mainly geared toward ensuring public safety and contained little to no guidance on the character of new construction. Grading ordinances soon became widespread, and today grading provisions are included in all three major model building codes.

So-called "slope/density" ordinances began to appear in the 1960s and were common by the 1970s. These ordinances represented the first efforts to link allowable density to the natural constraints of a site—in other words, the amount of allowable hillside construction on a parcel was limited by the ability of the site to handle the physical pressures of new development. Also in the 1970s, local governments began to enact erosion and sedimentation control ordinances, intended to improve water quality by reducing the amount of sediment in water runoff.

While it has been only in recent decades that jurisdictions have concerned themselves with the aesthetic implications of hillside development, today this goal predominates in many ordinances. The primary aesthetic goal generally is to protect important views. Hillside and ridgeline development is restricted or prohibited in order to preserve scenic views for the public of and from the undisturbed hillside or ridgeline.

Beyond this basic tenet, the ordinances vary widely in their approaches, as Olshansky describes. A jurisdiction might choose to encourage development while emphasizing public safety, thus requiring extensive mass grading and re-engineering of hillsides to provide high-quality roadways that allow quick access for public safety vehicles. Or a jurisdiction might require selective grading and improvements of hillsides for safety concerns, while also imposing development standards (e.g., setbacks from ridgelines, restrictions on removal of native vegetation) to protect important natural features. A third approach could be to prohibit hillside development altogether. A combination approach might require grading and other engineering techniques in certain areas targeted for development while prohibiting development altogether in other areas; the exact location and characteristics of these cluster developments (e.g., hilltops versus valleys) could vary depending on local conditions.

Regardless of the particular approach taken by an ordinance, communities should keep in mind the lesson illustrated by the *Corrigan* case discussed above: An ordinance must never be so restrictive as to deny the owner all reasonable economic value from his or her land. Such a complete denial would

While it has been only in recent decades that jurisdictions have concerned themselves with the aesthetic implications of hillside development, today this goal predominates in many ordinances. The primary aesthetic goal generally is to protect important views.

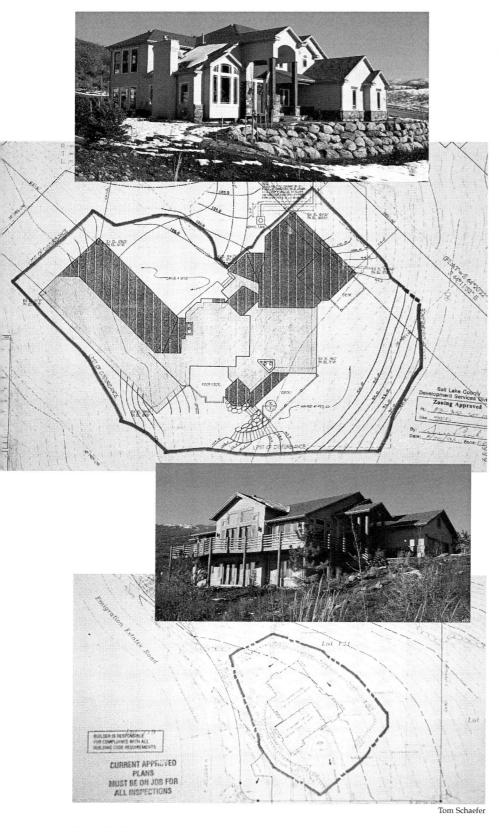

Tom Schaefer

Salt Lake County, Utah, employs a Foothills and Canyons Overlay Zoning District. A key feature of the ordinance for the district is that it defines limits of disturbance on the development site to preserve the "visual and aesthetic qualities" of the foothills.

constitute a taking under the Constitution (and perhaps under state constitutions, as well) and require payment of just compensation to the landowner. To avoid being so restrictive, wise jurisdictions should consider enacting provisions to allow escape valves from this type of situation, such as density transfer provisions.

Ordinances that do not prohibit hillside development altogether tend to vary widely in their areas of emphasis and scope of coverage. Increasingly, jurisdictions are adopting "sensitive lands protection" ordinances that include development standards in a number of different areas. Officials in Salt Lake County, Utah, for example, recently adopted a Foothills and Canyons Overlay Zoning District intended, in part, to "preserve the visual and aesthetic qualities of the foothills and the canyons, including prominent ridgelines." The ordinance's wide-ranging scope is typical of many modern hillside development ordinances. Development standards address:

- lot and density requirements;
- slope protection standards;
- grading standards;
- road and site access;
- access to trails and public lands;
- fencing;
- tree and vegetation protection;
- natural hazard protection;
- stream corridor and wetlands protection;
- wildlife habitat protection; and
- traffic.

A key feature of the Salt Lake County overlay zone is that, for every development subject to the ordinance, limits of disturbance must be established indicating the specific area(s) of the site in which construction and development activity must be contained. For single-family residential development, limits of disturbance include the area required for the principal structure, accessory structure(s), utilities, services, drainage facilities, and a septic tank. Area required for driveways and leach fields are not included. Limits of disturbance are designated individually for each development site, based on criteria such as minimization of visual impacts, erosion prevention and control, fire prevention and safety, and preservation of significant trees or vegetation.

Colorado Springs, Colorado, also has enacted a strong hillside protection program. This fast-growing city is facing intense development pressures in some of its spectacular hillside neighborhoods that back up onto Pike's Peak and the Front Range. Concerned about the potential destruction of its fragile foothills environment, Colorado Springs has adopted a Hillside Overlay Zoning District that applies in addition to the base zoning districts. The purpose of the overlay district is to allow people to "develop and maintain hillside properties in an environmentally sensitive fashion," while also ensuring that visual impacts of development are mitigated to the maximum extent possible.

The city has adopted both mandatory zoning regulations and recommended design guidelines to help achieve its twin goals of aesthetic and environmental protection. Performance standards for hillside development are contained in the zoning code (regulating basic things such as setbacks, maximum height, lot coverage, drive grades, access points). A separate manual supplements the code requirements with recommended design standards and guidelines.

The Colorado Springs review process for the development of hillside properties is typical of most local jurisdictions. The process encourages applicants to hold a preapplication conference with staff to review the proposed development and applicable local regulations. A separate session to discuss design review issues may supplement this conference. The formal application must include a site/lot grading plan for all proposed development, including an inventory of site features, an analysis of particular site constraints, and an evaluation of alternative development options. Building elevation drawings also must be submitted for all proposed structures. After a review and evaluation, city staff approves or denies the application. The applicant may appeal to a local hearing officer. Follow-up inspections occur during the construction phase to determine compliance with the approved plans.

A partial list of the criteria for approval of plans demonstrates the multiple objectives behind the Colorado Springs hillside development ordinance:

* Have applicable code development standards been met?

* Is terrain disturbance minimized?

* Have cuts and fills been minimized?

* Has the natural land form been retained?

* Have visually compatible stabilization measures been used for cut-and-fill slopes?

* Have visual impacts on off-site areas been avoided or reasonably mitigated?

* Have natural features such as slopes and rock formations been incorporated into the site design?

* Has the structure been sited off from the ridgeline?

> Limits of disturbance are designated individually for each development site, based on criteria such as minimization of visual impacts, erosion prevention and control, fire prevention and safety, and preservation of significant trees or vegetation.

Given the multiple objectives behind modern hillside development ordinances, it is understandable that potential conflicts may sometimes occur among competing goals. Minimum road-width standards, for example, may run counter to provisions protecting native vegetation. The potential for such conflicts underscores the importance of laying a solid foundation for new ordinances through careful planning and extensive public participation to ensure that any choices or trade-offs made among competing objectives accurately reflect the community's stated goals and preferences.

Regulating ridgeline development. Closely related to the hillside development ordinances are those ordinances limiting ridgeline development. Development atop ridgelines often may be seen from numerous locations throughout a community, and thus may even more dramatically infringe on special views than hillside development.

The Castle Rock, Colorado, ridgeline development ordinance defines "skyline areas" where development is controlled. The ordinance is designed to prohibit buildings like this one, located in a nearby community.

Clarion Associates

Castle Rock, Colorado, recently adopted one of the more progressive and sophisticated ridgeline protection ordinances in the country. The city's ordinance defines various "skyline areas" (any area in which all or part of a permanent structure would be visible along the skyline when viewed from one or more points on specially designated viewing platforms) and ridgeline areas (mapped areas having a major visual impact on the character of the town based on field observations). As part of the town's subdivision approval process, building envelopes must be defined to restrict the siting of improvements in these key areas. No primary or accessory structures may be constructed within the most sensitive skyline or ridgeline areas. Improvements that are allowed must mitigate their impacts on the visual landscape in several ways, including:

- *Color:* All primary and accessory structures must use predominant exterior wall colors that repeat the colors most commonly found in the land and vegetation around the building, and which have a light reflection value of no more than 40 percent.

- *Vegetation:* The area around each primary and accessory structure must include at least one tree of a species with a mature height of at least 35 feet for each 2,500 square feet of a lot or parcel area (maximum of eight required trees).

- *Floodlights:* Floodlights shall not be used to light all or any portion of any primary or accessory structure facade, and all outdoor lighting sources shall use full cutoff light fixtures.

- *Exposed Basements:* On the side of each primary and accessory structure facing the nearest designated viewing platform, no basement wall shall be exposed for more than one-half of its height, unless a vegetated berm at least three feet in height is constructed as a visual buffer.

Protecting Scenic Roadways

A fourth common type of view protection program focuses on scenic roadways.[4] More and more communities are recognizing how the aesthetic regulation of important roadways, such as entryways that provide first impressions to a city or town, can accomplish much in protecting the character of the overall community. Typical roadway protection programs emphasize restrictions on signs (e.g., no billboards), lighting (e.g., no neon, no excessive nighttime lighting), and landscaping (e.g., minimum landscaping of roadside areas is required in order to prevent broad expanses of concrete).

Because scenic roadways may be several hundred miles long—for example, the 252-mile long Blue Ridge Parkway—scenic roadway protection programs often extend beyond the boundaries of individual jurisdictions to the regional, state, and multistate levels. Indeed, as discussed below, scenic roadway protection is notable as one of the few types of aesthetic regulation practiced by all levels of government. A number of private, non-profit organizations also are heavily involved with roadway protection, including national groups such as Scenic America and state-level organizations like Scenic North Carolina.

The National Scenic Byway Program. The creation of the National Scenic Byway Program provided a strong boost to the protection of scenic roadways nationwide. Established by the Intermodal Surface Transportation Efficiency Act of 1991 (ISTEA) and administered by the Federal Highway Administration (FHWA), the program originally allocated $74 million for six years to establish a national initiative to support the development of existing and new state scenic byway programs, to provide improvements to byways and byway facilities, and to support technical assistance activities for scenic byways.

FHWA announced the first round of nationally designated roads in September 1996, based on nominations submitted by local communities and state and federal land management agencies. Federally designated byways are distinguished in one or more of six possible areas: archaeology, culture, history, nature, recreation, and scenic value. The top tier of byways, known as All-American Roads, are considered the "best of the best" by FHWA. The first six byways to receive the "All-American Road" designation included routes of major historical and cultural importance, such as the 43-mile Selma to Montgomery March Byway, along the trail of the famous march in 1965 led by Dr. Martin Luther King, Jr. Other All-American Roads include Route One, Pacific Coast Highway, along 72 miles of the spectacular California coastline near Monterey; and the San Juan Skyway, a 233-mile route in southwestern Colorado winding past numerous 14,000-foot mountains and attractions such as Telluride and Mesa Verde National Park.

FHWA created a second tier of nationally designated roadways, known as the National Scenic Byways, that "possess outstanding qualities that exemplify the regional characteristics of our nation." The 14 byways originally selected from across the nation demonstrate an impressive breadth of scenic, cultural, and historic diversity. Examples include the Creole Nature Trail on Lake Charles in Louisiana, the Ohio River Scenic Route in Indiana, and the Kancamagus Scenic Byway in New Hampshire.

Typical roadway protection programs emphasize restrictions on signs (e.g., no billboards), lighting (e.g., no neon, no excessive nighttime lighting), and landscaping (e.g., minimum landscaping of roadside areas is required in order to prevent broad expanses of concrete).

Scenic America

ALL-AMERICAN ROADS AND NATIONAL SCENIC BYWAYS

The following list and descriptions of All-American roads and National Scenic Byways were taken from the National Scenic Byways Program web site (www.byways.org). They are organized alphabetically by state and include the name of the road, the state where it is located, and the year the road was designated. The site contains information about the program's information clearinghouse, more detailed descriptions of the byways, maps, and thumbnail photos of the various roads described in this list. The phone number for the program is 800-4BYWAYS (800-429-9297).

All-American Roads

All-American roads are the United States' finest byways: the best of the best. They are destinations unto themselves and an exciting adventure for all ages.

NATCHEZ TRACE PARKWAY, ALABAMA (1996)
Native Americans, Kentucky boatmen, post riders, government officials, soldiers, and fortune seekers all moved across this 425-mile trail charting new territory and creating a vital link between the Mississippi Territory and the fledgling United States. The parkway also runs through Mississippi and Tennessee.

SELMA TO MONTGOMERY MARCH BYWAY, ALABAMA (1996)
Journey through history along the trail that marks one of the major historic events in twentieth century American history, the Selma to Montgomery March in 1965, led by Dr. Martin Luther King, Jr.

ROUTE 1, BIG SUR COAST HIGHWAY, CALIFORNIA (1996)
Travel the route that provides access to the austere, windswept cypress trees, fog-shrouded cliffs, and crashing surf of the Pacific Ocean as it traverses the California coast.

SAN JUAN SKYWAY, COLORADO (1996)
The San Juan Skyway snakes through Old West towns like Durango and picturesque Telluride, and Mesa Verde National Park--all in the shadow of impressive 14,000-foot peaks of the Rockies.

TRAIL RIDGE ROAD/BEAVER MEADOW ROAD, COLORADO (1996)
Trail Ridge and Beaver Meadow Roads connect the towns of Estes Park and Grand Lake as they cross through the Rocky Mountain National Park over a distance of 53 miles.

NATCHEZ TRACE PARKWAY, MISSISSIPPI (1996)
Since the late 1930s the National Park Service has been constructing a modern parkway that closely follows the course of the original Natchez, Chickasaw, and Choctaw Indian trail to the northeast, an unhurried route from Natchez to Nashville. The parkway also runs through Alabama and Tennessee.

BLUE RIDGE PARKWAY, NORTH CAROLINA (1996)
Providing spectacular mountain and valley vistas, quiet pastoral scenes, sparkling waterfalls, and colorful flowers and foliage displays, the Parkway extends through the Blue Ridge, Black, Great Craggy, Great Balsam, and Plott Mountains.

HISTORIC COLUMBIA RIVER HIGHWAY, OREGON (1998)
This byway traverses the Gorge, a scenic area that includes the Columbia River.

VOLCANIC LEGACY SCENIC BYWAY, OREGON (1998)
Volcanic features include Crater Lake National Park, wildlife, and a rich cultural history. These make the Volcanic Legacy Byway a spectacular adventure.

NATCHEZ TRACE PARKWAY, TENNESSEE (1996)
Native Americans, Kentucky boatmen, post riders, government officials, soldiers and fortune seekers all moved across this 425-mile trail charting new territory and creating a vital link between the Mississippi Territory and the fledgling United States. The parkway also runs through Alabama and Mississippi.

STATE ROAD 410: STEPHEN MATHER MEMORIAL PARKWAY, WASHINGTON (1998)
Follow SR 140 along the glacier-fed White River from Enumclaw to the fertile valleys of Naches in Central Washington.

ROADS AND BYWAYS *(continued)*

Scenic Byways

SEWARD HIGHWAY, ALASKA (1998)
Situated near Anchorage, the Seward Highway is a 127-mile drive through South Central Alaska which takes you through awesome natural beauty on the way to Seward.

TALLADEGA SCENIC DRIVE, ALABAMA (1998)
In northeast Alabama, the Talladega Scenic Drive is the best and easiest way to view the state's natural treasures from the comfort of your automobile.

CROWLEY`S RIDGE PARKWAY, ARIZONA (1998)
Crowley`s Ridge is the only known erosional remnant in North America. A mixture of plant communities and a diversity of species respond to abrupt changes in soil type, exposure, moisture, and slope.

KAIBAB PLATEAU-NORTH RIM PARKWAY, ARIZONA (1998)
This byway travels along the spectacular north rim of the Grand Canyon

DEATH VALLEY SCENIC BYWAY—ROUTE 190, CALIFORNIA (1998)
This State Scenic Highway crosses the sculptured landscape of Death Valley National Monument, a stark setting which contrasts the lowest elevation in North America with mountain ridges along the valley.

TIOGA ROAD/BIG OAK FLAT ROAD, CALIFORNIA (1996)
Observe a great diversity of flora and fauna as well as craggy mountains and ruffling meadows crossing the Yosemite National Park valley and ridges for 64 miles from east to west.

FRONTIER PATHWAYS SCENIC AND HISTORIC BYWAY, COLORADO (1998)
Historic homesteads, the pristine Wet Mountain Valley, romantic stage-stop ruins, and wildlife viewing pullouts highlight this unspoiled historic and scenic route. This byway is unique for its topographical diversity.

GRAND MESA SCENIC AND HISTORIC BYWAY, COLORADO (1996)
This "playground in the sky" climbs through the dusty canyon of Plateau Creek to the cool evergreen forests of the mesa top, 11,000 feet above sea level. This byway offers the visitor a peek at porcupines, mountain lions, coyotes, red fox, elk and deer.

SANTA FE TRAIL, COLORADO (1998)
This route lets you retrace Colorado's portion of the Santa Fe Trail. This historic trade route saw its heaviest use between 1820 and 1880, but in spring or early summer, the keen observer can still pick out wagon tracks in the prairie grasses.

TOP OF THE ROCKIES SCENIC AND HISTORIC BYWAY, COLORADO (1998)
With altitudes seldom dipping below 9,000 feet, this byway is worthy of its name. It crosses 10,424-foot Tennessee Pass en route to the historic mining town of Leadville, the highest incorporated community in the U.S.

STATE ROUTE 169, CONNECTICUT (1996)
This 32-mile, 25-town route traverses one of the last unspoiled areas in the northeastern United States, with rustic farmlands, forests, farmsteads, open spaces, and historic structures and features.

MERRITT PARKWAY, CONNECTICUT (1996)
Transportation buffs will especially enjoy this corridor`s significant design, which brilliantly integrates the craft of the engineer and the artist.

MEETING OF THE GREAT RIVERS SCENIC ROUTE, ILLINOIS (1998)
The Meeting of the Great Rivers Scenic Route is a 50-mile byway that travels through the southwestern area of Illinois, near Alton.

OHIO RIVER SCENIC ROUTE, ILLINOIS (1998)
This scenic byway travels along the Ohio River through the southern area of Illinois, near Golconda, Metropolis and Cairo.

North Carolina Travel and Tourism

Meg Maguire

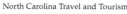
North Carolina Travel and Tourism

ROADS AND BYWAYS *(continued)*

OHIO RIVER SCENIC ROUTE, INDIANA (1996)

Traversing 303 miles through the lush hills and farmlands of southern Indiana and paralleling the mighty Ohio River, this route marks a time-worn and history-rich corridor linking historic villages and farms through a picturesque landscape.

THE NATIONAL ROAD, INDIANA (1998)

Running through the heart of Indiana, the National Road is a primary east/west route.

CREOLE NATURE TRAIL, LOUISIANA (1996)

Highlights of this route include four National Wildlife Refuges, salt and freshwater resources, Civil War and archaeological dig sites, and miles of natural beaches, marshlands, and prairie lands, yielding an abundance of wildlife and scenic appeal.

EDGE OF THE WILDERNESS SCENIC BYWAY, MINNESOTA (1996)

Leave the urban center of Grand Rapids and enter 47 miles of the natural wonders of upper Minnesota, including vistas of flat lowland meadows, swamps and lakes, rolling hills of hardwood forests, and remnants of glaciers long gone.

MINNEAPOLIS GRAND ROUNDS, MINNESOTA (1998)

The Grand Rounds Scenic Byway is a system of lovely trails, paths, and roadways in a totally unique urban setting.

CHEROHALA SCENIC BYWAY, NORTH CAROLINA (1998)

The Cherohala Skyway is located in the western area of the state near Robbinsville in North Carolina.

KANCAMAGUS SCENIC BYWAY, NEW HAMPSHIRE (1996)

This 45-kilometer "living museum" of trees and plants highlights the natural elements and their relationship with development, telling an ongoing story of forest regrowth and ecology.

WHITE MOUNTAINS TRAIL, NEW HAMPSHIRE (1998)

The White Mountains Trail guides the traveler through the North Country area in New Hampshire which possesses all of the intrinsic qualities.

BILLY THE KID SCENIC BYWAY, NEW MEXICO (1998)

Follow the ghosts of famous lawmen, outlaws and warriors through the rugged beauty of the million-acre Lincoln National Forest.

EL CAMINO REAL, NEW MEXICO (1998)

During colonial years, New Mexico was tied to the outside world by this one thoroughfare, El Camino Real, which descended the Rio Grande valley from Santa Fe on its way to Mexico City to the south.

JEMEZ MOUNTAIN TRAIL, NEW MEXICO (1998)

Just north of Albuquerque is one of New Mexico's most spectacular scenic drives. It is a journey through time. It takes you past amazing geologic formations, ancient Native-American ruins, a Native-American pueblo, and the area's logging, mining, and ranching heritage.

SANTA FE TRAIL, NEW MEXICO (1998)

The Santa Fe Trail was the first of America's great Trans-Mississippi routes.

LAKE TAHOE EASTSHORE DRIVE, NEVADA (1996)

The nearly 25 miles of Eastshore Drive skirt the edges of Lake Tahoe, providing visitors with breathtaking views of the Lake Tahoe Basin, while the visitor's center offers accounts of the pioneer and Native-American history of the area.

PYRAMID LAKE SCENIC BYWAY, NEVADA (1996)

As the only byway in the nation entirely within a tribal reservation, this route takes the visitor around one of the largest desert lakes in the world and provides a unique opportunity to interact with the Paiute tribe.

SEAWAY TRAIL SCENIC BYWAY, NEW YORK (1996)

This touring route along the coast of the eastern Great Lakes demonstrates the forces of nature through a landscape that was formed by glaciers and shaped by wind and water. Historic and picturesque lighthouses dot the trail throughout.

ROADS AND BYWAYS *(continued)*

OHIO RIVER SCENIC ROUTE, OHIO (1998)
The Ohio River Scenic Route is located in the south and eastern, near and comprising the entire southern border and part of the eastern border of Ohio.

CASCADE LAKES HIGHWAY (HIGHWAY 46), OREGON (1998)
Oregon`s Cascade Lakes Highway has interested visitors for over 50 years.

HIGHWAY 101—PACIFIC COAST SCENIC BYWAY-OREGON SECTION (1998)
This route follows the beautiful Oregon Coast. The drive offers beach and ocean views, rain forests, cliffs, farmlands, and quaint towns.

MCKENZIE PASS/SANTIAM PASS, OREGON (1998)
There are dramatic, close-up views of the most beautiful of the snow capped High Cascade Peaks, two Wild and Scenic Rivers and waterfalls.

OUTBACK SCENIC BYWAY, OREGON (1998)
One of the best routes in Oregon`s Great Basin region that captures all its diversity.

CHEROKEE FOOTHILLS SCENIC BYWAY, SOUTH CAROLINA (1998)
Following an ancient Cherokee path, this beautiful two-lane road leaves I-85 at Gaffney, makes a 130-mile arc through peach orchards and villages, past Cowpens Battlefield, past several state parks, and over Lake Keowee to meet I-85 again.

SAVANNAH RIVER SCENIC HIGHWAY, SOUTH CAROLINA (1998)
Winding along three major lakes, this road crosses four counties. Spring and fall colors are especially beautiful along this easy-traveling river route. Many recreation areas are along the way.

PETER NORBECK SCENIC BYWAY, SOUTH DAKOTA (1996)
The highlights of this byway include the spectacular Black Hills and Mount Rushmore. The rugged terrain, massive granite outcroppings, and diversity of the landscape are traversed by and through pigtail bridges and narrow tunnels.

THE NATIVE AMERICAN SCENIC BYWAY, SOUTH DAKOTA (1998)
The history of the Sioux and other indigenous peoples unfolds along this byway through cultural, historical, and archeological sites in the heart of the Sioux nation.

CHEROHALA SKYWAY, TENNESSEE (1996)
Cultural heritage and historic sites of the Cherokee tribe and early settlers are offered throughout the skyway in a grand forest environment in the southern Appalachian Mountains.

FLAMING GORGE-UINTAS SCENIC BYWAY, UTAH (1998)
Designated as the state's first National Forest scenic byway in 1988, this route known as "The Drive Through the Ages" travels through the Ashley National Forest and east of Uinta Mountains, one of the few east-west ranges in the country.

NEBO LOOP SCENIC BYWAY, UTAH (1998)
Connecting the cities of Nephi and Payson, this route offers breathtaking views of the Wasatch Mountains and 11,877-foot Mt. Nebo, the tallest mountain in the range. There are many scenic overlooks and the fall foliage is spectacular.

MOUNTAINS TO SOUND GREENWAY, WASHINGTON (1998)
The 101-mile drive along the Mountains to Sound Greenway is a popular traverse through the northwest area of Washington near Seattle.

COAL HERITAGE TRAIL, WEST VIRGINIA (1998)
Located in the southern part of the state between Beckley, Welch, and Bluefield.

HIGHLAND SCENIC BYWAY, WEST VIRGINIA (1996)
This highway in the Monongahela National Forest traverses through river valleys and up onto mountain ridges, providing breathtaking vistas as well as scenic walks through mountain bogs and cranberry glades.

Source: www.byways.org, 12/16/99

Scenic America

While several state-level byway programs existed prior to the national program, this new federal requirement has led to the formation and enhancement of state scenic byway programs across the country.

North Carolina has actively developed a scenic roadways program since the late 1980s, prior to the creation of the national program, and in that time has designated 38 scenic byways. Activities underway in the state demonstrate the wide range of byway-related activities made possible through ISTEA funding.

In June 1998 a major new piece of federal legislation, the Transportation Equality Act for the 21st Century (TEA-21), gave permanent status to the national byways program and doubled the program's funding. Whereas ISTEA had awarded $74.3 million to the national scenic byways program, TEA-21 allocated $148 million. All-American Roads and National Scenic Byways receive priority consideration for these funds, which are used to develop programs and services such as scenic pullovers, special signage, and additional lanes to handle increased traffic. TEA-21 also designated three new All-American Roads and 30 new National Scenic Byways.

The national byways program also provides a wealth of materials to assist state and local officials in managing byways. The Byways Clearinghouse Online is a national library and reference center on the Internet established to serve as a central source of information on scenic byway programs and issues (www.byways.org). The comprehensive website includes case studies, corridor management plan information, lists of frequently asked questions about scenic byways programs, and opportunities for on-line discussion.

State scenic roadway programs. Roads must first be recognized at the state level as important scenic highways before they can receive one of the national designations. While several state-level byway programs existed prior to the national program, this new federal requirement has led to the formation and enhancement of state scenic byway programs across the country.

Florida, for example, had no official state program prior to ISTEA but, in 1993, established the Florida Scenic Highway Program. Since then, the state has created an impressive system designed to encourage identification and protection of byways based on community-based consensus and partnerships. State transportation officials hope to use the program to promote economic development and recreational opportunities, as well as to protect and enhance scenic resources.

The program is a model of a bottom-up, grassroots approach to byway protection. Civic groups, businesses, and government leaders become "partners" to identify potential corridors for protection. These partners form a coalition officially known as a Corridor Advocacy Group (CAG). The CAG navigates the formal designation process, including working with the state to prepare an application and a Corridor Management Plan. Once a byway is designated, the CAG establishes a Corridor Management Entity to handle implementation of the plan and ensure long-term maintenance and monitoring. Annual reports are required to keep the state apprised of progress in implementing the plan and protecting the corridor. Tools are available from the state to assist with development and implementation of a management plan, and the state also provides marketing materials to help CAGs communicate the stories of their individual byway to the public.

North Carolina has actively developed a scenic roadways program since the late 1980s, prior to the creation of the national program, and in that time has designated 38 scenic byways. Activities underway in the state demonstrate the wide range of byway-related activities made possible through ISTEA funding. For example, under the leadership of Scenic North Carolina, the state program has produced a booklet, *North Carolina Scenic Byways*, which provides a guided tour along each designated byway in the state, plus historical information, geographical descriptions, and lists of cultural attractions. The state also has used ISTEA funds to promote handmade crafts in the state's western mountain region located near byways; improve access to the Nantahalah River, a popular spot for rafting; construct educational kiosks along byways; and develop audio tapes to guide travelers along the historically rich routes of the state's coast.

A continuing area of controversy in many states is the extent to which billboards should be allowed on state-designated scenic byways. Currently, the federal Highway Beautification Act prohibits new billboards along designated scenic byways that are interstate, part of the National Highway System, or federal-aid primary roads. However, in very limited circumstances, where areas contain none of the byway's intrinsic qualities, states may exclude such blighted portions of these roads from designation. Billboard companies attempt to exploit this provision in the hopes that scenic designation will have no effect on their ability to construct new billboards. Indeed, the industry has suggested that *all* commercial and industrial areas should be exempt from scenic designation. The issue leads to what scenic resource advocacy groups call "segmentation": a scenic byway disrupted by unsightly billboards that corrupt the continuous character of the roadway.

The problem of segmentation may be solved by encouraging your state to adopt legislation to erase the loophole in the federal law. States are free to adopt regulations on billboards that are more restrictive than the minimum standards set under the Highway Beautification Act. Scenic America has proposed the following model language for adoption at the state level: "State scenic byways shall be continuous in designation; no exclusions shall be permitted along the designated corridor." If complete continuity is not possible, the organization suggests the following language:

> The scenic byway corridor shall be as continuous as possible. Selected sections of a byway may be excluded if all of the following conditions are present:
>
> * The section of the roadway is zoned for commercial or industrial use;
>
> * The section of the roadway contains substantial and ongoing commercial or industrial use, and those uses are visible from the main traveled way;
>
> * The section of the roadway contains none of the intrinsic qualities for which a scenic byway may be designated; and
>
> * The local byway sponsor has requested the exclusion and demonstrated that the section of the roadway meets the three above conditions.

Scenic roadway protection at the local level. Local jurisdictions have been regulating roadside aesthetics for some time. The mountain resort community of Park City, Utah, for example, embarked in 1995 on a major effort to address concerns about its rapid growth. The continuing magnitude and increasing density of development in the city and its immediate environs had given rise to a growing fear that growth would irreversibly alter the community's distinctive character and informal way of life. As part of this larger growth management project, the city undertook a program to better define and protect its major entryways. Specifically, it installed tastefully designed entry signs at major gateways to announce that visitors are entering Park City, landscaped highway medians in strategic locations as prominent and tangible signals of the city's commitment to an attractive environment, and enacted special setback and landscaping controls on development in entryways.

RECENT DEVELOPMENTS

The field of view protection regulation is expanding as quickly as any of the topics addressed in this report (except, perhaps, regulation of telecommunications facilities). Increasingly, view protection is seen as an impor-

A continuing area of controversy in many states is the extent to which billboards should be allowed on state-designated scenic byways.

States are free to adopt regulations on billboards that are more restrictive than the minimum standards set under the Highway Beautification Act. Scenic America has proposed the following model language for adoption at the state level: "State scenic byways shall be continuous in designation; no exclusions shall be permitted along the designated corridor."

Increasingly, the public is coming to believe that the protection of important viewsheds and view corridors is a necessary component of efforts to protect and enhance rural and small-town character.

Successful programs to protect scenic resources—be they scenic rural highways, historic farmsteads, or urban view corridors—should be supported by adequate documentation of the resources' value. Perhaps the most useful advance in the field of view protection since the original edition of this report was published has been the refinement of various methodologies to assist in identifying and evaluating scenic resources.

tant aspect of rural preservation programs. Also, planners and legal experts are developing new tools, techniques, and programs at a rapid pace to assist communities in their efforts to identify and protect important scenic resources. This concluding section provides a brief review of recent developments.

Preserving Views to Protect and Enhance Rural Character

Jurisdictions are incorporating additional protections into their local development codes to protect features that contribute to rural character, such as undeveloped rolling hills, historic farmsteads, and other scenic features. Increasingly, the public is coming to believe that the protection of important viewsheds and view corridors is a necessary component of efforts to protect and enhance rural and small-town character. As Randall Arendt points out in *Rural by Design*: "Public perception of community character is based largely on what can be seen from an automobile. . . . 'The view from the road' is more than a phrase—for most of us it comprises virtually everything we know about the natural and human-made features of our towns" (Arendt 1994).[5]

Communities have an impressive set of tools already available with which they can protect scenic resources and other components of rural character. In zoning ordinances, for instance, local governments might create sensitive lands overlay districts to impose increased minimum lot sizes and increased setbacks along scenic roadways. Subdivision regulations can impose quality standards on new development to ensure compatibility with local rural character—perhaps, for example, by requiring landscaping in commercial development and larger subdivisions. Communities may use density bonus and density transfer programs to award developers who preserve sensitive lands, including view corridors.

Nonregulatory strategies could include pursuing an aggressive land acquisition program to purchase lands (either fee simple or through conservation easements) that have been prioritized based upon their environmental, scenic, and cultural value. Or local governments might work cooperatively with state agencies to target future highway expansion outside designated view corridors.

One especially noteworthy tool in this context is cluster development. Cluster zoning is accomplished by transferring development density to suitable portions of a parcel through on-site clustering. Sensitive areas on the site—traditionally farmland or important natural features such as wetlands or wildlife habitat—are protected from development. Increasingly, local governments are using clustering to protect scenic vistas.

The benefits of clustering are well-documented: Clustering can preserve land without severely limiting development rights, and it encourages innovative, environmentally sensitive design. There are disadvantages, however, most notably that sophisticated planning staffs are required to assess site layouts, and potential political opposition may emerge from landowners who do not want cluster developments as neighbors. Further, encouraging cluster development as a panacea to poor site design can actually promote development in areas where none should occur at all.

New Methodologies for Scenic Resource Assessment and Management

Successful programs to protect scenic resources—be they scenic rural highways, historic farmsteads, or urban view corridors—should be supported by adequate documentation of the resources' value. Perhaps the most useful advance in the field of view protection since the original edition of this report was published has been the refinement of various methodologies to assist in identifying and evaluating scenic resources. Manuals, regimes, and programs, both simple and sophisticated, are now available to allow for the accurate estimation, description, and management of scenic resources. Importantly, the development of these new methodologies helps to establish a much firmer legal basis for view protection because it makes the selection and evaluation of scenic resources more rational and less arbitrary.

One example is a recent Scenic America publication entitled "O, Say, Can You See: A Visual Awareness Tool Kit for Communities." Developed by Scenic America in conjunction with the landscape architecture faculty of the State University of New York at Syracuse, this booklet features 16 tools for promoting and enhancing visual awareness at the local level. One tool, for instance, is photographing visual awareness; the section includes a discussion of how, by taking photographs, people can record special places and landscape features to express their visual preferences about their community. The exercise provides an opportunity for participants to "vote with their eyes" about what features they value in their surroundings.

A simple evaluation process for scenic resources. Based on experience throughout the country, Scenic America also has developed and refined a more general, five-step approach for identifying and evaluating scenic resources. This approach consolidates much of the theory and practice developed over several decades by planners and landscape designers.[6] This straightforward method should prove useful to community groups, local officials, and others interested in studying scenic resources and evaluating their significance. The approach also provides an information base upon which decisions to protect scenic resources may be adequately defended inasmuch as courts look for factual and rational bases to support land-use regulations.

Because the Scenic America approach is so general, it should be applicable in a wide variety of contexts. Note, however, that the approach is somewhat sophisticated, and complete implementation may often demand more time and/or financial resources than are available. Nevertheless, the approach is presented in its entirety here to demonstrate the necessary thought process that a community should at least attempt to follow as it formulates its own view protection program.

The steps of the Scenic America approach to identifying and evaluating scenic resources include the following.

Step One: Organize the project. The initial phase involves basic organizational tasks, such as developing goals, a workplan, and a timetable for action. Assemble a working group that is small enough to work efficiently, yet large enough to ensure all necessary interests are represented, including landowners and local officials. This group will consider basic tasks, such as defining preliminary study area boundaries, and also more complex tasks, such as identifying the types of information necessary to complete the project and developing a preliminary working definition of what they consider to be "scenic." For example, in one community effort, scenic resources were defined to mean the "shared images of what is special or unique about the region's landscape." Most importantly, the group should agree on the project goals: Why are they conducting the study and how will they apply the results?

Step Two: Understand the regional landscape. After completing initial organization tasks and determining project goals, the working group must develop a better understanding of the natural context in which the project is taking place. Specifically, they must do the following.

- *Map the bioregion.* The working group (or perhaps a technical subgroup) should identify and map the physiographic regions and subregions (the "bioregions") within the study area in order to provide an objective

FOR MORE INFORMATION

Scenic America cites several useful reference works to assist in compiling inventories of bioregions, including:

N.M. Fenneman, *Physiography of the Western United States* (New York: McGraw-Hill, 1931);

N.M. Fenneman, *Physiography of the Eastern United States* (New York: McGraw-Hill, 1938); and

Erwin Raisz, *Landforms of the United States*, 6th ed., 1957.

Most states also have reference works describing their particular bioregions.

look at the larger area within which the specific study area may be examined. Focus not just on the landscape (e.g., major landforms, dominant vegetation), but also on the major uses to which the land has been put (e.g., agricultural patterns, historic and cultural resources).

- *Map landscape districts.* Subdivide the overall bioregion into smaller units, known as landscape districts, based on natural boundaries like watershed boundaries or major landforms.

- *Map place units.* If possible, further subdivide landscape districts into place units, which are smaller areas of distinct visual character that are spatially enclosed by landforms, vegetation, or other features. Whereas landscape districts may be an appropriate unit of analysis for large scenic byways extending hundreds of miles, place units may be more appropriate for analyzing, for example, an individual farmstead.

- *Record features and document community interests.* Document key features of the landscape using maps and photography. Interviews with residents will help pinpoint the most locally significant visual resources and their cultural context.

Step Three: Identify key resources. Following Step Two, identify the key features that make the scenic resources valuable to the local community. Key tasks during this part of the process are listed here.

- *Review district and place unit boundaries.* Boundaries and place names selected by the working group should be verified with the public, ideally in a workshop setting with ample opportunity for discussion.

- *Finalize maps and review resources.* The public should elaborate upon why they find the scenic resources at issue to be significant, what makes them distinct, and how they fit into the larger environmental context of the bioregion and the historical context of the local culture. What specific features are important? Such features, known as the primary or intrinsic landscape resources of the study area, are what will be evaluated to determine the scenic quality of the place units. These features should be reflected on final maps of the place units (or landscape units, if that scale is more appropriate to the project).

Step Four: Determine scenic value. The most important step is an evaluation of the scenic value of the key resources that have been identified. This step includes the following tasks.

- *Choose evaluation criteria and develop a rating scale.* Based upon the project goals developed in Step One, select criteria upon which to evaluate the key resources. Sample categories of inquiry include:

  - magnitude (How expressive or abundant are the resources?);

  - distinctiveness (How unique or representative are they of the region?);

  - intactness (How disturbed are they compared to a natural state?);

  - draw (How much of a draw are they for tourist-related activities, education and interpretation, or economic development; how important are they to community identity?);

  - opportunity (Are there opportunities of the moment for protection or restoration that might suggest action? Would they be important as scenic resources if improved?); and

IDENTIFYING AND EVALUATING SCENIC RESOURCES

- **Step One:** Organize the project.

- **Step Two:** Understand the regional landscape.

- **Step Three:** Identify key resources.

- **Step Four:** Determine scenic value.

- **Step Five:** Develop an action plan.

• preference (Do people prefer certain place units over others? How do they value the characteristic features that are commonly found in these place units?);

• *Evaluate the place units.* Evaluate each of the key resources within each place unit identified in Step Three against the criteria selected. Values should be added to each criterion, and sum totals should be developed for each place unit. The sum score represents the scenic quality of an individual place unit as compared to other place units in the study area. A higher score represents a higher level of scenic quality. The total scores obtained should be analyzed to determine the scenic quality of each landscape district or place unit (i.e., which resources are most scenic, and which are less so). If possible, attempt to discern patterns in the rankings that may allow for prioritization in development of an action plan.

Step Five: Develop an action plan. Once the scenic resources have been systematically identified and evaluated, the final stage is the development of a plan for action—in other words, a plan by which the scenic resources may be managed and protected for the long term. Successful implementation depends upon making protection of the resources a key factor in the decision making of the governments and individuals that control the resources.

The strongest action plans will include a judicious blend of both regulatory and nonregulatory tools. As already noted, potential regulatory mechanisms might include overlay zoning districts, which layer enhanced restrictions (e.g., building height limits) on top of existing base zoning regulations in designated scenic areas, and tree and vegetation conservation ordinances that restrict the amounts and types of trees and vegetation that can be removed during new construction. Nonregulatory tools might include an optional density transfer program or a public education campaign. Extensive and continuing citizen involvement, both from the public and private sectors, is the key to success for the Scenic America approach and other similar methodologies.

The Scenic America approach provides a highly useful, generalized framework for identifying and evaluating scenic resources. A recent project in Adirondack State Park, New York, provides a more specific example of how planners may gather and manage visual resource information using Geographic Information System (GIS) technology.[7]

In 1996, with a grant from the New York State Scenic Byways Program, the Adirondack Park Agency funded the development and testing of a methodology to document and assess visual resources along roadways in the huge Adirondack Park (more than 6 million acres).[8] The project was considered crucial because of spotty identification of scenic resources in the past, and a continuing need to conserve and protect the park's scenic corridors to maintain its unique natural features and the local tourism-based economy. The project resulted in the creation of a Visual Resource Inventory that the agency hopes will be a valuable tool for collecting data for road corridor management planning, establishing a database for scenic byway designations, and identifying and maintaining a record of Regional Vistas on the park's land-use map.

The heart of the Adirondack Park project involved gathering data along all roadways within the study area at increments of one-tenth mile. Data were collected in several formats, including a geographic point indicator (based on highway mile markers), a visual inventory form, photographs of the road corridor, and supplementary photographic views. Resource information characteristics were gathered in the following categories.[9]

FOR MORE INFORMATION

The Visual Resource Inventory and Assessment Methodology for Adirondack Road Corridors was produced by the Adirondack Park Agency Scenic Byways Project. Contact:

New York State Adirondack Park Agency
P.O. Box 99
Ray Brook, NY 12977
518-89-4050.

Natural Features

● General considerations (view size, view length, accessibility, orientation, view framing)

● Landform considerations (elevation, slopes, number of peaks visible to viewer, rock form, shape variation)

● Vegetation considerations (quantity and diversity, and size of fields)

Human Disturbances

● Utility poles (e.g., visibility, pole type, number)

● Signs (visibility, number)

● Land disturbance (location, size)

● Human structures (number of structures and proximity to vantage point)

Each resource information characteristic was ranked on a scale of 1 to 10 (10 being highest), and these scores were in turn grouped into high, medium, and low categories. Data was collected manually in the field, and entered in laptop computers at the time of observation. A total score equaled a composite of both positive (e.g., picturesque mountain streams) and negative (e.g., utility poles) features. The resulting total scores were incorporated into a computerized GIS program that created a new data layer featuring important visual resources, categorized by relative scenic value. This data layer now may be combined with other data layers (e.g., wildlife habitat). Park planners may use the information when making future land-use decisions, and private citizens will find it useful in to prepare future scenic road applications and to promote tourism.

The Adirondack experience demonstrates the tremendous possibilities involved in incorporating scenic resources into GIS systems. GIS allows planners to create new data layers of scenic resources, to be studied and applied alongside other important areas of concern, including sensitive environmental resources (e.g., steep slopes, wildlife habitat, wetlands), current land uses and zoning, and proposed future land uses. Planners may use this increasingly multifaceted body of information to make much more sophisticated and knowledgeable recommendations about how future development should occur.

Notes

1. The Virginia Advisory Commission on Intergovernmental Relations is undertaking the study in response to House Joint Resolution No. 477, February 1997. The study aims to determine the effect of view protection efforts on the economy and quality of life in the state.

2. For an in-depth discussion of the use of police power to protect scenic landscapes, including a discussion of the position of a minority of states (i.e., aesthetic value alone is not sufficient justification to invoke the police power), see Mark Bobrowski, "Scenic Landscape Protection Under the Police Power," *Boston College Environmental Affairs Law Review* 22, 697.

3. In one case involving a challenge to height controls imposed by a view protection ordinance, the court ruled that aesthetic considerations alone were enough to uphold the provision of a shoreline management act that limited the height of buildings to 35 feet so as not to obstruct the view of certain lakes. See *State Dept. of Ecology v. Paceset-*

ter Construction Co., 571 P.2d 196 (Wash. 1977). For other examples, see *Wilkinson v. Board of County Commissioners of Pitkin County*, 872 P.2d 1269 (Colo. App. 1993); *Arkules v. Board of Adjustment of Town of Paradise Valley*, 728 P.2d 657 (Ariz. Ct. App. 1986); and *Ross v. City of Rolling Hills Estates*, 238 Cal. Rptr. 561 (Cal. Ct. App. 1987) (unsuccessful challenges involving viewshed ordinances).

4. A different set issues is raised by the protection of historic roads and are beyond the scope of this report. For a good discussion, see Paul Daniel Marriott, *Saving Historic Roads: Design and Policy Guidelines* (New York: Preservation Press and John Wiley and Sons, Inc., 1998).

5. In addition to *Rural by Design*, see Fred Heyer, *Preserving Rural Character*, Planning Advisory Service Report No. 429 (Chicago: American Planning Association, 1990) and American Farmland Trust, *Saving American Farmland: What Works* (Washington, D.C.: American Farmland Trust, 1997).

6. For detailed information on the Scenic America approach outlined in this section, see Scenic America, "Evaluating Scenic Resources," *Technical Information Series* 3, No.1, 1996.

7. For another recent example, see "A Process for Scenic Quality Analysis Along the Blue Ridge Parkway," March 1997, available from the Community Planner of the Blue Ridge Parkway, Asheville, North Carolina.

8. For a complete summary of the project, see New York State Adirondack Park Agency, *Demonstration of a Visual Resource Inventory and Assessment Methodology for Adirondack Road Corridors*, Scenic Byways Project SBNY-94-09, September 1996.

9. These objective categories were supplemented with one subjective question, asked purely for quality control purposes. This supplemental question asked the field inspector to provide a general impression of the quality of the visual resource, based upon purely personal judgment.

Chapter 4

Tree and Vegetation Protection

The tree which moves some to tears of joy is in the eyes of others only a green thing which stands in the way. . . . But by the eye of a man of imagination, nature is imagination itself.

WILLIAM BLAKE

TREES AND OTHER GREENERY, WHICH DO SO MUCH TO SOFTEN THE ROUGH EDGES OF DEVELOPMENTS, BUILDINGS, AND STREETS, ARE OFTEN OVERLOOKED WHEN CONSIDERING COMMUNITY AESTHETICS. Many citizens do not realize the aesthetic importance of trees until they are gone, felled by disease, neglect, or, more commonly of late, by intensive development. Moreover, increasing evidence suggests that trees contribute in many ways to a more pleasing, safer environment. They help to moderate effects of sun, cold, and wind, and they reduce pollution. They serve as screens against noise, act to stabilize soil, and reduce erosion and run-off, besides being a haven for birds and animals.

There is also growing evidence that tree protection and good landscaping can add greatly to the value of a project by making it more attractive to consumers. In one survey in Hampton, Virginia, more than 80 percent of the respondents said they preferred shopping at a business that had substantial landscaping.

Across the United States, interest is growing in protecting existing trees, particularly in urban areas, for both aesthetic and environmental purposes. A number of local governments have adopted a specific species of street tree as a community hallmark. Tallahassee, Florida, for example, is becoming known as the dogwood capital of the South for its aggressive program of planting dogwoods along streets throughout the city. Other communities have gone farther, adopting tree preservation ordinances and detailed landscaping requirements.

Indeed, protecting trees, woodlands, and vegetation through municipal ordinances is one of the fastest-growing areas of land-use law, and local governments are enacting increasingly strict and sophisticated regulations. No longer satisfied with saving publicly owned street trees or large specimen trees on private property, these new regulatory regimes often require protection of smaller trees or large tracts of woodlands, and even require off-site mitigation if trees are destroyed during construction. In practice, these regulations affect the development process every step of the way, from subdivision to site design, through construction to long-term maintenance.

Based on experience to date, it is clear that an increasing number of communities will adopt tree and vegetation protection laws to preserve visual character, environmental resources, and quality of life. Their actions are triggered by the very real threat that, if steps are not taken immediately, irreplaceable losses of trees and vegetation will occur in many parts of the country. Abundant evidence can be found in the U.S. Department of Agriculture's recently released National Resources Inventory, a report on the health of America's private land, which accounts for about 70 percent of the land in the United States. According to the report, the country is now losing 3 million acres of agricultural and forest land to development each year—double the amount lost each year from 1982 to 1992. Nearly 2 billion tons of soil are eroding into waterways each year, and gross wetland losses have increased to 54,000 acres annually on agricultural land (though some wetlands protection programs are beginning to stem the tide). A summary and the complete text of the USDA's National Resource Inventory report may be found at the department's web site, www.nrcs.usda.gov. In addition, tree and forest cover is declining rapidly. A recent survey conducted by American Forests found that, between 1973 and 1997, more than 1.9 million acres were cleared of heavy forest in the lower Chesapeake Bay watershed (17 percent of the 11.4 million-acre region). The lost trees would have removed 9.3 million pounds of air pollutants annually, and the loss has resulted in an estimated 19 percent increase in runoff from major storms.

This chapter discusses some of the more interesting aspects of municipal tree and vegetation protection ordinances.[1] The first section addresses the key legal questions that tree conservation ordinances can pose, primarily relating to the specificity of review standards and the taking issue. The second section provides an overview of important issues to consider when drafting an effective ordinance and summarizes the wide variety of local regulatory approaches in place throughout the country. While varying widely by jurisdiction, these approaches have some common elements. Protection is often based on size, species, percent lot cover, and similar considerations. Replacement and mitigation requirements are often part of these local laws.

KEY LEGAL ISSUES

Early legal decisions involving trees almost invariably dealt with negligence and valuation issues—a tree limb falling on a neighbor's house causing serious damage, or instances where workmen had erroneously chopped trees down on the wrong property.[2] Few of these cases have much relevance today. The situation has changed dramatically, however, as more and more jurisdictions are adopting tough tree protection ordinances that are being challenged in court.

Courts have been very supportive of these ordinances if drafted in a careful manner. A recent case from Atlanta provides a typical example (*Parking Association of Georgia, Inc. v. City of Atlanta*, 450 S.E.2d 200 (Ga.

Indeed, protecting trees, woodlands, and vegetation through municipal ordinances is one of the fastest-growing areas of land-use law, and local governments are enacting increasingly strict and sophisticated regulations.

The country is now losing 3 million acres of agricultural and forest land to development each year—double the amount lost each year from 1982 to 1992. Nearly 2 billion tons of soil are eroding into waterways each year, and gross wetland losses have increased to 54,000 acres annually on agricultural land (though some wetlands protection programs are beginning to stem the tide).

1994)). The city had adopted a zoning ordinance that imposed landscaping and tree planting requirements on surface parking lots with 30 or more spaces in several downtown and midtown zoning districts. The ordinance required landscaping areas equal to at least 10 percent of the paved area within a lot, ground cover (shrubs, ivy, pine bark, or similar landscape materials), and at least one tree for every eight parking spaces. The Supreme Court of Georgia upheld the ordinance, noting that it was a reasonable exercise of the police power and that "the means adopted have a real and substantial relation to the goals to be attained." Also, while noting that several legitimate purposes underlay the ordinance—including promoting public safety, regulating temperature, and addressing air-quality and water-runoff problems—the court emphasized that aesthetic goals alone would be enough to justify such an ordinance (at 202).

In general, tree protection ordinances tend to raise the same legal issues as the other local land-use controls discussed in this report. Experience shows that they are likely to be challenged primarily on two grounds: vagueness of review standards and the taking issue.

Standards for Permit Reviews

As tree protection regulations become stronger and broader in scope, they are coming under greater scrutiny and will be the focal point of more court challenges. While the trend among most local ordinances is for greater specificity in permit review standards, some still are quite vague. For example, one community's tree preservation law simply says that permits can be issued if steps by an applicant to protect trees are in accord with the intent of the ordinance. Another has rigorous tree replacement requirements but contains no guidance about where those trees are to be replaced on a site. Staff is given total discretion in this area.

While courts in tree preservation cases and most other areas of land-use law have been very favorable to local governments in upholding rather broad review standards, fairness and regulatory efficiency dictate that local ordinances contain clear standards that result in predictable decisions by staff and review commissions and that limit administrative discretion. This is not always an easy task, given the recurring tension between using detailed, precise review standards and the need for flexibility and administrative discretion in dealing with developments that can vary greatly from case to case.

Most modern tree protection ordinances require a developer or landowner to obtain a permit before undertaking specified activities, such as vegetation clearance or tree removal. As discussed throughout this report, courts are generally quite deferential to local governments in setting and applying environmental regulatory standards or design regulations (e.g., those involving the protection of historic resources). For example, in *Watson v. City of St. Petersburg*, 489 So.2d 138 (Fla. App. 1986), the property owner brought an action challenging the constitutionality of a tree ordinance on the grounds that permit review standards to be applied by the city manager were vague and did not provide any guidelines to aid in interpreting key terms. Specifically, the ordinance stated that the permit had to be denied if the tree removal had a "significant adverse impact" on the environment in eight listed areas. For example, the permit was to be denied if the tree removal "will substantially alter the water table adversely . . ." or "will significantly increase ambient noise levels. . . ."

The plaintiff argued that terms such as "significantly" and "substantially" were deficient and that the ordinance failed to provide any standards or guidelines to interpret them. The court disagreed, however, pointing out that the ordinance contained eight specific grounds for denial,

> While courts in tree preservation cases and most other areas of land-use law have been very favorable to local governments in upholding rather broad review standards, fairness and regulatory efficiency dictate that local ordinances contain clear standards that result in predictable decisions by staff and review commissions and that limit administrative discretion.

including ground and surface water stabilization, water quality and aquifer recharge, ecological impacts, noise pollution, air movement, air quality, wildlife habitat, and aesthetic degradation. Thus, the relatively vague terms found clear definition and explanation in more detailed criteria for assessing the impacts of removal.

A vagueness challenge to tree harvesting performance standards also failed in *Town of Freeport v. Brickyard Cove Associates*, 594 A.2d 556 (Me. 1991). Brickyard Cove, a development company, owned a heavily wooded, 24-acre waterfront parcel in a zone designated Resource Protection District under the town's zoning ordinance. The district regulations allowed timber harvesting subject to performance standards, which included the requirement that harvesting leave behind a "well-distributed stand of trees" and that harvesting not create "single openings greater than 7,500 square feet in the forest canopy." Harvesting operations also had to be conducted in such a manner and at such a time to minimize soil disturbance. The ordinance furthermore dictated adequate measures to prevent soil erosion and sedimentation.

Brickyard Cove sought permission for timber harvesting and was informed that such harvesting was a permitted use subject to the performance standards. The developer proceeded to clear-cut most of the site, causing serious soil erosion and silt in the stream and cove areas where trees and vegetation had been clear-cut. After Brickyard Cove refused to implement a proposed restoration plan, the town sued.

The trial court entered judgement for the town, holding that the activity constituted clear-cutting, not timber harvesting. The court imposed the maximum civil penalty of $2,500, awarded attorney's fees, and ordered the developer to implement the town's restoration plan. On appeal, Brickyard Cove argued, among other things, that the absence of a definition for the performance standard term "well-distributed stand of trees" left the ordinance too vague to be enforceable because there was no way for its employees to know that clear-cutting was not permissible as timber harvesting.

Repeating the common test in such cases—that the ordinance must be sufficiently clear that a person of ordinary intelligence understands what it means—the court explained: "The absence of a definition of a term in an ordinance does not compel a finding of invalidity; it means only that the term will be given its common, everyday meaning unless the context dictates otherwise" (at 558). Applying this rule, the court reasoned that "[T]imber harvesting that left behind a well-distributed stand of trees would leave behind at least *some* trees. . . . It is also consistent with the common sense meaning of 'timber harvesting' as the cutting of timber trees of merchantable size, not clear-cutting" (at 558, emphasis in the original.) The court also ruled that Brickyard Cove had failed to meet the performance standard relating to maximum canopy openings of 7,500 square feet.

This is not to say that local governments should ignore the standards issue or that courts have granted them carte blanche in designating individual trees or portions of sites for preservation or unlimited discretion in reviewing permit applications. The case of *Morristown Road Associates v. Borough of Bernardsville*, 394 A.2d 157 (N.J. Super 1978) discussed above in the chapter on design review, is a good example of what happens when review standards are excessively vague. In that case, the city had adopted a site plan ordinance with standards that a citizen design review committee and the planning board were to apply in reviewing development proposals. Troubled by the lack of definitions in the ordinance for key operative terms, the court struck down the regulations for vagueness.

The Taking Issue

The "taking" issue, familiar to almost anyone involved in local land-use planning and regulation, is a shorthand reference to the Fifth Amendment to the U.S. Constitution's prohibition regarding public use of private property: "nor shall private property be taken for public use without just compensation." This limitation on federal power has been extended to states and local governments through the Fourteenth Amendment. But can a *regulation* of private property, such as a tree-protection ordinance, give rise to a taking?

As noted already in this report, the answer is that, in certain circumstances where a regulation denies an owner of all reasonable economic use of the property or significantly interferes with his or her distinct, investment-backed expectations, the regulation may be recognized as a taking.[3] Several important decisions have been rendered by state supreme courts demonstrating that the new generation of tough tree control ordinances may indeed spark constitutional controversy in the takings context. These decisions, discussed below, stand as a sober caution to local governments considering strict tree protection provisions and emphasize the need for careful thinking in drafting regulations.

Early taking/tree protection decisions. Although few courts dealt with tree protection regulations before the 1980s, two decisions do stand out that provide an important historical context for modern decisions. The first, *Miller v.*

Several important decisions have been rendered by state supreme courts demonstrating that the new generation of tough tree control ordinances may indeed spark constitutional controversy in the takings context. These decisions . . . stand as a sober caution to local governments considering strict tree protection provisions and emphasize the need for careful thinking in drafting regulations.

Schoene, 276 U.S. 272 (1928), was decided by the U.S. Supreme Court in 1928. The facts of the case are interesting. Faced with the destruction of the state apple crop by a fungus carried by red cedar trees, the State of Virginia enacted legislation authorizing the destruction of any cedars located on private property within two miles of an apple orchard *without* compensation. Noting that apples were one of the principal agricultural products of the state generating millions of dollars for the economy and many jobs and that red cedars had little commercial value, the Court held that the state had not exceeded its constitutional authority by declaring red cedars a public nuisance subject to being destroyed and prohibiting their planting.

The second case involved an advisory opinion to a state legislature considering tree protection legislation. In *re Opinion of the Justices,* 69 A.627 (Me. 1908), the Maine Senate asked whether it could regulate the cutting or destruction of trees on private land for a variety of environmental purposes without paying compensation. Focusing on the goal of the proposed legislation, which would be to prevent use of private property that would be injurious to citizens generally, the court concluded "We think it a settled principle, growing out of the nature of well-ordered civil society, that every holder of property, however absolute and unqualified may be his title, holds it under the implied liability that his use of it may be so regulated that it shall not be injurious . . . to the rights of the community."

In sum, these early cases supported strong tree protection efforts by government through police power regulation without payment of compensation.

Modern taking/tree protection decisions. While a significant majority of decisions involving tree and vegetation protection and related issues, such as open space preservation, have been strongly favorable to local governments, one important decision does sound a warning note. For that reason, it is discussed first, followed by an examination of those more typical cases in which takings claims are rejected.

Probably the most important adverse decision is *Allingham v. City of Seattle*, 749 P.2d 160 (Wash. 1988). The facts of the case are all-important and deserve detailed discussion. The City of Seattle enacted a Greenbelt Ordinance in 1984 that regulated development in numerous designated greenbelt areas throughout the community. The greenbelts were primarily linear bands of undeveloped, treed hillsides covering approximately 900 acres, about half of which were privately owned.

The ordinance created an overlay zone that imposed new regulations upon existing zoning restrictions. It required that owners of lots in excess of 5,000 square feet reserve 50 percent of their site in an undisturbed state called a "greenbelt preserve," and replant an additional 20 percent of the lot to create a restored greenbelt preserve. Lots less than 5,000 square feet and those in industrial districts were subjected to lesser, but still substantial, open space and restoration requirements. The ordinance also set forth criteria for determining the specific locations of the greenbelt preserves, primarily to ensure contiguity of the entire greenbelt. Under certain limited circumstances, the size of the greenbelt could be reduced administratively.

A group of landowners affected by the ordinance commenced an action seeking to have it declared invalid as a taking of private property and in violation of the due process and equal protection requirements of the state and federal constitutions. At trial, it came to light that the city had actually adopted a policy in 1954 to acquire greenbelts throughout the community. A number of parcels were acquired, but funds from a bond issue proved inadequate. Thereafter, the city adopted a regulatory approach.

In addition to this fact, which weakened the city's case by calling into question the "character" of the government's action, the situation of sev-

eral of the plaintiffs clearly had an impact on the trial court judge. One such plaintiff was a 74-year old woman on a fixed income who worked at McDonald's restaurant to make ends meet. She wanted to sell her property but could not because of the new ordinance and could not afford the cost of filing a variance application. She had paid taxes on the property for 50 years. The named plaintiffs, the Allinghams, had purchased their property in 1955 as a nest egg for retirement. The land was located in a lower-middle-class neighborhood where people wanted yards for their kids to play and to store recreational vehicles and boats. The Allinghams testified that the property had no value without a cleared yard, yet the ordinance required them to leave potential yard space as an undisturbed, dense thicket. Additionally, crime in the area was high, and homeowners wanted cleared open space around their houses to deter burglars.

Not surprisingly, the trial court judge held for the plaintiffs. Pointing out that the city regulated only when it ran out of money, the court ruled that a taking had been effected because the ordinance destroyed 70 percent of all value and had only narrow exemptions. Moreover, the judge railed against the ordinance's practical effect: "The requirement that children must play in an area covered with brambles and thickets is oppressive."

The trial court also ruled that the clustering of development permitted under the ordinance did not save the ordinance since there was little demand for high-density projects, and the state environmental policy act would thereby be triggered, further complicating any proposal. Instead, the court suggested a number of less restrictive ways to accomplish the city's goals, including purchase of easements, tax incentives, socioeconomic exceptions, taking a smaller percentage of the property, or adopting less intrusive restrictions.

On appeal, the city argued that the plaintiffs should have applied for administrative relief before commencing a lawsuit. While there was ample legal authority supporting this position, the Supreme Court of Washington ruled that the "available administrative remedies are patently inadequate to relieve the hardship imposed by the ordinance." The court then found that, while there was no doubt that the ordinance served a host of legitimate public interests, it constituted a taking of property in violation of both the state constitution and the U.S. Constitution:

> . . . the ordinance deprives certain landowners of all profitable use of a substantial portion of their land. Under the ordinance, 50 to 70 percent of certain lots must be preserved in or returned to a natural state. . . . Although he still holds title to the property reserved as greenbelt land, he is denied the control over his property typically accorded landowners.

In response to the decision, the city adopted new greenbelt regulations that substituted performance standards for the specific open space retention percentages.

Legal commentators were highly critical of one aspect of the decision: the refusal of the Washington Supreme Court to consider the city's argument that the remaining 30 percent of any lot could be put to profitable use, and therefore the owner had not been deprived of *all* profitable use as was generally thought to be required by prior federal and state court decisions. Indeed, in a landmark U.S. Supreme Court taking decision decided in 1978, the Court laid down this rule:

> Takings jurisprudence does not divide a single parcel into discrete segments and attempt to determine whether rights in a particular segment have been entirely abrogated. In deciding whether a particular governmental action has effected a taking, this Court focuses both on the character of the action and on the nature of the interference with rights *in the parcel as a whole.* . . . (*Penn Central Transportation Co. v. New York City*, 438 U.S., at 130–131, emphasis added)

Interestingly, just two years later in a case rejecting a challenge to regulations protecting wetland vegetation, the Washington Supreme Court overruled the *Allingham* decision to the extent that it suggested the taking analysis did not view the economic impact on the parcels in question in their entirety, only on the 70 percent restricted area (*Presbytery of Seattle v. King County*, 787 P.2d 907 (Wash. 1990)).

> With the exception of this court's recent decision in *Allingham v. Seattle*, neither state nor federal law has divided property into smaller segments of an undivided parcel of regulated property to inquire whether a *piece* of it has been taken. . . . Rather, we have consistently viewed a parcel of regulated property in its *entirety.* . . . To the extent that *Allingham* is inconsistent with the foregoing analysis, it is hereby overruled. Additionally, to the extent that *Allingham* equates a physical taking of an owner's land with a regulation upon its use, it is also expressly overruled. (at 915, emphasis in the original)

Notwithstanding these second thoughts, the *Allingham* case teaches some important lessons:

- Any hint that a tree protection regulatory scheme is being adopted as a substitute for a public acquisition program can be deadly in a legal challenge.

- Inflexible standards, coupled with a lack of administrative relief provisions, are a recipe for judicial intervention. Variance provisions should provide realistic opportunities for development. Incentives, such as allowing transfer of development rights or reductions in property taxes, might help take the sting out of regulations in extreme cases.

- Local ordinances should contain some sort of procedure to help ascertain when the regulatory impact is close to effecting a taking.

While the *Allingham* decision is troublesome to local governments in these regards, it does not reflect the strong view in a majority of states towards tree protection ordinances with respect to the taking issue. Cases like *Glisson v. Alachua County, Florida,* 558 So.2d 1030 (Fla. App. 1 Dist. 1990) are more in the mainstream.

In *Glisson*, Alachua County (Gainesville, Florida) undertook an extensive study of the Cross Creek area, which contains the site of the Marjorie Kinnan Rawlings home (a state historic site) and is punctuated with lakes, wetlands, upland habitat, and hammock zones. Most of the area is undeveloped and is home to much wildlife and many species of birds, including bald eagles. The area is surrounded by a state wildlife management area and two large lakes that have been designated as Outstanding Florida Waters.

As a result of the study, the county adopted an extensive vegetation protection and development control plan to address increasing growth and subdivision of land in the area. Construction in wetland areas was prohibited, with minor exceptions. One dwelling unit per five acres was permitted in sections designated as upland conservation areas; lot sizes could not exceed one acre and the remaining four acres had to be protected in their natural state. Removal of native vegetation was severely restricted except for bona fide agricultural purposes, and vegetated buffer zones were established around lakes, critical wildlife habitat, and scenic roads. In the vil-

lage periphery zone, one dwelling unit per five acres was permitted, again with clustering to preserve the most sensitive or unique areas. Active use zones were designated as areas having comparatively little ecological value and were to be the focus of future development. A system to allow transfer of development rights to sites outside the Cross Creek area also was created.

The plaintiffs, all of whom had expended substantial sums seeking development approval prior to adoption of the ordinance, sued. They claimed the regulations were not valid police power enactments and resulted in an unconstitutional taking of their property because they required the owners to maintain the status quo with regard to present uses of the property in order to preserve an area as a benefit to be enjoyed by the public at large.

On appeal from a lower court ruling for the county, the appellate court had little trouble holding that the vegetation protection provisions and other land-use regulations were valid police power enactments. This was despite the fact that evidence at trial revealed that areas designated for preservation were not unique but found throughout the county and that many had been disturbed either by timbering or agricultural activities.

With regard to the taking issue, while recognizing that the regulations significantly diminished the value of the properties in question, the court ruled this was not enough to establish a taking: "[B]ecause the regulations permit most existing uses of the property and provide a mechanism whereby individual landowners may obtain a variance or transfer of development rights, the regulations on their face do not deny individual landowners all economically viable uses of their property." Indeed, the court pointed out that one of the plaintiff property owners had received development approval after filing suit and that his sub-divided lots were sold for a substantial profit.[4]

In sum, the taking issue should be of paramount concern in drafting tree protection regulations, particularly those that may result in a large portion of any site being put off limits to development. Procedures should be included in any such ordinance to elicit information about the economics of development with regard to the regulations as applied. Moreover, incentives, development rights credits, and other similar techniques should be considered to help alleviate any potential hardship.

DRAFTING CONSIDERATIONS
Enabling Authority

An essential first step in drafting any type of local land-use ordinance is to confirm that the locality has adequate enabling authority. In the context of tree and vegetation protection, such authority generally can emanate from the following sources.

Specific enabling legislation. Increasingly, state legislatures are enacting legislation that either empowers or requires local governments to adopt tree protection laws. For example, in Hawaii, state law requires that each county enact laws to designate and protect "exceptional" trees (HRS Sec. 58-1 et. seq.). Also, the Maryland legislature has adopted strong tree protection legislation that requires each county to enact comprehensive development review and regulatory programs that are set forth in detail in the state law (Maryland Natural Resources Section 5-1606 (1991)).

Environmental protection. Many states have enacted enabling legislation authorizing or directing local governments to adopt measures necessary to conserve soil, prevent water pollution, protect wildlife habitat and coastal wetlands, and similar environmental goals.[5] While these laws may omit specific mention of tree protection, they often serve as a perfect vehicle for adopting tree preservation ordinances. After all, the link between these goals and tree protection is easily established.

Planning/zoning/subdivision laws. Many communities rely on state enabling legislation for local planning, zoning, subdivision, and other land-use activities in enacting tree protection ordinances. For example, the new Utah state planning and zoning legislation specifically mentions "aesthetics" as a proper purpose of zoning enactments, thus creating wide latitude for local action (Utah Code Annotated Sec.10-9-102 (1991)). Other state laws authorize the regulation of "landscaping," which arguably can be interpreted to cover tree protection. Generally, courts in most jurisdictions have liberally interpreted state land-use enabling legislation to allow a wide variety of local initiatives.[6]

Home Rule/Charter Authority

In the absence of specific enabling legislation or related statutory sources, some local governments will be able to fall back on their general home rule authority to enact a wide range of police power regulations to justify tree protection regulations (Rathkopf 1975, Sec. 13.02 [1] and Sec. 27.04 [3]). Typically, state home rule enabling legislation allows local governments to legislate unless specifically preempted by the state legislature. Similarly, counties and cities with constitutionally or legislatively granted charters may find adequate power there. To illustrate, Broward County, Florida, has enacted extensive tree preservation provisions based on a county charter provision allowing it to establish "minimum standards protecting the environment by prohibiting . . . the destruction of resources of the County."

Sidebar notes:

In sum, the taking issue should be of paramount concern in drafting tree protection regulations, particularly those that may result in a large portion of any site being put off limits to development.

Broward County, Florida, has enacted extensive tree preservation provisions based on a county charter provision allowing it to establish "minimum standards protecting the environment by prohibiting . . . the destruction of resources of the County."

Overall, finding enabling authority to justify extensive local tree protection legislation should not be difficult in most jurisdictions. However, making a conscious effort to define the scope of the preferred legislative program and then identifying the proper authority is a critical first step in any drafting effort.

Establishing a Valid Public Purpose

Because tree protection serves so many important public goals, communities typically invoke a number of purposes in establishing their ordinances. Environmental objectives tend to dominate, although aesthetic rationales are common. From a legal perspective, the purpose/authority section of an ordinance is critical from one very important perspective: Do the purposes for which the ordinance is being enacted comport with available enabling authority? In some jurisdictions, this issue is all-important.

The list of benefits from trees generally break down into four broad categories: aesthetics/livability, environmental values, real estate values, and health benefits. Ample technical information is available in each of these categories to substantiate a valid public purpose (Ebenreck 1989; Scenic America 1992a). Some of the material is quite intuitive and has been documented extensively—the aesthetic benefits of trees on the environment, for example (Arnold 1980; Spirn 1984; Whyte 1980). Also, numerous justifications may be found linking tree preservation to the promotion of various environmental values, including soil erosion (Clark et al 1985; Grey and Deneke 1978), air pollution (Schwab 1992), energy conservation (EPA n.d.), noise buffering (Grey and Deneke 1978), water conservation, and wildlife habitat and ecosystem protection (Rodbell 1991). Too, numerous studies have linked higher home prices to the presence of trees on a site (Fletcher 1991).

While the health benefits of tree preservation is a newer area of inquiry, it nevertheless has been the source of some interesting study in recent years (Hiss 1990). Researcher Roger S. Ulrich, for example, has documented various ways in which the incorporation of natural features into design can promote wellness and stress reduction (Ulrich 1986; Rodbell 1990; Ulrich 1991). Ulrich has demonstrated that, for stressed individuals, viewing natural scenes, such as trees, can trigger broad shifts in feelings toward more positive mental states. Notes Ulrich, "visual exposure to everyday nature scenes produces significant recovery from stress within only about five minutes, as indicated by reduced blood pressure and muscle tension." Trees and vegetation also can play a role in accelerating the recovery of hospital patients. Following one long-term study of such effects, Ulrich (1992) made these observations:

> I found that patients recovering from gallbladder surgery had more favorable postoperative courses if their windows overlooked a small stand of trees rather than a brick wall. Compared to those with the wall view, those with the natural window view had shorter postoperative hospital stays, elicited far fewer negative comments ("patient is upset") in nurses' notes, tended to have lower scores for minor postsurgical complications such as persistent headache or nausea, and needed fewer doses of narcotic pain drugs.

General Regulatory Approaches to Tree Protection

Tree and vegetation protection ordinances usually take one of the following regulatory approaches.

Specimen and special trees. Many jurisdictions require permits for removal or alteration of "special" trees on private property. "Special" is typically defined as those exceeding a certain diameter, size, or other physical parameter. Terms such as "champion" or "monarch" trees may be the operative nomenclature in the local ordinance. Additionally, "special" trees

The list of benefits from trees generally break down into four broad categories: aesthetics/livability, environmental values, real estate values, and health benefits. Ample technical information is available in each of these categories to substantiate a valid public purpose.

may be defined to include those with special historical associations (for example, a treaty may have been signed under a tree's boughs).[7] Some communities maintain big-tree registries much like lists of landmark buildings. Others rely on identification through surveys required during the site planning process as outlined in the previous section.

Size. Probably the most common approach to protecting significant trees is to require protection of all specimens that exceed certain physical specifications. In Austin, Texas, for example, a "protected tree" means "any tree having a trunk circumference of 60 inches or more, measured four-and-one-half feet above natural grade level." Other ordinances are similar, but use *diameter* at 4.5 feet above the ground instead of circumference (what is commonly known in the trade as diameter at breast height, or DBH). In Thousand Oaks, California, review is triggered for oak trees exceeding just two inches DBH.

While trunk size specification is a simple and straightforward way of protecting trees, it can be very imprecise and result in protection of some trees not worthy or miss others that are. Thus, while an oak with a DBH of one foot is not particularly unusual, a dogwood of that size is quite remarkable. To deal with this issue, an increasing number of jurisdictions are establishing variable size specifications depending on the species of the tree.

Species. Another protection criterion, although far less common than size, is tree species. Some communities, like Thousand Oaks, California, concentrate their protection efforts on only one species of tree—needless to say, in this instance, oak trees. Tampa, Florida, focuses its specimen tree protection efforts on 12 species, although others can be protected by the parks department upon adoption of appropriate standards. A variation on this approach gaining more adherents is to protect all native vegetation to the maximum extent possible.

In 1994, species protection provisions were upheld in a case involving a Beaufort, South Carolina, tree conservation ordinance (*Sea Island Scenic Parkway Coalition et al. v. Beaufort County Board of Adjustments and Appeals*, 449 S.E.2d 254 (S.C. 1994)). The ordinance established a procedure for the local development review committee to evaluate the impact of any new development on local trees, including trees in general, trees over eight inches in diameter, and specific "endangered or valued" trees, including all live oaks. The ordinance required that a tree survey accompany applications for development permits, showing the "trees proposed for removal." Approval to remove endangered trees would "not normally" be granted, and "every effort" was to be made "in the design and layout of development projects to conserve as many trees as possible."

The development review committee denied a proposed supermarket a development permit in part because the members found its development plan "required excessive tree removal." The plan in fact required the removal of 52 percent of the protected live oak trees on the site. The local Board of Adjustment reversed the denial, however, finding that the number of trees to be removed was not "excessive" and that the development could thus go forward. On appeal, the South Carolina Court of Appeals again reversed the decision, finding that the Board's decision to permit the tree removal was "arbitrary" and "clearly erroneous."

Woodland protection/percent tree cover. Another technique for delineating which resources to protect focuses less on individual trees and more on entire stands or woodlands. While only a few ordinances written prior to 1970 took this approach, it is quickly becoming the method of choice in most jurisdictions that have adopted comprehensive tree protection programs and often is combined with protections for specimen trees. However, because this approach can have a significant economic impact, it is being subjected to increasing judicial scrutiny.

There are various ways of implementing such a requirement. Lake County, Illinois, for instance, requires that a flat 70 percent of mature woodlands on a site and 40 percent of young woodlands be protected as open space. Definitions for mature and young woodlands are provided in the ordinance. Other jurisdictions have adopted milder standards that take into consideration the proposed type of development and specific site constraints. In Fairfax County, Virginia, for instance, a sliding scale is used to determine how many trees and how much natural vegetation (combined) must be preserved: 10 percent minimum cover retention in commercial and industrial districts, 15 percent in high-density residential areas, and 20 percent in lower-density residential areas.

Many communities incorporate such techniques into a comprehensive protection scheme. For instance, a system could be developed in which a minimum percentage of trees and natural vegetation is preserved, subject to the sliding scale requirements, and supplemented by a requirement that all significant trees over a certain size be preserved.

Another popular technique in these ordinances is the delineation of so-called *limits of disturbance*, a very flexible approach that nevertheless provides specific guidance in selecting areas to preserve. For example, Park City, Utah, has adopted a sensitive lands protection ordinance that establishes minimum open space or development setback requirements depending on the type of terrain (e.g., steep slopes) or natural resources (e.g., wetlands) found on a site. The planning staff is then given a good deal of discretion and flexibility to work with the developer to determine limits of disturbance—that is, where development should take place on the site and

Another technique for delineating which resources to protect focuses less on individual trees and more on entire stands or woodlands. While only a few ordinances written prior to 1970 took this approach, it is quickly becoming the method of choice in most jurisdictions that have adopted comprehensive tree protection programs and often is combined with protections for specimen trees.

how much of the parcel should be left undisturbed. Specific criteria, such as erosion control, view protection, and water conservation considerations, are contained in the ordinance to help guide this process.

Hudson, Ohio, also has recently adopted tree and vegetation protection regulations that incorporate the limits of disturbance concept. In brief, the Hudson regulations prohibit the removal of all trees and vegetation outside the approved limits of disturbance except as specifically exempted. Within the limits of disturbance, all trees and vegetation must be preserved to the maximum extent feasible. When site development causes any disturbance outside the limits of disturbance to any vegetation, the disturbed area must be revegetated to preexisting conditions.

Distance/buffer requirements. Another common technique used in determining what to protect involves establishing distance or buffer requirements. For example, some communities adopt regulations requiring a buffer zone (e.g., 100 feet) between major roadways and any buildings on adjacent private property. Within the buffer, all trees and vegetation must be retained, with certain limited exceptions. Existing trees and vegetation retained may be counted toward bufferyard landscaping requirements.

Special area protection. A growing number of communities are focusing their tree and vegetation protection activities on what might be called "special areas": lands with important aesthetic or environmental values that warrant special protection. One of the advantages to this approach is that it is usually easier to garner political support for strong protection measures in areas with unique qualities.

Natural areas, such as rivers and coastal zones, are targeted for protection in some communities. In Fulton County, Georgia, the Chattahoochee River Corridor Tributary Protection Act requires active tree protection in an area "ex-

tending outward 35 horizontal feet from the tops of the banks on both sides of all flowing tributaries of the Chattahoochee River." Disturbed areas within the buffer must be replanted to county standards using indigenous riparian vegetation.

In Sanibel, Florida, native vegetation that contributes to beach stability cannot be removed seaward of a coastal construction control line. Strict controls also are placed on vegetation trimming and stump removal. Where undesirable, nonnative species such as Australian Pine are removed, a revegetation plan must be submitted in order to reduce soil movement caused by wind or water (Sanibel 1991)

Replacement/mitigation standards. Another increasingly common feature of local tree preservation laws are provisions requiring replacement of any trees removed on site, or other mitigation measures such as off-site planting or cash-in-lieu contributions. Most such requirements are based on very specific numerical standards governing the number of trees to be replaced. Fulton County, Georgia, for example, offers specific guidance regarding replacement and mitigation. The quantity of replacement trees must be sufficient to produce a total "site-tree density factor" of no less than 15 units as defined in administrative guidelines (Fulton County 1992). Detailed standards are provided for transplanting and selecting quality replacement stock. Specimen trees must be replaced by species with potential for comparable size and quality.

To the extent that these replanting requirements bear some reasonable relationship to the number of trees removed (for example, more but smaller replacement trees may be required that, when mature and accounting for inevitable losses, will compensate for removal of larger trees), they should withstand challenge.[8] However, such requirements must not be unclear about *where*

the replacement trees should be located and what kind and size they should be.

Construction Protection Measures

Most sophisticated local governments have come to realize that designating trees for protection by strong standards is only half the battle. The best standards being implemented by the most sympathetic developer can be undermined in an afternoon of careless construction activities on a site. Bulldozing near a large tree's roots, digging utility trenches, dumping construction wastes close to a tree—all of these actions can result in the de facto removal of a tree that was designated for preservation. The death may be slower, but it can be just as sure. For example, just a few years ago, it was commonly accepted practice to protect a tree by forbidding any construction activities or excavation within its so-called dripline (a vertical line extending from the outermost edge of the tree canopy to the ground). The latest thinking is that this old standard may not be sufficient given the fact that most trees do not have a single large tap root, but rather a large network of smaller, shallower roots that extend far beyond the dripline.

Local ordinances typically address four critical impacts that construction activities might have on trees:

- *Impact injuries/accidental cutting.* The most common requirement is to use construction fences or barricades around the trunk of the tree or stands of trees.

- *Excavation.* An increasing number of ordinances require tunneling under major tree roots or masses rather than trenching. If trenches are used, then roots must be cut with sharp instruments to reduce potential damage.

- *Grade changes.* Many local ordinances restrict severe grade

changes around trees to prevent damage to roots by smothering their water and oxygen supplies.

- *Other hazards.* Other construction hazards, such as dumping toxic substances or setting fires to clear vegetation, are often addressed in local ordinances.

Maintenance After Development

Once development is complete, the next step in the tree preservation process is continuing maintenance—ensuring that trees protected by the local ordinance survive and flourish. This may entail replacing protected trees that die after construction is completed or requiring periodic fertilizing and pruning until their survival is ensured. Other ordinances require protected and replacement trees to be maintained in a healthy condition with proper fertilization, pruning, and irrigation as necessary for a prescribed period.

While the number of ordinances dealing with the tail-end of the development process is relatively small, more are recognizing that modest measures at this point are important supplements. The ordinances that do address this issue are instructive. The requirements of the tree protection ordinance in Columbia, Missouri, are fairly typical:

> If any of the trees required to be retained or trees planted as part of the landscaping plan should die within a period of eighteen (18) months after completion of the activities associated with the land disturbance permit, the owner of the property shall replace the trees within six (6) months at a ratio of one-to-one with an approved tree having a minimum diameter of two (2) inches measured at a point one foot above natural grade. Shrubbery or other plantings which die within eighteen (18) months of completion of the activities shall be replaced in kind within six (6) months. (City of Columbia, Missouri, Code of Ordinance, Chapter 12A–49 (e))

Given the fact that it takes at least one growing season and typically three years or longer for a tree to show signs of stress and die after construction nearby, 18 months would be a minimum replacement period. In recognition of this fact, Lake County, Illinois, requires posting of a performance bond that is applied "toward the replacement of any trees which should die within three years of the completion of construction" (Lake County Development Code, Section 4401.F.4.)). As an alternative, the developer may establish a tree nursery on site with a specified minimum amount of stock per residential lot and use such stock to replace any trees that die on site within three years.

Exemptions

Most tree protection ordinances provide a variety of exemptions, largely to reduce administrative burdens. Some of the more common are noted here.

- *Residential.* Small-scale and single-lot residential developments are typically exempted. Baton Rouge, Louisiana, for example, exempts all single-family residential development from its tree protection regulations.

- *Agricultural/commercial forestry operation.* Many ordinances exempt, in varying degrees, farming and forestry activities. An increasing number, however, require buffers to be retained and restrict commercial development on a site cleared for agricultural or silvicultural purposes.[9]

- *Parcel size.* Most ordinances have a compliance cut-off based on the size of the proposed development (e.g., two acres or less).

- *Diseased/dangerous trees.* Ordinances almost universally exempt removal of diseased or dangerous trees from regulatory requirements.

- *Other regulations.* Sight distance requirements, sidewalk clearance, or safety measures might also be grounds for exemptions.

For each one of these exemptions, its particular circumstance may make eminent common sense, but communities should think carefully about the overall cumulative impact. If a wooded area is already subdivided into small residential lots, but not yet developed, a blanket exemption for sites less than five acres may result in severe deforestation and loss of habitat. Similarly, wholesale exemption of silvicultural practices may result in the destruction of trees along scenic byways, when a modest buffer requirement that would not unduly hamper forestry operations might have been preferable.

Enforcement

The vast majority of developers will faithfully carry out tree preservation plans. Many will exceed their requirements. However, a few "cowboys" will always test the limits, making it essential that local tree protection ordinances include strong provisions that promise fair but certain enforcement. In practice, very few tree protection enforcement cases go to court, and most are settled through negotiation and compliance or mitigation. One survey revealed that, in the typical program, five violations are detected per year with only an average of one prosecution annually (Coughlin, Mendes, and Strong 1984). Still, enforcement must be a credible probability if potential violators are to be deterred.

Local ordinances take a variety of approaches to enforcement. The most common is to use misdemeanor prosecutions to assess fines and perhaps seek a jail sentence.[10] A second approach, gaining increasing popularity, is to require replacement of felled trees and other mitigation measures. Fur-

Most tree protection ordinances provide a variety of exemptions, largely to reduce administrative burdens. . . . For each one of these exemptions, its particular circumstance may make eminent common sense, but communities should think carefully about the overall cumulative impact.

ther, some communities withhold certificates of occupancy until the property owner complies with tree protection measures.[11]

Finally, some localities are backing up their enforcement provisions by requiring developers to establish conservation escrow accounts up front to ensure completion of tree protection and planting requirements.[12] For instance, Hudson, Ohio, allows developers to make cash payments in lieu of complying with tree replacement standards, and the city places all monies received in an individual conservation escrow account (such funds must be refunded within one year from the completion of construction) (City of Hudson, Land Development Code, Section 1207.02, September 1997)).

Complements to Regulation

Practitioners know that regulations are the backbone of any effective tree protection program. However, experience also shows that companion provisions and programs, including incentives and educational efforts, can help smooth otherwise sharp or rough edges of mandatory controls and standards. Indeed, the most successful tree protection programs are a judicious mix of supplementary approaches.

Local governments have become increasingly savvy in using incentives to take the sting out of tough controls and reward exemplary performance. These include:

- *Landscaping requirement credits.* The most common incentive is to give credit for all trees preserved towards meeting local landscaping requirements.

- *Zoning and planning incentives.* A growing number of communities offer zoning and planning incentives, such as increased densities, reduced setbacks, and density clustering to encourage tree protection.

- *Differential assessment.* Some localities give property tax breaks for protecting large woodlands.

- *Land acquisition.* Some local governments have established aggressive programs to purchase key woodland parcels and forests as complements to regulatory programs.

In addition to these incentive programs, educational efforts can help bring citizens, local government representatives, and the development community together to better understand how best to implement tree protection ordinances. Such efforts can focus on voluntary, as well as regulatory, programs.

For example, East Baton Rouge Parish in Louisiana has created a "Tree Registry of Ancient, Historic, and Unique Trees" in an effort to encourage the voluntary protection of special trees. The parish has enlisted the public to help designate such trees in an effort "to improve public awareness and attitudes regarding the importance of trees and their environment" (East Baton Rouge Parish 1991). The parish defines ancient trees as those that "can be assumed to be a minimum of 100 years of age" and historic trees as those "that can be shown to be of special historic importance by virtue to some connection to a historic or notably important event, person, place, or occasion of significance." Unique trees are those "recognized for a unique quality or qualities which make [them] recognizably special. Determinants include the only known member of a species, exceptional physical character, aesthetic value, or some similar combination of factors." Nominations for inclusion on the registry may be made by any citizen and are reviewed by the local Office of Landscape and Forestry. Announcement ceremonies are held each year on Arbor Day to honor new inductees into the register.

Practitioners know that regulations are the backbone of any effective tree protection program. However, experience also shows that companion provisions and programs, including incentives and educational efforts, can help smooth otherwise sharp or rough edges of mandatory controls and standards.

Notes

1. For an extended discussion of tree and vegetation ordinances, see the document on which this chapter is based, Christopher Duerksen, *Tree Conservation Ordinances: Land-Use Regulations Go Green*, Planning Advisory Service Report No. 446 (Chicago, American Planning Association, 1993).

2. See, for example, *Annotation: Liability of Public Utility to Abutting Owner for Destruction or Injury of Trees In or Near Highway or Street*, 64 A.L.R. 2d 866.

3. See *Pennsylvania Coal Co. v. Mahon*, 260 U.S. 393 (1922). For a historical perspective on the taking issue, an excellent source is Fred P. Bosselman, David Callies, and John Banta, *The Takings Issue* (Washington, D.C.: GPO, 1973). For a current discussion of legal aspects of the taking issue, see Christopher J. Duerksen and Richard Roddewig, *Takings Law in Plain English* (Washington, D.C.: American Resources Information Network, 1994).

4. A sampling of other similar cases in accord with *Glisson* include *Presbytery of Seattle v. King County*, 787 P.2d 907 (Wash. 1990); *Kinzli v. City of Santa Cruz*, 620 F.Supp. 609 (D.C. Cal.1985); and *Pecora v. Gossin*, 356 N.Y.S.2d 505 (N.Y. Sup. Ct. 1974).

5. For example, see Del. Code Ann. tit. 7 ch. 7508 (protection of ecological functions); Me. Rev. Statutes Sec. 12:681 (preservation of ecological and natural values); Mich. Compiled Laws Ann. ch. 103F (protection of shorelands).

6. An example is *Swanson v. City of Bloomington*, 421 N.W.2d 307 (Minn. 1988). But for an example of a court being less permissive in interpreting state enabling legislation, see *Dunbar v. City of Spartanburg*, 221 S.E.2d 848 (S.C. 1976).

7. In addition to these local enactments, the American Forestry Association in Washington, D.C., has an interesting Famous and Historic Trees program that can provide useful information to communities interested in this subject. This program also provides seeds and small trees that are descendants of famous and historic trees such as a Mount Vernon Red Maple and Washington, D.C., Tidal Basin Japanese Cherries.

8. From a practical standpoint, each community should carefully consider what constitutes a rational replacement standard in light of the species involved, specimen size, local survival rate of smaller stock, time required for trees to grow to maturity, and similar considerations. This may vary markedly depending on the region of the country in which the community is located.

9. Some landowners have attempted to clear-cut their property under cover of this exemption, saying such action is necessary to prepare the land for an agricultural or farming use. Courts, however, generally hold that large-scale clear-cutting is not of the same character as the farming or agricultural activities the exemption is intended to protect. For a typical case illustrating the issue, see *Cannata v. Department of Environmental Protection*, et al., 680 A.2d 1329 (Conn. 1996).

10. See, for example, *Freeport v. Brickyard Cove Associates*, 594 A.2d 556 (Me. 1991), upholding a fine of $2,500 and requiring the offending developer to restore the damage caused by illegal clear-cutting by replanting 24 acres of land.

11. This approach is used by Fulton County, Georgia. See the discussion in Macie (1989).

12. The Fairfax County Erosion and Sedimentation Control and Conservation Ordinance, ch. 104-1-1, requires the establishment of a conservation escrow account to insure the installation, maintenance, and adequate performance of conservation measures on a project.

Chapter 5

Billboards, Signs, and Newsboxes

The problem addressed by this ordinance—the visual assault on the citizens of Los Angeles presented by an accumulation of signs posted on public property—constitutes a significant substantive evil within the city's power to prohibit.

CITY OF LOS ANGELES V. TAXPAYERS FOR VINCENT
104 S.CT. 2118 (1984), AT 2130

WHILE THE BULK OF THIS REPORT IS CONCERNED WITH *PRESERVATION* OF THE UNIQUE NATURAL, SCENIC, AND CULTURAL RESOURCES THAT CONTRIBUTE TO LOCAL AESTHETIC CHARACTER, THERE ARE IMPORTANT ISSUES OF *PREVENTION* TO DISCUSS AS WELL. This chapter summarizes some of the complex legal issues surrounding the control of billboards, signs, and newsboxes, focusing on how local governments can prevent an accumulation of outdoor advertising from overwhelming and obscuring community character.

Anyone who has traveled the nation's highways over the last several years would suspect—correctly—that the number of billboards in the country has been steadily rising. Indeed, a 1997 Scenic America study conservatively estimated that between 425,000 and 450,000 billboards now line the nation's federal-aid highways, up from 300,000 in 1965. Moreover, signs and billboards are taking on newer and more intrusive forms, becoming more technologically sophisticated (computerized screens are just one example), more portable, more garish, and larger. Indeed, one New Jersey beachfront store has even begun selling ad space on its sand—calling the mammoth ads "environmentally friendly" since they disappear when walked on. Further, billboard content continues to trumpet the baser aspects of our consumer culture. Remarks Meg Maguire, president of Scenic America, "A drive down an American highway looks like a ride through Vice Valley, with ads for giant-sized booze, strip joints, and casinos. It's sky trash—litter on a stick.

Scenic America

These pictures are visible evidence of the noxious effect of sign clutter or a billboard "alley" (this one in Houston) on a local environment. While local governments must be especially cautious in their regulations because of the free speech issue, aesthetic concerns have clearly been recognized by the courts as a valid basis for controls on signs and billboards.

Scenic America

How do most Americans view the proliferation of billboards? The answer is surprisingly consistent across numerous national and state polls. Most people surveyed agree that billboards degrade scenic beauty and their communities in general. Sixty-nine percent of Missourians, for instance, believe that fewer billboards would make their state more attractive to tourists, while just 26 percent disagreed. In another recent survey, 96 percent of Houstonians agreed that it is important to make major improvements in the beautification of their city, and 79 percent supported maintaining or strengthening the city's ordinance removing all billboards by 2013. A 1997 Michigan poll found that most state residents surveyed desire stronger billboard controls, and 60 percent favor banning new billboards altogether along state highways. Noted the state's Attorney General, who supports a ban on billboards: "Michigan citizens have had enough of outdoor advertisers stealing our landscape"(Scenic America 1997). According to those surveyed, individual communities, rather than the state, should dictate whether to impose such controls: 77 percent said that local governments should have the first option in regulating or banning billboards.

Polls also indicate that the public overwhelmingly disapproves of the practice of allowing billboard operators to cut down trees on public land to improve the visibility of their private billboards (allowed in 24 states), which leads to the destruction of tens of thousands of public trees each year. Further, surveys in Rhode Island, Florida, and Missouri all have found that people obtain little or no useful information about products or services from billboards.

Not surprisingly, many communities are beginning to enact bans, or at least strict regulations, of billboards, especially along state highways. Asheville, North Carolina, is a recent example. In November 1997, the Asheville City Council voted unanimously to ban all new billboards, and voted 4-3 to require about 70 existing billboards to be removed within seven years. The councilman who spearheaded the proposal noted that the intent of the bill was to help preserve the city's unique aesthetic character: "Billboards make us less attractive to tourists and potential new businesses looking to move into the area. They send a message that we don't appreciate the unique natural environment we live in here in the mountains, that we are content to look like just another city." The action also was taken in response to an extensive grassroots lobbying effort by local volunteer groups. Asheville's action is part of a trend in a state that has long been afflicted with some of the worst billboard clutter in the nation (*Charlotte Observer* 1997). An informal 1996 survey found that at least 75 North Carolina towns, cities, and counties have banned new billboards (*Scenic North Carolina News* 1998).

Other communities also are taking aggressive steps to prevent the aesthetic blight associated with signs and billboards. Supported by favorable U.S. Supreme Court and state court decisions, these communities are enacting new aesthetic regulations or strengthening existing ones. While some have adopted traditional controls relating to size and placement, a number have gone farther to regulate design, landscaping, spacing, and other features of outdoor advertising, sometimes according to sophisticated formulas. Many areas (e.g., Asheville; Houston; San Diego; Little Rock, Arkansas; Fairfax County, Virginia; and Montgomery County, Maryland) have simply banned all new billboards. Too, many other cities like Los Angeles and Baltimore are restricting billboards containing advertising that may be detrimental to children. Four states with tourist-oriented economies are billboard free, including Alaska, Hawaii, Maine, and Vermont. The Alaska ban was reinforced through a November 1998 statewide ballot initiative in which 72 percent of voters chose to protect the natural beauty of their state by keeping billboards off the state's roads—the first time that all the citizens of any state have had the opportunity to vote on the billboard issue.

Even some sign companies are getting into the act, proposing tough new restrictions on themselves. In Reading, Pennsylvania, for example, the dominant local sign company is helping the city to author tough new billboard restrictions in order to prevent new competitors from entering the market.

This chapter summarizes some of the complex legal issues involved in the regulation of signs, billboards, and other forms of outdoor communication. In addition, guidelines are presented for drafting sign and billboard controls. Finally, a review of recent developments discusses ongoing attempts to restrict local authority in this area by amending state enabling legislation, as well as efforts to restrict alcohol and tobacco advertising in urban areas.

LEGAL ISSUES

In the past, the legal battle over sign and billboard controls focused on the validity of aesthetics as a basis for land-use regulation. As we have seen throughout this report, however, most courts are now favorably inclined toward accepting aesthetics as a justification for regulation, and most state legislatures have specifically granted local governments the power to control signs and other items affecting community aesthetics.

However, that does not end the legal inquiry, because the regulation of signs and other forms of outdoor communication raises potential freedom of speech issues under the First Amendment to the U.S. Constitution.[1]

> Supported by favorable U.S. Supreme Court and state court decisions . . . communities are enacting new aesthetic regulations or strengthening existing ones. While some have adopted traditional controls relating to size and placement, a number have gone farther to regulate design, landscaping, spacing, and other features of outdoor advertising, sometimes according to sophisticated formulas.

Generally, the government may not regulate the *content* of speech, but may attach reasonable time, place, and manner restrictions on its exercise. Thus, controls on the size and location of signs, for example, are routinely upheld, although care must be taken in designing acceptable controls. These regulations can also raise constitutional issues of just compensation under the Fifth Amendment when attempts are made to remove existing, nonconforming structures.

The 1981 landmark case of *Metromedia, Inc. v. City of San Diego,* 453 U.S. 490 (1981), continues to illustrate key principles regarding the ability of local governments to regulate signs and billboards. In that case, the city of San Diego had enacted a nearly total ban on billboards within city limits, with exceptions for on-site commercial signs; political campaign signs; historic and religious markers; time, temperature, and news signs; and a few others. The California Supreme Court sustained the measure, but the U.S. Supreme Court reversed the state court, holding that the San Diego ordinance was in several respects an unconstitutional interference with the freedom of speech protected by the First Amendment. The primary objection of the justices in *Metromedia* was that the San Diego ordinance regulated the *content* of signs by allowing some exceptions and not allowing others.

Yet, despite the fact that the ordinance was struck down for this reason, a majority of the justices agreed on several issues supportive of local sign regulation, including the fact that the promotion of aesthetic objectives alone is sufficient basis for use of the police power to control signs. Further, controls on size, shape, color, and so forth—so-called "time, place, and manner" restrictions—are permissible so long as they are reasonable and do not discriminate based on content. The justices also agreed that *a complete prohibition of off-premises commercial signs (i.e., billboards) is constitutional*, and that a sign control ordinance is not void even though it may put sign companies out of business.

State courts have generally followed the Supreme Court's lead in upholding sign controls and other aesthetic regulation. Thus, the traditionally conservative Arkansas Supreme Court upheld Fayetteville's strict regulations, which prescribe maximum size and height limits, setbacks, and a four-year amortization (noncompensatory removal) period for nonconforming signs *(Donrey Communications Co., Inc. v. City of Fayetteville,* 660 S.W.2d 900 (Ark. 1984)). The court attached particular importance to tourism and protection of scenic resources in the community.[2]

Despite widespread legal acceptance, however, courts still have not granted communities *carte blanche* to impose unlimited restrictions based on weak rationales. Several recent decisions indicate that communities still must pay careful attention when drafting and administering controls on signs and billboards. Some of the most important considerations are discussed below.

Commercial Versus Noncommercial Speech

For purposes of determining whether a particular sign restriction will be upheld, the law distinguishes between "commercial speech" and "noncommercial speech." Signs such as billboards that advertise goods or services for economic gain are considered commercial speech, while signs that communicate ideological messages (such as political or religious signs) are considered noncommercial speech. Both types enjoy protection under the Constitution, but noncommercial speech receives more protection, since the goals it furthers (e.g., self-expression, political discourse) are core democratic principles that the Founding Fathers directly sought to protect through the First Amendment.[3]

Sidebar (left margin):

Generally, the government may not regulate the content of speech, but may attach reasonable time, place, and manner restrictions on its exercise. Thus, controls on the size and location of signs, for example, are routinely upheld, although care must be taken in designing acceptable controls.

For purposes of determining whether a particular sign restriction will be upheld, the law distinguishes between "commercial speech" and "noncommercial speech." Signs such as billboards that advertise goods or services for economic gain are considered commercial speech, while signs that communicate ideological messages (such as political or religious signs) are considered noncommercial speech.

Billboards and Other Commercial Speech

Communities frequently target their strictest regulations at commercial speech, since billboards and other roadside advertising are one of the most pervasive threats to local aesthetic character. What are the rules regarding how communities can and cannot regulate commercial speech? The basic principles, from *Metromedia,* are clear: so-called "time, place, and manner" controls are generally permissible. Thus, restrictions on size, shape, color, height, flashing, placement, orientation, number, and so forth are acceptable, so long as they are reasonable and advance a significant government interest, such as the protection of aesthetic character.[4] Also, governments should not draft regulations that affect the content of commercial speech.

Beyond these basic rules, courts decide the constitutionality of commercial sign controls by applying a four-part test on a case-by-case basis. This important test is known as the *"Central Hudson* test" after the case in which it was first announced (*Central Hudson Gas & Electric Corp. v. Public Serv. Commission,* 447 U.S. 557, 100 S.Ct. 2343 (1980)). The inquiry is as follows.

1) As a threshold concern, commercial speech must concern lawful activity and not be misleading in order to be entitled to First Amendment protection.

If commercial speech is entitled to protection, governments may nevertheless regulate that speech if:

2) the regulation seeks to implement a substantial governmental interest;

3) the regulation directly advances that interest; and

4) the regulation reaches no further than necessary to accomplish the given objective, and leaves open ample alternative means of communication.

In a court challenge, the governmental body seeking enforcement must demonstrate that the regulation meets each of these elements.

A 1996 case from Moreno Valley, California, illustrates how the *Central Hudson* test is generally applied by the courts (*Desert Outdoor Advertising v. Moreno Valley,* 103 F.3d 814 (9th Cir. 1996)). Moreno Valley had enacted a sign control ordinance that included, among other features, locational and structural restrictions on off-site signs, and a requirement that applicants obtain a conditional use permit prior to erecting an off-site sign. The ordinance was challenged by local advertisers as a violation of the First Amendment but was upheld by a federal district court.

The Ninth Circuit Court of Appeals, however, found the ordinance unconstitutional. The ordinance passed the threshold consideration since the commercial speech at issue concerned lawful activity and was not misleading. As to the next three elements of the test, however, there were problems. While aesthetics and traffic safety were the ostensible goals of the Moreno Valley ordinance, the document itself contained no actual statements of purpose regarding those interests. Noted the court, "...the City has not shown that it enacted its ordinance to further any interest in aesthetics and safety. Furthermore, the City provided no evidence that the ordinance promotes those interests" (at 819).

The ordinance thus failed the second and third elements of the *Central Hudson* test because the city failed to provide any evidence that it had a substantial governmental interest in safety and aesthetics, or that the ordinance directly advanced those interests. The city could easily have withstood this part of the challenge simply by drafting explicit purpose statements listing aesthetics and traffic safety as the substantial governmental interests the restrictions were intended to promote and by demonstrating how the restrictions would directly advance those interests.

Other cases have emphasized the third prong of the *Central Hudson* test: the regulation must *directly advance* a substantial governmental interest. Long Hill Township, New Jersey, ran afoul of this principle in 1997 with an ordinance banning all neon signs, even those inside stores, in order to prevent the look of "highway commercial signage" (*State of New Jersey v. Calabria, Gillete Liquors*, 693 A.2d 949 (1997)). A court found the ordinance to be unconstitutional since the township had offered no evidence as to how the particular restriction—the banning of neon—would directly advance the stated goal of protecting aesthetic character. The court acknowledged that municipal regulations generally are presumed valid even in the absence of detailed findings by lawmakers. This presumption of validity doesn't excuse the local government from making *any* effort to justify its action, however. Explained the court:

> [T]here must be shown a factual basis for a particular regulatory scheme, namely, a reason for a total municipal-wide ban. A record cannot be devoid of evidence of how a ban advances the interest of aesthetics. The record is devoid of evidence, facts, or analysis why the mere existence of neon is offensive to that goal. There is no evidence that there are unusual problems in the use of neon that cannot otherwise be regulated as other forms of lighting, specifically, as to degree of illumination, amount of light used within a given space or structure, . . . or number of lights used on the interior of the store.

Because the township failed to provide *any* evidence in its ordinance as to why a total ban on neon signs was necessary in order to avoid "commercial highway appearance," and why more limited regulations (e.g., controls on degree of illumination) would not suffice in place of a total ban, the court found the ordinance unconstitutional.

Communities also run into trouble with the fourth prong of the *Central Hudson* test: the requirement that the restriction be *narrowly tailored.* Regulation of For Sale signs presents some intriguing constitutional issues in this context. A number of courts have held that total bans of on-site For Sale signs in residential areas are unconstitutional because they do not allow for adequate alternative means of communicating real-estate sales information to the public. In other words, total bans in some instances may not be sufficiently tailored and thus violate the fourth prong of the *Central Hudson* test (*Linmark Associates v. Township of Willingboro* 431 U.S. 85, 97 S.Ct. 1614 (1977); *Cleveland Area Bd. of Realtors v. City of Euclid*, 833 F.Supp. 1253 (N.D. Ohio 1993)). In 1995, the Supreme Court of Vermont found just such an ordinance, enacted by the Town of Manchester, to be unconstitutional (*In re Deyo*, 670 A.2d 793 (Vt. 1995)). The court noted that "a more finely tuned ordinance would . . . [prevent] the proliferation of signs while allowing limited forms of real estate advertising" (at 795).

The holding in the Vermont case was based, in part, on a U.S. Supreme Court case in which a similar ordinance was invalidated on grounds that it was not designed to regulate or promote aesthetic values or any other value unrelated to the suppression of free expression (*Linmark Associates v. Township of Willingboro*, 431 U.S. 85 (1977)). The court also noted that the ordinance was not enacted in response to an emergency, panic-selling situation. If it had, the court said, the ordinance might have been constitutional. Interestingly, in another case, restrictions on For Sale signs were invalidated, but those on Sold and garage sale signs passed muster (*Schoen v. Township of Hillside*, 382 A.2d 704 (N.J. Super 1997)). The court ruled that

Sold signs serve no purpose except personal advertising and thus are not related to the free flow of commercial information.

Most sign ordinances distinguish between on-site and off-site commercial signs, a key distinction that has been upheld by the courts. Generally, strict regulations—including total bans—on off-site commercial signs (i.e., billboards) will be upheld, while courts look much more carefully at restrictions of on-site commercial signs. A total ban on all commercial signs within a community (both on- and off-site) probably would be found unconstitutional because it would be unnecessarily restrictive and would not leave open ample alternative channels of expression. Under a complete ban, no one could tell what services were being provided or what goods were being sold in a particular commercial building (Ziegler 1995). *Again, however, a total ban on billboards would probably be acceptable, and a ban on offensive signs in special areas, such as a historic district, may pass judicial muster.*

What about requiring sign permits? Recall that in the *Moreno Valley* case, discussed above, the city required all applicants for off-site signs to obtain a conditional use permit. The issuance of a permit was subject to some objective criteria involving locational and structural standards, but local officials also had tremendous discretion in deciding whether to grant permits. Specifically, the ordinance conditioned the issuance of a permit upon findings by local officials that, "Such a display will not have a harmful effect upon the health or welfare of the general public and will not be detrimental to the welfare of the general public and will not be detrimental to the aesthetic quality of the community or the surrounding land uses" (Moreno Valley Ordinance No. 133, quoted in *Moreno Valley*). Based on such broad, ambiguous language, local officials conceivably could have relied upon practically any excuse to deny issuing a permit. For this reason, the court said that the permit requirement violated the First Amendment. Relying on an earlier Supreme Court case, the court noted that: "a law subjecting the exercise of First Amendment freedoms to the prior restraint of a license, without narrow, objective, and definite standards to guide the licensing authority, is unconstitutional" (at 818, quoting *Shuttlesworth v. City of Birmingham*, 394 U.S. 147, 150-151 (1969)).

The lesson is clear: any conditional permit system for signs must be guided by clear, definite, objective standards that prevent unbridled discretion in the hands of local officials in order to avoid being overturned for vagueness. As seen throughout this report, this is a fundamental principle of land-use law and applies to sign controls just as it does to design review, view protection, tree preservation, and other areas of aesthetic regulation.

Political Signs and Other Noncommercial Speech

Signs not containing advertising—including political, religious, and ideological signs—are considered noncommercial speech. Noncommercial speech generally is afforded a higher degree of protection than commercial speech, and the U.S. Supreme Court clearly indicated in the *Metromedia* case that noncommercial speech cannot be more stringently regulated than commercial speech.

To examine the constitutionality of restrictions on noncommercial speech under the First Amendment, courts employ a balancing test similar to the *Central Hudson* test used for evaluating restrictions on commercial speech. Under the *O'Brien* test (*United States v. O'Brien*, 391 U.S. 367, 88 S.Ct. 1673 (1968)), content-neutral regulation of noncommercial signs will be upheld if: 1) the regulation is within the constitutional power of government; 2) the regulation directly advances a substantial governmental interest; and 3) the regulation does not unnecessarily restrict freedom of expression in order to advance that interest. While the *O'Brien* test is sim-

A total ban on all commercial signs within a community (both on- and off-site) probably would be found unconstitutional because it would be unnecessarily restrictive and would not leave open ample alternative channels of expression. Under a complete ban, no one could tell what services were being provided or what goods were being sold in a particular commercial building.

The lesson is clear: any conditional permit system for signs must be guided by clear, definite, objective standards that prevent unbridled discretion in the hands of local officials in order to avoid being overturned for vagueness. As seen throughout this report, this is a fundamental principle of land-use law and applies to sign controls just as it does to design review, view protection, tree preservation, and other areas of aesthetic regulation.

Content-neutral regulation of noncommercial signs will be upheld if: 1) the regulation is within the constitutional power of government; 2) the regulation directly advances a substantial governmental interest; and 3) the regulation does not unnecessarily restrict freedom of expression in order to advance that interest.

ilar in concept to the *Central Hudson* test, its application by the courts is different because courts are much more suspicious of restrictions on noncommercial speech, as noted above.

Because of the high degree of protection afforded noncommercial speech, a strict ban on noncommercial signs most likely will be found unconstitutional, as was vividly illustrated in the 1994 case of *City of Ladue v. Gilleo*, 114 S.Ct. 2038 (1994). In that case, the U.S. Supreme Court found that a ban on most forms of noncommercial signs in Ladue, a suburb of St. Louis, violated the First Amendment.

During the period leading up to the Persian Gulf war, Margaret Gilleo, a homeowner in Ladue, placed a large sign in her yard reading, Say No to War in the Persian Gulf, Call Congress Now. Informed that her sign violated the local sign ordinance, Gilleo petitioned for a variance but was denied. Gilleo then placed a relatively small, 8.5" by 11" sign inside the window of her home, with the words: For Peace in the Gulf. The city responded by enacting a new sign ordinance that prohibited all signs except those falling within one of 10 exemptions. The exemptions included certain types of noncommercial signs, such as signs for churches and schools, but window signs of the type erected by Gilleo were specifically prohibited. The purpose of the new ordinance, stated the city, was to prevent the:

> Proliferation of an unlimited number of signs in private, residential, commercial, industrial, and public areas of the City of Ladue [that] would create ugliness, visual blight and clutter, tarnish the natural beauty of the landscape as well as the residential and commercial architecture, impair property values, substantially impinge upon the privacy and special ambience of the community, and may cause safety and traffic hazards to motorists, pedestrians, and children. (at 2041)

Gilleo challenged the new ordinance in court as a violation of her First Amendment rights. A federal district court, and later the Court of Appeals, found the ordinance to be unconstitutional, in part because it was a content-based regulation that favored some types of noncommercial speech over others—church signs were favored over political yard signs, for instance. The city claimed the ordinance merely imposed content-neutral time, place, and manner restrictions, and that other outlets were available for Gilleo's speech, such as handbills. But the U.S. Supreme Court, on appeal, disagreed, expressing concern over how the ordinance prohibited an entire type of noncommercial speech. In an eloquent opinion, the court observed:

> *Ladue* has almost completely foreclosed a venerable means of communication that is both unique and important. It has totally foreclosed that medium to political, religious, or personal messages. Signs that react to a local happening or express a view on a controversial issue both reflect and animate change in the life of a community. Often placed on lawns or in windows, residential signs play an important part in political campaigns, during which they are displayed to signal the resident's support for political candidates, parties, or causes. They may not afford the same opportunities for conveying complex ideas as do other media, but residential signs have long been an important and distinct medium of expression. (at 2045)

Thus, *Ladue* demonstrates that communities may not draft sign controls that are so strict they prohibit entire avenues of speech—most especially, controversial political statements, such as Ms. Gilleo's, that are highly valued in a democratic society.

Despite the high level of protection afforded noncommercial speech, restrictions on the time, place, and manner of such speech will nevertheless be upheld so long as they are reasonable and advance significant government interests. This lesson was underscored in 1984 as part of a challenge to a Los Angeles ordinance that banned the placement of both commercial and noncommercial signs on public property (*City of Los Angeles v. Taxpayers for Vincent*, 104 S.Ct. 2118 (1984)). The plaintiffs, who had their political campaign posters removed from utility poles pursuant to the ordinance, sued on First Amendment grounds. In reversing an appeals court decision striking down the ordinance, the U.S. Supreme Court found that the ordinance's restrictions on noncommercial speech were narrowly tailored to accomplish the city's objectives and that ample alternative modes of communication still existed for noncommercial speech. Further, the court reiterated its support of local sign control efforts—and the use of aesthetics as a justification for such efforts—saying:

> [M]unicipalities have a weighty, essentially aesthetic interest in proscribing intrusive and unpleasant formats for expression. . . . We reaffirm the conclusion of the majority in *Metromedia.* The problem addressed by this ordinance—the visual assault on the citizens of Los Angeles presented by an accumulation of signs posted on public property—constitutes a significant substantive evil within the city's power to prohibit. "The city's interest in attempting to preserve (or improve) the quality of urban life is one that must be accorded high respect." (at 2130, quoting *Young v. American Mini Theatres, Inc.*)

Other restrictions on noncommercial speech that have been upheld have included controls on the placement and size of political signs on public property (*Candidates Outdoor Graphic Service v. City of San Francisco*, 574 F.Supp. 1240 (N.D. Cal. 1983)) and similar controls on private property. Note that such restrictions quickly can become "unreasonable" in the eyes of a court, however. In 1993, a federal district court found that an Arlington County, Virginia, sign ordinance that prohibited more than two temporary signs on private property was unconstitutional (*Arlington County Republican Comm. v. Arlington County*, 983 F.2d 587 (4th Cir. 1993)). The court found that the restriction interfered with the ability of residents to communicate support for more than two political candidates at one time or for households with two or more voters to adequately express support for a range of candidates.

The distinction between commercial and noncommercial speech forms the conceptual background for most legal issues involving the regulation of signs and billboards. Several other issues that have received significant attention from the courts and/or state legislatures are discussed in the following sections, including temporary and portable signs, fees and amortization provisions, and the Federal Highway Beautification Act.

The distinction between commercial and noncommercial speech forms the conceptual background for most legal issues involving the regulation of signs and billboards.

Temporary and Portable Signs

While not as visually obtrusive as billboards, temporary and portable signs nevertheless are viewed by many as an unappealing form of outdoor advertising. Such signs run the gamut from gigantic floating balloons to blinking trailers. They tend to be poorly designed, garish, and are often located illegally on public rights-of-way. They can contain either commercial or noncommercial speech, but usually feature some type of advertisement. They are also extremely difficult to regulate because they can be moved quickly to avoid enforcement action. In response to these concerns, many communities have either banned such signs or imposed very strict regulations upon them.

Meg Maguire

Stricter regulation of portable signs is possible if a local community can show that such signs pose greater safety and aesthetic problems. In this case, the character that a bed-and-breakfast operator is trying so hard to create with other touches is completely undercut by the use of a portable sign.

Courts will strike down strict regulations on temporary and portable signs if localities fail to present any valid reason for treating such signs differently from other signs (*Dills v. Cobb County*, 593 F.Supp. 170 (N.O. Geo. 1984); *All American Sign Rentals v. City of Orlando*, 592 F.Supp. 85 (M.D. Fla. 1983)). However, stricter regulations have been upheld when communities adequately demonstrate that such signs pose greater aesthetic and safety problems than do other types of signs (*Messer v. City of Douglasville*, 975 F.2d 1505 (11th Cir. 1992); City of *Hot Springs v. Carter*, 310 Ark. 405, 836 S.W. 2d 863 (1992); *Rent-A-Sign v. City of Rockford*, 406 N.E.2d 943 (Ill. 1980); *Sign Supplies of Texas v. McConn*, 517 F.Supp. 778 (S.D. Tex. 1980)). For example, in 1997 a federal district court upheld a Louisville, Kentucky, ordinance that restricted the use of small freestanding signs within the city limits by:

1) reducing the maximum allowable size from 32 square feet to eight square feet;

2) reducing the maximum allowable height from nine feet to four feet; and

3) limiting the hours of display to the hours of the business conducted at the site (*Wilson v. City of Louisville*, 957 F.Supp. 948 (1997)).

The court had little difficulty upholding the restrictions, despite the fact that they were specific to portable signs, noting that the planning commission had specifically found the prohibited signs "were unattractive and constituted safety hazards." Also, noted the court, business owners still had adequate alternative modes of communication available to them under the ordinance (e.g., through distribution of flyers, using smaller portable signs or larger permanent signs).

In light of the mixed case law in this area, communities would be well-advised to have adequate documentation to support more stringent regulations on temporary and portable signs, or else to regulate them in the same manner as off-site commercial signs. Thus, restrictions on materials, location, size, landscaping, and so forth could be applied to these signs to make their use more compatible with surrounding areas, so long as such restrictions apply equally to off-site commercial signs.

Fees and Amortization

Many communities impose fees on the issuance of sign permits. Generally, if such fees are reasonable and related to the cost of administration, enforcement, and removal, they should withstand judicial scrutiny, especially if applied to commercial signs (see, for example, *Outdoor Media Dimensions, Inc. v. State*, 945 P.2d 614 (1997), which upholds removal fee provisions, and *Union City Bd. of Zoning Appeals v. Justice Outdoor Displays, Inc.*, 467 S.E.2d 875 (Ga. 1996), which upholds permit and fee exemptions for temporary signs, small signs, and residential signs). However, fees imposed on political signs, even to ensure removal after an election, are suspect unless they can be shown to relate to the actual cost of administration and removal. Moreover, if the fees are set too high, they will be struck down for having a "chilling" effect on freedom of speech (*People v. Middlemark*, 420 N.Y. S.2d 151 (1979)).

In addition to imposing fees to defray the cost of administration and removal, many communities have adopted a process, known as amortization, that allows the local government to remove legally erected billboards that no longer comply with local zoning controls; no cash compensation is provided, yet the billboard operator is given a grace period that allows him to recoup his investment and still make a reasonable profit. The rationale is that, if nonconforming signs are allowed to remain, a community's efforts to improve its aesthetic character will be stymied.

While a few states, such as Indiana, New Hampshire, and Tennessee, have prohibited amortization based on state statutory and constitutional limitations, a majority of state courts have upheld reasonable amortization periods that allow the sign owner to recoup his investment. Thus, amortization periods ranging from 3 to 10 years have been approved in many recent cases (see *Naegele Outdoor Advertising v. City of Durham*, 803 F.Supp. 1068 (M.D.N.C. 1992); *Georgia Outdoor Advertising v. City of Waynesville*, 900 F.2d 783 (4th Cir. 1990); and *National Advertising v. Board of Adjustment Co.*, 800 P.2d 1349 (Colo. App. 1990)). These amortization periods appear reasonable in light of the fact that most signs are depreciated for federal tax purposes in five years or less. An ominous trend, however, is for state legislatures—at the behest of the billboard lobby—to forbid amortization without cash compensation (see the discussion of Utah's new legislation below).

Federal Highway Beautification Act

In 1965 Congress passed legislation that established a national policy and program for the control of outdoor advertising along federally funded interstate and primary highways. Under the Federal Highway Beautification Act, the Federal Highway Administration (FHWA) oversees a program that requires each state to develop a billboard control program restricting the construction of new signs except in commercial or industrial zones, and requiring the removal of nonconforming and illegal signs. Cash compensation must be paid if legal, nonconforming signs are forcibly removed by the state.

In light of the mixed case law in this area, communities would be well-advised to have adequate documentation to support more stringent regulations on temporary and portable signs, or else to regulate them in the same manner as off-site commercial signs.

Many communities impose fees on the issuance of sign permits. Generally, if such fees are reasonable and related to the cost of administration, enforcement, and removal, they should withstand judicial scrutiny, especially if applied to commercial signs.

Scenic America

Despite widespread public opposition to the practice, loopholes in the Federal Highway Beautification Act have allowed billboard owners to cut down trees blocking the view of billboards.

The critics call the Act a "loophole-riddled disaster," pointing out, for example, that the federal legislation fails to define "commercial or industrial area," opening the door for individual gas stations and other small-scale roadside developments to allow adjacent billboard construction.

While courts have uniformly upheld state regulation of billboards pursuant to the Act (see *Newman Signs v. Hjelle,* 268 N.W.2d 741 (N.D. 1978) and *State v. Mayhew Products Corp.,* 281 N.W.2d 753 (Neb. 1979)), the Act had little impact upon local sign control efforts in its first years. In 1978, however, the billboard lobby secured passage of an amendment that *forbids* the use of local police power regulations to force removal of nonconforming signs along *federal highways* in their jurisdiction *unless cash compensation is paid.* As a result, local governments have been severely hampered in their regulation of signs along such highways no matter what state courts have said about noncompensable amortization. The visual result has been billboard "alleys" running along federal roadways through cities that themselves have billboard controls.

In recent years, environmental and scenic conservation groups have strongly criticized the Act, saying it has lost its "teeth," and that the billboard industry has eviscerated the Act through litigation. The critics call the Act a "loophole-riddled disaster," pointing out, for example, that the federal legislation fails to define "commercial or industrial area," opening the door for individual gas stations and other small-scale roadside developments to allow adjacent billboard construction. In addition, critics argue that the billboard lobby has succeeded in persuading many states to permit the cutting of trees that block signs on private property, despite widespread public opposition to this practice. Critics ultimately point to the continuing proliferation of billboards along the country's highways as proof that the Act is broken and should be fixed (Phillips 1997).

In response, several efforts to reform the Act to deal with these shortcomings have been proposed. The most recent attempt was the 1998 introduction in both the House of Representatives and the Senate of the Scenic Highway Protection Act, which would have accomplished several key reforms of the 1965 Act. It would:

- prohibit new billboard construction in unzoned areas to protect rural character;

- prohibit tree-cutting to improve billboard visibility on federal-aid highways;

- remove federal influence from local decision making on the removal of billboards under local ordinances; and

- require the federal Department of Transportation to conduct an annual, comprehensive inventory of all billboards on federal-aid highways.

Although the proposed Scenic Highway Protection Act enjoys wide, bipartisan support, it did not advance during the 1998 legislative season, and supporters expect a protracted effort over several years before full adoption of the measure.

GUIDELINES FOR DRAFTING LOCAL SIGN AND BILLBOARD CONTROLS

Clearly, the law in this area is highly complex, and local governments attempting to draft new, or to tighten existing, regulations should keep in mind some important legal considerations. Nevertheless, remember that tremendous public support exists for stronger sign and billboard controls, and that many local governments already have successfully responded to citizen concerns by enacting new, increasingly tough ordinances that go far beyond traditional sign regulations. These ordinances should pass judicial muster if the following broad guidelines are kept in mind.

- First Amendment restrictions must be observed. Restrictions on speech are valid only if the regulation seeks to implement a substantial government interest, directly advances that interest, and reaches no further than necessary to accomplish the given objective.

- Time, place, and manner restrictions generally are valid. Examples of potentially appropriate subjects for regulation include size, shape, color, height, flashing, placement, orientation, and number.

- A sign ordinance should clearly state the purposes for which it is being adopted. The promotion of aesthetic objectives alone is sufficient justification for regulating signs.

- An ordinance that is part of a comprehensive city beautification effort (including, for example, preservation, scenic roadway protection, or street tree planting) is more likely to withstand judicial scrutiny than an ordinance disconnected from other city policies and regulations.

- A distinction can be made between on-premises and off-premises signs (billboards), and the latter may be banned entirely, but care should be taken in carving out exceptions within those two categories. Unexplained differences in treatment of different kinds of noncommercial signs has been particularly troublesome to some courts.

- A prohibition of all off-premises commercial signs (e.g., billboards) is likely to be constitutional.

- A total communitywide ban on political and ideological signs is likely to be unconstitutional.

- All signs can be prohibited in special areas in a community, such as historic districts, but great care should be taken in doing so, particularly in commercial zones and with respect to noncommercial signs.

- Conditional permit systems for signs must be guided by clear, definite, objective standards that prevent unbridled discretion in the hands of local officials.

Remember that tremendous public support exists for stronger sign and billboard controls, and that many local governments already have successfully responded to citizen concerns by enacting new, increasingly tough ordinances that go far beyond traditional sign regulations.

Clarion Associates

When devising sign controls, local governments need to be careful to not prohibit "artistic" signs, like this one. Rather, planners drafting regulations might want to find a way to encourage creativity and designs that fit the character of the community, the district, and the building.

• Post-campaign and post-event removal requirements are permissible, as are inspection and removal fees, if reasonably related to actual administrative costs.

• "Problem" signs, such as portable signs, can be regulated strictly, but the grounds for the special treatment should be rooted in the public welfare and should be made explicit.

• A sign and billboard control ordinance is not void even though it may put sign companies out of business.

• When drafting amortization provisions, be sure the amortization period selected is long enough to allow the sign owner to recoup his investment and make a profit; five- to eight-year periods have been upheld by the courts.

Keep in mind that courts generally are supportive of local regulations that restrict signs and billboards. However, important constitutional limits exist regarding how far local governments may go, and care when drafting sign ordinances is essential. In particular, local governments must avoid content-based controls that violate the First Amendment and focus instead on merely regulating the time, place, and manner of speech.

As has been noted throughout this chapter, keep in mind that courts generally are supportive of local regulations that restrict signs and billboards. However, important constitutional limits exist regarding how far local governments may go, and care when drafting sign ordinances is essential. In particular, local governments must avoid content-based controls that violate the First Amendment and focus instead on merely regulating the time, place, and manner of speech. Nevertheless, in spite of these cautionary notes, remember that there are hundreds of communities nationwide successfully regulating signs and billboards. There is plenty of room within the legal boundaries to craft tough, creative restrictions to curb visual pollution.

RECENT DEVELOPMENTS

In the wake of favorable federal and state court decisions, a flurry of new sign control ordinances have been enacted at the local level. This section discusses two of the more interesting recent developments in the field of sign and billboard control: the continuing debate in state legislatures over how much authority to grant local governments to regulate outdoor advertising, and increasing efforts in larger cities to restrict alcohol advertising.

Efforts to Restrict Local Authority at the State Level

The authority of most communities to regulate signs and billboards comes from the state; thus, the billboard industry and local governments continue to vigorously lobby state legislatures to either reduce or increase the amount of permissible local regulatory control. Missouri provides an interesting example of how some states are responding to this pressure.

Missouri has long restricted the ability of local governments to regulate billboards, and, as a result, has some of the most visually cluttered highways in the country. In late 1997, however, in an effort to clean up the state's roads, the legislature passed a bill granting local governments limited authority to restrict billboards and even adopt moratoriums. Oddly, this authority was restricted to cities with a city engineer who served on the local planning and zoning commission. Local governments that did choose to adopt their own regulations could set rules on height, spacing, and lighting, and could charge a modest fee to cover administrative costs. Or, they could choose to adopt less-restrictive regulations enacted by the state and charge higher fees. In other words, the state forced communities to choose between adopting stronger controls or collecting higher revenues.

Karl Kruse

Scenic Missouri, appalled by strips of billboards like this one in the state, launched a petition drive to encourage the state legislature to allow greater local control over billboards. The campaign was successful in getting some positive change when new legislation was passed in August 1998.

Not satisfied with this slippery approach toward a major aesthetic problem, Scenic Missouri, a nonprofit organization, launched a petition drive to put before state voters an amendment to the state constitution that would have given all cities clear authority to regulate or ban billboards, without restrictions on fees. The proposal struck a strong, positive chord in the state. Commenting in a favorable editorial, the *St. Louis Post-Dispatch* (October 6, 1997) remarked: "Maybe the walnut bowl industry would suffer, but at least a drive in the country wouldn't be an assault on the senses."

Scenic Missouri was forced to abandon their campaign in mid-1998 when it became clear they would have a difficult time, because of financing and time constraints, obtaining the necessary signatures to put the amendment before the voters. The organization ultimately achieved some success, though. Reacting favorably to the petition drive, the state legislature passed a new law in August 1998 granting local governments more authority to regulate billboards and giving the scenic conservation community some of what they had sought in the amendment (Senate Bill 883). The new law makes two key changes. First, any city or county in Missouri now has the authority to regulate the size, lighting, and spacing of billboards more restrictively than state law. Second, no city or county may charge more than a $500 initial inspection fee for billboards, or a business tax of over more than 2 percent of the gross annual revenue generated by the billboard. In other words, while communities gained authority to enact stronger billboard controls, they still are somewhat restricted in their collection of fees. As this report went to press, however, Scenic Missouri is underway with its Save Our Scenery 2000 initiative (see sidebar).

While local governments in Missouri achieved some success in expanding local regulatory authority in their state, a few other states are moving in the opposite direction. Nationwide, the billboard industry is aggressively lobbying states to limit local powers, with some success. One especially troubling situation for scenic conservation advocates is Utah. In recent years, Utah has prohibited local governments from using amortization to remove nonconforming billboards. Instead, state law allows for the termination of such billboards only through voluntary agreement and/or purchase from the billboard owner, or eminent domain. Further, if a municipality prevents a billboard company from maintaining, repairing, or restoring a billboard structure damaged by casualty, act of God, or vandalism, the municipality's actions constitute eminent domain and require full cash compensation be paid to the billboard company (Utah Code Ann., Sections 10-9-408 and -409).

More recently, the Utah state legislature passed the comprehensive Outdoor Advertising Act (Utah Code Ann., Section 72-5-501). While addressing a variety of relatively noncontroversial issues (e.g., permitting requirements, spacing requirements from federal and state highways), the Act also includes specific provisions that are highly favorable to the billboard industry and potentially highly expensive for local governments. For instance, all communities that require the removal of nonconforming billboards must pay the billboard owners just compensation, which is defined very broadly under the new statute to include damages to all remaining properties owned by the billboard company which constitute "an economic unit," both adjacent and nonadjacent to the billboard site. Thus, the statute theoretically requires local governments to pay damages resulting from loss of business experienced at a retail store in one part of a city because of the removal of a billboard in an altogether different part of the city.

Some of the most far-reaching language in the Act relates to the consequences of road widening. Utah currently is undertaking a significant amount of road construction and widening, especially in the Salt Lake City area, in part to prepare for the 2002 Winter Olympics. Since road construction and widening forces the removal of many billboards, the sign industry has lobbied aggressively for action by the state legislature.

In response, the legislature included in the Act provisions requiring that, if a billboard is removed pursuant to road widening, the owner shall be allowed to relocate the billboard to another location on the same property, on adjacent property, on the same highway within a certain distance, or to a location mutually agreed upon by the owner and the county or municipality (Utah Code Ann., Section 72-5-510(6)). Strikingly, the county or municipality must pay all costs related to relocation and remodeling and, if it refuses to allow the relocation, must pay just compensation as described above. In other words, at least in the context of road widening, Utah's Outdoor Advertising Act shifts major costs associated with billboard regulation onto local communities—probably the entities least able to afford such costs, yet which stand to lose the most in terms of aesthetic character.

SCENIC MISSOURI SAVE OUR SCENERY 2000 INITIATIVE

Scenic Missouri's initiative petition campaign, if successful, would amend the Missouri billboard statute in four important ways.

1. New billboard construction on interstate and primary highways would be prohibited.

2. The destruction of trees and other vegetation on highway right-of-ways to improve billboard visibility would be prohibited.

3. Existing billboards could not be rebuilt, replaced, or relocated and, therefore, would slowly begin to dwindle in number.

4. The authority of local governments to regulate billboards would be reaffirmed.

The measure will appear on the ballot in November 2000.

Regulation of Alcohol and Tobacco Advertising

Over the last decade, many major urban centers have been working to ban alcohol and tobacco advertising, citing the effect such ads have on underage drinking and cigarette smoking and the disproportionate emphasis placed on siting this advertising in minority communities. In support of such bans, communities draw upon numerous studies showing direct correlations between advertising and product usage, and cite crime statistics demonstrating the involvement of alcohol in many violent crimes. In September 1997, for instance, the Chicago City Council voted 44-1 to ban alcohol and tobacco billboards in some areas of the city. Other jurisdictions have enacted similar bans, including Los Angeles, Oakland, and Detroit. Importantly, the bans regulate the *location* of alcohol and tobacco billboards, rather than the *content* of the copy contained on the boards.[5]

Baltimore is the trendsetter in this area, since that city's tobacco and alcohol advertising controls are among the strongest such restrictions and have been tested the furthest in court. In 1993, the Maryland legislature

Scenic America

Ray Foote

Many cities have successfully fought the battle of regulating the siting of billboards advertising alcohol, and the recent national settlement between states and major tobacco companies has meant that billboards like this one advertising Marlboros are now being used to deliver anti-smoking messages.

passed a law authorizing the City of Baltimore to adopt an ordinance restricting the placement of signs that advertise alcohol and cigarettes in "publicly visible locations," including "outdoor billboards, sides of buildings, and freestanding signboards" (Md. Code, Art. 2B, Section 222). Ten limitations in the law specify areas where such restrictions may not be enforced, including on buses and taxicabs and at businesses licensed to sell such products, including sports arenas.

In 1994, Baltimore enacted two ordinances to take advantage of this new authority, one aimed at alcohol ads and one aimed at cigarette ads. First, however, the city examined numerous studies demonstrating a strong correlation between such ads and alcohol and cigarette usage by minors, as well as the involvement of alcohol in many youth crimes. For instance, alcohol use was involved in one-half of all major causes of death among youth in Baltimore, and one-third of all juvenile males arrested in Baltimore in a given period said they had consumed alcohol within the previous 72 hours. Tobacco and alcohol advertisements were the first and second most prevalent types of ads in the city, respectively. The city council noted that children are exposed to such advertising "simply by walking to school or playing in their neighborhood," and that children's "attitudes favorable to alcohol are significantly related to their exposure to alcohol advertisements."

> Baltimore enacted restrictions prohibiting alcohol and cigarette advertising in certain targeted locations within the city where "minors . . . live, attend school, attend church, and engage in recreational activities."

With these and other findings as support, Baltimore enacted restrictions prohibiting alcohol and cigarette advertising in certain targeted locations within the city where "minors . . . live, attend school, attend church, and engage in recreational activities." The prohibitions are subject to the 10 exemptions listed in the state law and also are exempt in areas zoned for commercial and industrial use.

In 1995, the brewing company Anheuser-Busch and a local sign company filed suit against the city on the grounds that the ordinances violated their freedom of speech under the First Amendment. A federal district court upheld the ordinances, saying they were valid restrictions on commercial speech because they passed the *Central Hudson* four-part test, discussed above.

On appeal, the Fourth Circuit Court of Appeals agreed with the lower court that the ordinances do not violate the First Amendment (*Anheuser-Busch, Inc. v. Schmoke*, 63 F.3d 1305, 1309 (4th Cir. 1995); *Penn Advertising of Baltimore, Inc. v. Mayor and City Council of Baltimore*, 63 F.3d 1318 (4th Cir. 1995), a parallel case with the same result and analysis, deals with cigarette advertising). The court concentrated its analysis on the last two prongs of the *Central Hudson* analysis: Do the regulations directly advance the governmental interests asserted and are they narrowly tailored to reach no further than is necessary to serve those interests? Regarding the first question, the court agreed with other courts that have addressed the issue and found it reasonable for a community to conclude that an advertising ban directly and materially advances a local interest in promoting the welfare of minors.

> . . . [W]e find that it was reasonable for the Baltimore City Council to have concluded that [the ordinance's] regulation of the outdoor advertising of alcoholic beverages directly and materially advances Baltimore's interest in promoting the welfare and temperance of minors. . . . There is a logical nexus between the City's objective and the means it selected for achieving that objective, and it is not necessary . . . to prove conclusively that the correlation in fact exists, or that the steps undertaken will solve the problem. (*Anheuser-Busch v. Schmoke*, at 1314; similar language appears in *Penn Advertising*, dealing with cigarette advertising)

As to the second question, the court found that the advertising bans were narrowly tailored to a sufficient degree so as to prevent excessive regulation. Because, for example, the restrictions exempt all commercial and industrial zones, they are not overly restrictive. The court was sympathetic to Baltimore's plight: "In the face of a problem as significant as that which the City seeks to address, the City must be given some reasonable latitude" (*Anheuser-Busch, Inc. v. Schmoke*, at 1316).

Some cities are broadening their justifications for enacting these types of restrictions. Chicago's ban, for example, enacted in September 1997, is targeted primarily at billboards in minority neighborhoods. When asked the reason for this, the local pastor who spearheaded the drive remarked:"We have targeted them because they have targeted us. They target children and they saturate black and Hispanic communities." The ban is considered a first step toward billboard control in a city with historically few meaningful outdoor advertising regulations—and many unsightly and illegal billboards as a result. In fact, a survey showed that nearly 25 percent of the city's billboards are illegal (*Chicago Sun Times* 1997; *Chicago Tribune* 1997).

As this report went to press, regulating tobacco advertising on billboards had become a moot issue throughout most of the country. As part of a $206 billion nationwide settlement between five major tobacco companies and 46 states, the companies agreed to remove all their outdoor advertising of tobacco products in those states, including billboards at stadiums and along highways, by April 23, 1999. The companies must continue to pay for the advertising space, however, until their leases expire, so that anti-smoking groups may use the spaces. In addition to the ban on outdoor advertising, the settlement also ends the distribution and sale of clothing and merchandise (e.g., baseball hats) with tobacco brand-name logos; and the use of cartoons in the advertising and packaging of tobacco products.

NEWSBOXES

Communities increasingly are interested in minimizing the visual clutter caused by the proliferation of newsboxes.[6] Aggressive marketing by newspapers, such as *USA Today,* seems to have placed a rack of such newsboxes on every street corner in the country. In fact, in some larger cities, it is not unusual to find two dozen or more boxes jammed together at one corner. These newsboxes, particularly the brightly colored ones placed in historic areas, are obtrusive, and the methods used to anchor them to public light poles and street furniture can be damaging as well as unattractive. Moreover, too many newsboxes can lead to overcrowded sidewalks and related safety concerns (e.g., blocking wheelchair access). Many communities have reacted by limiting the number and placement of such boxes, as well as requiring that they be painted muted colors (in *Gold Coast Publications v. Corrigan,* 42 F.3d 1336 (11th Cir. 1994)), a court upheld the Coral Gables, Florida, uniformity requirements for newboxes specifying make, color, and size of lettering). In other cities, such as New York City, business improvement districts require that newspapers in downtown areas be distributed through attractive, comprehensive newsboxes where multiple publications are available, rather than through individual boxes.

However, just as with signs, communities must use care in drafting regulations since newsboxes are protected by the First Amendment guarantee of freedom of speech. While a newsbox itself is not a form of speech, it is a mechanism for the distribution of speech and as such receives protection under the First Amendment (*Lakewood v. Plain Dealer Publishing Co.,* 486 U.S. 780, 108 S.Ct. 2138 (1988)). Thus, the same general rules that apply to signs, billboards, and other forms of outdoor communication also apply to newsboxes. Restrictions must be content-neutral. They may reasonably

As this report went to press, regulating tobacco advertising on billboards had become a moot issue throughout most of the country. As part of a $206 billion nationwide settlement between five major tobacco companies and 46 states, the companies agreed to remove all their outdoor advertising of tobacco products in those states, including billboards at stadiums and along highways, by April 23, 1999.

Just as with signs, communities must use care in drafting regulations since newsboxes are protected by the First Amendment guarantee of freedom of speech. While a newsbox itself is not a form of speech, it is a mechanism for the distribution of speech and as such receives protection under the First Amendment

Meg Maguire

Arcadia, California, has launched a streetscape improvement program that includes designs for newsboxes. Courts look favorably on newsbox regulations that are part of a broader set of aesthetic regulations.

regulate the time, place, and manner of box placement but must be narrowly tailored so as to restrict no more speech than is necessary and must leave open alternative means of communication. While courts look favorably upon newsbox regulations that are part of a comprehensive aesthetic regulatory scheme, recent cases indicate that this is not a prerequisite in order for regulations to be upheld (*Globe Newspaper Co. v. Beacon Hill Architectural Commission,* 100 F.3d 175, 191 (1st Cir. 1996)).

An outright ban on newsboxes, as was attempted by New Jersey in the early 1980s (*Southern New Jersey Newspaper v. State,* 542 F.Supp. 173 (D.N.S. 1982) will probably be struck down as an overly broad restriction on the distribution of speech. Yet bans that are confined to a special area, such as a historic district, have been upheld. In 1996, for instance, a "Street Furniture Guideline" enacted by Boston's Beacon Hill Architectural Commission was the subject of just such a challenge. The regulation effectively prohibits newsboxes on sidewalks within the Beacon Hill historic district (*Globe Newspaper Co.,* at 80). Although a lower court found that the regulation violated the First Amendment, the First Circuit Court of Appeals disagreed, explaining that the legislation was a constitutional, content-neutral restriction on distribution, that aesthetic concern was a significant government interest that supports such a ban, and that newspapers had ample alternative channels for distribution in the district.

As in the context of sign regulations, any restriction on newsboxes must advance a significant governmental interest (which can include aesthetics), must directly advance that interest, and must be narrowly tailored so as not to prohibit too much speech. In 1993, the U.S. Supreme Court overturned a Cincinnati ordinance that failed to meet these basic rules (*City of Cincinnati v. Discovery Network,* 113 S.Ct. 1505 (1993)). In the interests of promoting aesthetics and traffic safety, the ordinance banned newsboxes that distributed commercial handbills, but not newsboxes that distributed newspapers. Only about 5 percent of the city's newsboxes would have been affected by the ban. As the court explained, the restriction was not narrowly drawn to achieve its purported goals:

> The fact that the city failed to address its recently developed concern about newsracks by regulating their size, shape, appearance, or number indicates that it has not "carefully calculated" the costs and benefits associated with the burden on speech imposed by its prohibition. The benefit to be derived from the removal of 62 newsracks while about 1,500-2,000 remain in place was considered "minute" by the District Court and "paltry" by the Court of Appeals. We share their evaluation of the "fit" between the city's goal and its method of achieving it. (at 1510)

The Cincinnati case also demonstrates how—as with sign controls—content-based regulations will be carefully scrutinized by the courts and usually found invalid. The Cincinnati ordinance clearly was content-based in that the ban only applied depending upon the type of material inside the newsbox. Content-based regulations are not *per se* unconstitutional; rather, they are subject to strict scrutiny by the courts and must overcome a strong presumption of unconstitutionality. The city failed to overcome this presumption. Concluded the court:

The Cincinnati case also demonstrates how—as with sign controls— content-based regulations will be carefully scrutinized by the courts and usually found invalid.

> Cincinnati has enacted a sweeping ban that bars from its sidewalks a whole class of constitutionally protected speech. . . . [W]e conclude that Cincinnati has failed to justify that policy. The regulation is not a permissible regulation of commercial speech, for on this record it is clear that the interests that Cincinnati has asserted are unrelated to any distinction between "commercial handbills" and "newspapers." Moreover, because the ban is predicated on the content of the publications distributed by the subject newsracks, it is not a valid time, place, or manner restriction on protected speech. For these reasons, Cincinnati's categorical ban . . . cannot be squared with the dictates of the First Amendment. (at 1517)

Not all content-based newsbox regulations are overturned, however. Contrast the Cincinnati case with *Crawford v. Lungren*, 96 F.3d 380 (9th Cir. 1996), in which a content-based restriction on newsboxes was upheld. A California state statute limited minors' access to pornography by prohibiting coin-operated vending machines (including newsboxes) from distributing "harmful matter" in public places unless supervised by an adult. The regulation was clearly content-based, yet the Ninth Circuit Court of Appeals upheld the regulation in 1996, finding that the physical and psychological well-being of children were compelling state interests, and the statute was narrowly drawn to advance those interests.

As with sign regulation, the local government enacting the newsbox control regulations should take care to do studies to document the public benefits to be achieved by the regulation. The approach taken by Salt Lake City continues to provide a good model. In the mid-1980s, the city undertook a study of the number and location of newsboxes in the central business district and found that they were obstructing pedestrian passage on sidewalks and detracting visually from the downtown. The study also documented damage being done to public fixtures in the process of anchoring the boxes. Based on this evidence, the city enacted comprehensive regulations for newsboxes that require owners to register each newsbox and its location with the city; prescribe the size of the newsboxes, the maximum number at any one location, and the method of anchoring; and impose a number of other restrictions designed to balance dissemination of news with community aesthetics, protection of public property, and maintaining unobstructed use of public sidewalks. The positive results of the legislation are noticeable to anyone who strolls the wide, uncluttered streets of downtown Salt Lake City.

As with sign regulation, the local government enacting the newsbox control regulations should take care to do studies to document the public benefits to be achieved by the regulation. The approach taken by Salt Lake City continues to provide a good model.

Notes

1. The First Amendment provides: "Congress shall make no law . . . bridging the freedom of speech, or of the press. . . ." The Fourteenth Amendment makes this limitation applicable to the states.

2. For other state court cases upholding sign regulations based on aesthetic concerns, see: *City of Lake Wales v. Lamar Advertising Ass'n*, 414 So.2d 1030 (1982) (Florida); *State v. Diamond Motors, Inc.*, 429 P.2d 825 (1967) (Hawaii); *Temple Baptist Church v. City of Albuquerque*, 646 P.2d 505 (1982) (New Mexico); *People v. Goodman*, 290 N.E.2d 139 (1972) (New York); *Goodman Toyota, Inc. v. City of Raleigh*, 306 S.E.2d 192 (1983) (North Carolina); *Sun Oil Corp. v. City of Upper Arlington*, 379 N.E.2d 266 (1977) (Ohio).

3. For a useful background discussion on this distinction, see Ziegler (1995).

4. See, for example, *National Advertising Co. v. City of Denver*, 912 F.2d 405 (10th Cir. 1990), upholding a ban on off-premises commercial signs within 660 feet of a freeway. Note that the ability to impose reasonable time, place, and manner restrictions on commercial signs does not allow local governments to force a company to modify a registered trademark (*Blockbuster Videos v. City of Tempe*, 141 F.3d 1295 (1998)).

5. Federal laws preempt some state and local regulation of the content of alcohol and cigarette advertisements. See the Federal Alcohol Administration Act, 27 USC, Sections 201-219a; and Federal Cigarette Labeling and Advertising Act, 15 USC, Sections 1331-1340.

6. Newsboxes are known by many names throughout the country, including "newspaper vending machines" and, in New York City, "honor boxes." Two helpful background articles on this subject are Floyd and Reed (1997) and Fletemeyer (1997).

Chapter 6

Telecommunications Facilities

There is no evidence that the City Council had any intent to favor one company or form of service over another. In addition, the evidence shows that opposition to the application rested on traditional bases of zoning regulation: preserving the character of the neighborhood and avoiding aesthetic blight.

AT&T WIRELESS PCS, INC. V. CITY COUNCIL OF THE
CITY OF VIRGINIA BEACH, 155 F.3D 423 (4TH CIV. 1998), AT 427

WRITTEN JUST 13 YEARS AGO, THE ORIGINAL EDITION OF THIS REPORT WAS ABLE TO COVER THE RELATIVELY NEW ISSUE OF SATELLITE DISHES, AND AESTHETIC CONCERNS, IN JUST A FEW PAGES TUCKED INTO A CHAPTER DEALING WITH THE MUCH MORE TRADITIONAL TOPIC OF SIGN AND BILLBOARD CONTROLS. Thanks to the booming growth of the multi-billion dollar telecommunications industry, however, local governments today are increasingly worried about the aesthetic impacts of thousands of new wireless communications towers, dishes, antennas, and related facilities springing up all across the country.

The tension between scenic resources and telecommunications facilities is not a new phenomenon. For most of the century, telephone poles and wires have been strung through our neighborhoods and along roadways, disrupting picturesque views. Indeed, these wires and poles have been around for so long that, today, few of us stop to consider how visually dominant they are in our communities.

Since the introduction of wireless phone service in 1984, the aesthetic concerns associated with telecommunications facilities have increased exponentially, as millions of Americans have begun taking advantage of convenient new technologies such as personal communication services (PCS). Almost one-third of American adults were using wireless phone service by the end of 1998. While many people make the majority of wireless calls from their cars, the percentages of those calling from home and offices is rising, possibly suggesting the eventual replacement of "landline" service by wireless service. Most calls take place in dense urban areas and along heavily trafficked transportation corridors, with far fewer taking place outside such areas because of lack of coverage. This is changing, though, as telecommunications providers erect more and more towers.

Today, there are around 35,000 towers throughout the country, and there may be four times that many in existence in just a few years as the wireless industry matures. Often reaching several hundred feet tall and placed in elevated, highly visible public spaces, such facilities may have substantial communitywide aesthetic impacts. The towers infuriate nearby residents concerned about the visual impacts on their neighborhoods and threaten tourism by marring visually sensitive areas and resources. As a result, many governments are attempting to regulate communications facilities much more aggressively than they have before.

In the past, local regulation of satellite dishes and other telecommunication facilities posed few legal difficulties, and reasonable restrictions that related to proper zoning were upheld by the courts. Today, however, because of the passage of major new federal legislation, the law regarding local government siting, placement, and maintenance of such towers has become significantly more complicated. In February, 1996, Congress passed the Telecommunications Act of 1996, which makes clear that telecommunications infrastructure *will* be built within specified time frames in order to provide all Americans with access to new technologies and to accommodate healthy competition within the telecommunications industry. Many states, too, have passed their own legislation limiting local control.

The bottom line for local governments is that, while compliance with federal and state laws is necessary, and while this area of land-use regulation has become much more complicated in recent years than it was in the past, *it is still possible to draft regulations that minimize the effects of wireless towers on local community character and visual resources.*

This chapter discusses how communities can draft such regulations. First is an overview of the law regarding three principal types of telecommunications facilities: personal wireless service facilities, satellite dishes and television antennas, and amateur radio antennas. The second half of the chapter examines tools local governments can use to regulate such facilities, including advance planning techniques, zoning controls, and development standards.

GENERAL LEGAL ISSUES

As with the other forms of local land-use regulation discussed in this report, courts generally uphold restrictions on telecommunications towers so long they are reasonably related to a valid public purpose, which may include the protection of aesthetic resources and/or community character. Thus, local controls that regulate the siting, appearance, and height of antenna towers generally will be acceptable so long as they are reasonably crafted to accomplish specific aesthetic goals of the community.[1]

Beyond this basic principle, however, the field of telecommunications is tremendously influenced by recently adopted federal and state statutes, and by regulations that set limits on local government action. In other words, federal and state law either fully or partially "preempts" local regulation. Knowledge of these statutes and regulations is crucial for communities looking to craft regulations that will withstand judicial scrutiny.[2]

Federal involvement in the area of communications technology has a long history, dating back to the 1910s and 1920s when Congress first at-

> In the past, local regulation of satellite dishes and other telecommunication facilities posed few legal difficulties, and reasonable restrictions that related to proper zoning were upheld by the courts. Today, however, because of the passage of major new federal legislation, the law regarding local government siting, placement, and maintenance of such towers has become significantly more complicated.

Frank Vespe

As is obvious from this photo, telecommunications towers can have a jarring effect on the landscape and the view. Communities that are concerned about such effects need to carefully craft their regulations, making sure not to run afoul of the provisions set out in the Telecommunications Act of 1996.

tempted to impose order on the telegraph and rapidly developing radio and telephone industries. In 1934, the Communications Act, which is still in place today, solidified federal control of the airwaves and gave the federal government the ultimate authority to regulate telecommunications in interstate commerce. These early statutes were passed principally to provide order to the airwaves, but they also responded to the confusing patchwork of state and local regulations that had developed to control utility poles, telephone wires, and other such devices. Congress specifically preempted state and local control whenever state and local regulations conflicted with the new federal statutes or attempted to inhibit competition or the development of new technologies. Heverly (1996) provides a useful discussion of the history of telecommunications law.

Recently, Congress again fundamentally altered the legal landscape in this area by passing the Telecommunications Act of 1996 (TCA), which became law on February 8, 1996 (Pubic Law No. 104-104, 47 U.S.C. Section 332(c)(7)). Recognizing telecommunications technology as a major emerging force in the American economy, the TCA outlines in general terms a new national policy that encourages competition—and discourages government regulation—in the industry, to the maximum extent possible. According to Congress, the TCA is designed "to provide for a pro-competitive, de-regulatory national policy framework designed to accelerate rapid private sector deployment of advanced telecommunications and information technology and services to all Americans and by opening all telecommunications markets to competition" (H.R. Conf. Rep. No. 104-458, 104th Cong., 2d Sess. 113 (1996)). The TCA makes a host of changes in the way communications providers operate and are regulated, in areas as wide ranging as taxation, use of the public rights-of-way, and cable television rates. The TCA itself is broad and conceptual, and the Federal Communications Commission (FCC) has subsequently set rules clarifying exactly what many of the TCA's provisions mean and how they are to be implemented.

This chapter concentrates on those provisions of the TCA and the FCC rules, as well as other laws, that affect *local planning and zoning authority*—the area in which communities may most directly influence the aesthetic aspects of telecommunications facilities. Given the billions of dollars at stake, it is not surprising that companies already have begun to litigate the key provisions of the act, and the most significant of these cases are discussed below. The law surrounding three distinct types[3] of facilities is discussed: (1) personal wireless service facilities, (2) satellite dishes and television antennae, and (3) amateur radio antennas.

PERSONAL WIRELESS SERVICE FACILITIES

"Personal wireless service facilities" is an umbrella term encompassing a broad range of wireless communication technologies that transmit information almost instantaneously, primarily including cellular telephones (which use analog technology) and the newer personal communication services (PCS, which use digital technology).

Both cellular and PCS technologies require an interconnected network of antennas to function effectively. Such a network involves a large geographical area divided into "cells," each of which has an antenna that broadcasts to subscribers. As a subscriber travels from cell to cell, the signal is handed off from antenna to antenna, providing uninterrupted service. If the subscriber travels outside the permissible range, however, the call is disconnected. Wireless providers, wanting to provide uninterrupted service, attempt to place antennas strategically to meet customer demand. As customer usage increases, a correspondingly larger number of towers is needed. These new towers may be placed anywhere from elevated, highly visible sites to secluded forests, and from dense urban areas to rural highways. The new, popular PCS technology generally requires more towers to function than does cellular technology, although the digital towers may be somewhat shorter than the analog towers. Antennas for all personal wireless service facilities may be affixed either to freestanding towers or to existing buildings, with freestanding towers generally having a far greater visual impact, as is discussed later. For both cellular and PCS facilities, there are three types of hardware to be considered: the antennas themselves, the mounting structures upon which the antennas are placed (including towers), and the equipment shelters in which the controls for the antennas are located.

General Legal Issues

Regulation of personal wireless service facilities is considerably restricted by the TCA. Section 704 of the TCA, the primary provision dealing with local planning and zoning authority, generally preserves local control over siting, construction, modification, and use of wireless facilities, but imposes significant limitations upon that control. The key *substantive* limitations include the following:

- Local zoning may not "unreasonably discriminate among providers of functionally equivalent services."

- Local zoning may not "prohibit or have the effect of prohibiting the provision of wireless services."

Regulation of personal wireless service facilities is considerably restricted by the TCA. Section 704 of the TCA, the primary provision dealing with local planning and zoning authority, generally preserves local control over siting, construction, modification, and use of wireless facilities, but imposes significant limitations upon that control.

- No state or local government may regulate personal wireless service facilities based on the environmental effects of radio frequency emissions, to the extent that such facilities comply with the Federal Communications Commission (FCC) regulations concerning such emissions.

In addition, Section 704 contains important *procedural* limitations on local authority, including the following:

- Local governments must act on applications "to place, construct, or modify personal wireless service facilities within a reasonable period of time."

- Local government decisions denying personal wireless service facility applications "shall be in writing and supported by substantial evidence contained in a written record."

- Any person adversely affected by a state or local decision concerning personal wireless service facilities may commence an action in federal or state court.

To ensure compliance with the TCA, communities should review their zoning ordinances and determine whether current or future activities would violate either the general intent of Section 704—promotion of competition whenever possible—or any of the specific substantive or procedural limitations listed above. Specific guidance on each of the limitations is provided below.

Unreasonable Discrimination

The first substantive limitation is that local actions may not "unreasonably discriminate" among providers of functionally equivalent services. This provision does not mean that all providers or all proposed sites must be treated exactly alike; it does mean, however, that any distinctions made must be reasonable and legally defensible. For example, a community might legitimately approve towers proposed in industrial areas and deny towers proposed for residential areas if it finds that the impacts on surrounding properties will be demonstrably less intense in industrial areas, and that denial of towers in residential areas will not inhibit the provision of wireless services to any residents of the community.

The few courts to have examined this limitation have found that a variety of local zoning activities can constitute unreasonable discrimination, including actions that increase one provider's costs, therefore make competition with other providers more difficult, or actions that favor existing technologies over the introduction of new services.

A 1997 case from New Mexico illustrates one common situation: A court found the denial of a local conditional use permit to be unreasonably discriminatory (*Western PCS II Corporation v. Extraterritorial Zoning Authority of the City and County of Santa Fe*, 957 F.Supp 1230 (D.N.M. 1997)). The City and County of Santa Fe denied Western PCS's request to mount a wireless telecommunications antenna array to a water tank. The array, to be located in the Hondo Hills area near a federal interstate highway, would introduce digital technology into an area previously served only by analog service. In addition, the array would allow Western to offer uninterrupted digital service along the I-25 corridor; Western's competitors already offered uninterrupted analog service along that corridor. After considering Western's request at three meetings that took place over five months, the local zoning authority denied the permit, in part because no residents of the subdivision to be served had ever spoken in favor of the application.

The first substantive limitation is that local actions may not "unreasonably discriminate" among providers of functionally equivalent services. This provision does not mean that all providers or all proposed sites must be treated exactly alike; it does mean, however, that any distinctions made must be reasonable and legally defensible.

The court found that Santa Fe's denial of the permit constituted unreasonable discrimination under the TCA. The court explained:

> It does not take a telecommunications engineer or a marketing expert to recognize that an inability to provide uninterrupted service along the I-25 corridor would seriously impede Western's ability to compete with its competitors in the Santa Fe area. While Western provides a digital technology, rather than the analog service that its competitors provide, they are "functionally equivalent services." The . . . denial of Western's exemption either denies Western the opportunity to compete with its competitors along the I-25 corridor (and arguably throughout Santa Fe as a result), or it significantly increases Western's costs, and thereby reduces its ability to compete, by requiring it to provide an alternative site. (at 1237–38)

The case demonstrates that local officials must examine the effects their decisions will have on an applicant's competitive ability. This is, of course, not the only factor to be considered in local decision making, but the community must demonstrate that it took such considerations into account.

Communities often have suitable, existing sites for mounting telecommunications antennas. One of the most likely sites is a community water tower.

Jenifer Eggleston

Contrast the Santa Fe case with one from Virginia Beach, which illustrates how a municipality can deny an application yet not be guilty of "unreasonable discrimination." In 1997, the Virginia Beach City Council refused to issue a conditional use permit for new telecommunications monopoles (AT&T Wireless PCS, Inc. v. City Council of the City of Virginia Beach, 155 F.3d 423 (4th Cir. 1998)). The monopoles were to provide PCS service to the Little Neck peninsula, a residential area then equipped only for cellular service. Because the Little Neck area is highly wooded, the local planning staff, working with the two providers seeking to erect the towers, determined that construction of new towers, rather than use of existing facilities, would be necessary to provide PCS service in the area. A local church agreed to lease some of its land for construction of two new 135-foot monopoles that would accommodate antennas for all the providers, both digital and analog, licensed to service the Little Neck area.

Construction of the monopoles required a conditional use permit under the Virginia Beach zoning ordinance. The church's permit application included supportive supplemental materials (e.g., a letter from an appraiser stating that the proposed towers would have not adverse impact upon surrounding residential property values), yet many in the community voiced strong opposition to locating the towers in a residential area. Despite this opposition, the planning commission recommended approval. The city council, however, recognized mounting community opposition, which culminated in the presentation of petitions with more than 700 signatures in opposition to the towers. The city council rejected the planning commission's recommendation and voted unanimously to deny the application.

The federal district court found that the city council's denial violated the TCA, since it amounted to discrimination against new digital service providers in favor of existing analog service providers. The Fourth Circuit Court of Appeals, however, reversed and upheld the city council's rejection of the permit application. The court noted first that there was no unreasonable discrimination among providers of functionally equivalent services because both forms of wireless service (digital and analog) and all providers then operating in the Little Neck market would have benefitted from the new towers. Further, said the court, even if there had been some discrimination, it was not unreasonable.

> There is no evidence that the City Council had any intent to favor one company or form of service over another. In addition, the evidence shows that opposition to the application rested on traditional bases of zoning regulation: preserving the character of the neighborhood and avoiding aesthetic blight. If such behavior is unreasonable, then nearly every denial of an application such as this will violate the [TCA], an obviously absurd result. (at 427)

In spite of the ultimate result in the Virginia Beach case, which is quite favorable to municipalities, the case law nevertheless demonstrates that courts have found a variety of actions to constitute unreasonable discrimination. Communities are thus cautioned to examine their ordinances, policies, and procedures to ensure that all providers of functionally equivalent services (which is defined broadly) are treated in the same manner. *All applications for personal wireless service facilities do not have to be approved, and distinctions may be made among providers, but communities must justify that any distinctions made are reasonable.* Ideally, communities should have procedures and policies in place that identify rational distinguishing characteristics (e.g., proximity to sensitive resources, presence of existing towers that could support additional antennas) before applications are submitted to give providers fair warning about the types of applications most likely to be approved. Also, as is discussed in detail below, communities should ensure that substantial evidence supports any distinctions made and that such evidence is entered into the official written record of all decisions.

Prohibition of Service

Section 704's second substantive limitation on local zoning authority is that communities may not enact regulations that prohibit, or have the effect of prohibiting, the provision of personal wireless services. Congress's comments here are instructive: "It is the intent of this section that *bans or policies* that have the effect of banning personal wireless services or facilities not be allowed and that decisions be made on a case-by-case basis" (H.R. Conf. Rep. No. 104-458). In other words, this limitation bars actions that prohibit entire classes of service or affect entire geographic areas.[4]

All applications for personal wireless service facilities do not have to be approved, and distinctions may be made among providers, but communities must justify that any distinctions made are reasonable. Ideally, communities should have procedures and policies in place that identify rational distinguishing characteristics (e.g., proximity to sensitive resources, presence of existing towers that could support additional antennas) before applications are submitted to give providers fair warning about the types of applications most likely to be approved.

The City and County of Santa Fe ran afoul of this provision in the 1997 case mentioned above when it denied the application to mount a wireless telecommunications antenna array to a water tank. The array would have introduced digital service into an area that previously had only analog service. The court found that the denial constituted an effective prohibition of the provision of personal wireless services. The court explained: "Denial of Western's request has the effect of denying the provision of this new technology and its advantages to the Hondo Hills area. Most significantly, it denies this new technology to the I-25 corridor, as Western is the only provider of digital technology in the Santa Fe area." (Recall that the court also overturned the permit denial because it was unreasonably discriminatory; one action may easily run afoul of both limitations.)

Yet, this provision does not require a community to approve each and every application it receives. Communities vary greatly in terms of geography, population distribution, transportation networks, and other factors, and thus widely varying numbers and types of telecommunications facilities will be required to serve different areas. Therefore, as Congress noted, courts considering whether local regulations or decisions effectively prohibit the provision of personal wireless services must make their determinations on a case-by-case basis. And keep in mind this important point: *It is the provision of personal wireless services that must be allowed under the TCA, not necessarily the siting of towers.* Depending upon circumstances, a community might be able to deny most or all applications for towers that it receives and still not deprive its residents of personal wireless services.

Wireless companies alleging that individual permit denials have violated this provision of the TCA have, in the absence of an outright ban or the introduction of a new technology, generally been unsuccessful. For example, in 1997, the City of Ferrysburg, Michigan, denied a request by a provider to build a new 230-foot tower to improve existing service (*Century Cellunet of Southern Michigan v. City of Ferrysburg,* 993 F.Supp. 1072 (W.D. Mich. 1997)). The provider sued, alleging the denial amounted to a prohibition of service. A federal district court upheld the denial, noting that the provider had itself admitted there were other options available for improving customer service, and thus the denial did not amount to a ban on the provision of personal wireless services.[5]

Decision in Writing and Supported by Substantial Evidence

A number of communities have run afoul of Section 704's procedural limitations. The main procedural requirement is that denials of permit applications for personal wireless service facilities must be in writing and based upon substantial evidence contained in a written record. The idea is that sufficient written documentation must exist in order to allow a reviewing court to understand the reasoning behind a decision and whether that reasoning comports with the evidence presented.

A few jurisdictions have litigated the seemingly simple requirement that denials must be in writing. In the Virginia Beach case, for instance, the city council notified an applicant of its denial of his permit application by sending only a copy of the agenda item concerning the application with "Denied" stamped at the bottom. The city cited a copy of the official minutes of the council meeting as written evidence of the decision. A federal district court found the city's actions to be insufficient to meet the "in writing" requirement and suggested that the city should have produced written findings of fact to accompany its denial. The Fourth Circuit Court of Appeals disagreed, however, believing the rubber stamp notification to be sufficient, and also holding that "The simple requirement of a 'decision...in

Keep in mind this important point: It is the provision of personal wireless services that must be allowed under the TCA, not necessarily the siting of towers. Depending upon circumstances, a community might be able to deny most or all applications for towers that it receives and still not deprive its residents of personal wireless services.

writing' cannot reasonably be inflated into a requirement" that formal findings of fact be produced (at 430).[6]

The Virginia Beach holding is in line with most decisions on this issue, which have stated that the "in writing" requirement should not be difficult to satisfy. Note, however, that a few courts have held that a transcript of a hearing in which a permit is denied is, by itself, insufficient to meet the "in writing" requirement (e.g., *Western PCS*, at 1236). Rather, these courts have found that, in order to comply with Section 704, communities must supplement written denials of applications for personal wireless service facilities with written findings of fact that articulate the reasons behind the decision, based upon the evidence presented.

Most cases involving this provision of Section 704, however, revolve around the more complex question of what constitutes "substantial evidence," which is defined by the courts as sufficient, relevant evidence, such as "a reasonable mind might accept as adequate to support a conclusion" (*Universal Camera Corp. v. NLRB*, 340 U.S. 474, 477 (1952)). Communities attempting to make sense of this legalese have met with mixed success in court.

Of the cases in which local decisions were overturned because of a lack of substantial evidence, one common theme is apparent: generalized community concerns, unaccompanied by supporting documentation, do not constitute substantial evidence under Section 704. A 1996 Georgia case provides a good example. The Gwinnett County Board of Commissioners denied a permit for a 197-foot monopole in a commercial area (*BellSouth Mobility v. Gwinnett County*, 944 F.Supp. 923 (N.D. Ga. 1996)). In support of its application, the provider had produced numerous supporting materials, including an appraiser's report showing that communication monopoles did not affect surrounding residential property values in nearby neighborhoods and would not present air safety concerns. In addition, several county review agencies had no objections to the application. In contrast, opponents of the monopole had merely spoken for five minutes at the public hearing, voicing vague concerns about safety and property values, but offering no supporting documentation. The commissioners denied the permit without any discussion.

On appeal, a federal district court overruled the denial. In view of the readily apparent disparity in the provider's evidence and the county's evidence, the court found that it could not "conscientiously" side with the commissioners. Noted the court, "The only record evidence supporting the board's decision is the content of Mr. Nelson's five minute testimony. In light of the compelling evidence presented by the plaintiffs, however, the court finds that Mr. Nelson's generalized concerns do not constitute substantial evidence supporting the board's decision."

The lesson, from this and several similar cases, is clear: the mere existence of generalized opposition to a proposal, without supporting documentation, will usually be insufficient to counter reasoned, expert opinion under the substantial evidence standard.[7]

Contrast other cases in which permit denials were upheld because the communities could point to substantial evidence in a written record to back up their decisions.[8] In the Ferrysburg, Michigan, case cited above, for example, a federal district court upheld the city's decision to deny a permit for a proposed 230-foot tower. The court noted that the city's decision was supported by adequate substantial evidence in at least two areas, both of which were summarized in formally adopted findings of fact. First, the city found that the tower would pose an unreasonable risk to adjoining properties. The city had expressed concern during hearings about the possibility that the tower might fall onto adjoining properties; the provider

Of the cases in which local decisions were overturned because of a lack of substantial evidence, one common theme is apparent: generalized community concerns, unaccompanied by supporting documentation, do not constitute substantial evidence under Section 704.

The lesson, from this and several similar cases, is clear: the mere existence of generalized opposition to a proposal, without supporting documentation, will usually be insufficient to counter reasoned, expert opinion under the substantial evidence standard.

had assured the city that the tower would buckle in upon itself and not fall erect upon adjoining properties, but had offered no supporting documentation as proof. Noted the court, "If the tower were to fail and fall erect, surrounding properties would be affected. Thus, . . . the 'unreasonable risk' finding was supported by substantial evidence."

Second, the city found that the tower would not be "in harmony" with adjoining residences or the surrounding area. The court agreed, noting:

> The tower was to be over 230 feet tall. Also, the tower was to be lighted with white flashing lights during the day, and red lights at the top and middle. Since Ferrysburg is a small city, the land surrounding the tower would be the whole city. None of the buildings or structures surrounding the tower are alleged to be over 230 feet tall with flashing lights. Thus, the . . . finding, regarding the harmony with existing areas, was supported by substantial evidence. (at 1077)[9]

Reasonable Time

Section 704 also requires that decisions on applications for personal wireless service facilities be made within a "reasonable period of time." Rather than imposing a specific time limit, this provision simply means that such decisions should be processed in roughly the same amount of time required for other applications of a similar nature. Noted Congress: "It is not the intent of this provision to give preferential treatment to the personal wireless service industry in the processing of requests, or to subject their requests to any but the generally applicable time frames for zoning decision" (H.R. Conf. Rep. No. 104–458, 104th Conf., 2d Sess. 208 (1996)).

This usually should not be a difficult standard to meet, especially if local staff process the application with diligence, even though a final decision may be months away. In a case from Peoria County, Illinois, for example, a federal district court found that a review period lasting six months was reasonable, even though similar requests in the county took about three months to process, and the "usual duration" of zoning procedures in the community was two to three months (*Illinois RSA No.3, Inc., v. County of Peoria*, 963 F.Supp. 732 (C.D. Ill. 1997)). Explained the court:

Jenifer Eggleston

The roofs of buildings may provide the means to ensure an adequate distribution of antennas to serve community needs. The antennas on this building are clearly less obtrusive than a new tower.

The Court cannot say that taking six months, compared to three months, is per se unreasonable, and nothing in the record suggests that the County simply ignored or refused to process Plaintiff's request. Additionally, the Department issued its first report slightly more than one month after Plaintiff filed the Petition, suggesting that the Department began to work on (or acted upon) the Petition almost as soon as the Plaintiff filed it. Furthermore, the record reveals that Plaintiff did not object to several continuances, and generally took a permissive approach to scheduling (no doubt to foster local good will). (at 746)[10]

Note that courts take seriously the TCA's mandate that applications for telecommunications facilities be processed expeditiously. In several cases, courts overturning permit denials have refused to send the cases back to the communities for reconsideration (the usual course of action), instead directing the communities to issue permits immediately. Noted the judge in one such case: ". . . [S]imply remanding the matter to the [community] would frustrate the TCA's intent to provide aggrieved parties full relief on an expedited basis" (*Bell South Mobility v. Gwinnett County*, at 929).

Personal wireless service facilities, which may reach several hundred feet tall and thus have substantial communitywide aesthetic impacts, are the major focus of this chapter. Other types of facilities do trigger some aesthetic concerns, however, and the remainder of this section touches on some of the most common: satellite dishes and television antennas, and amateur radio antennas.

SATELLITE DISHES AND TELEVISION ANTENNAS

A decade ago, the aesthetic issues associated with earth-satellite receiving stations (or "satellite dishes") were a major issue of concern since a typical dish could measure from 6 to 12 feet in diameter and, if placed in a front yard, could substantially detract from the character of the street and surrounding neighborhood. Today, however, the aesthetic concerns associated with satellite dishes are less worrisome, not only because the dishes themselves are being made smaller and thus much less obtrusive, but also because new, competing technologies, such as digital cable television, have reduced the overall market demand for dishes. This section discusses the law relating to satellite dishes and television reception antennas. The two types of devices are treated together since they are covered by the same provisions of the TCA.

Legal Issues

The TCA deals with satellite dishes and television antennas in a completely different fashion than it does personal wireless service facilities. Section 207 of the TCA directs the FCC to adopt regulations that prohibit restrictions on viewers' ability to receive video programming services through satellite dishes and television antennas.[11] In August 1996, pursuant to this directive, the FCC identified three classes of dishes and antennas and adopted different rules for each. In general, these rules, which replace previous FCC preemption rules, are much more restrictive of local zoning authority than the restrictions related to personal wireless service facilities discussed above. Few cases have been litigated so far on these rules.

Small satellite dishes. This class includes satellite receiving dishes of one meter or less in diameter (or of any size in Alaska) and also includes television broadcast antennas and multichannel mulitpoint distribution services (MMDS), which are also known as "wireless cable" (47 C.F.R. Section 1.4000). *Generally, any restriction that impairs the installation, maintenance, or use of any of these devices is prohibited.* This rule applies to both gov-

> Note that courts take seriously the TCA's mandate that applications for telecommunications facilities be processed expeditiously. In several cases, courts overturning permit denials have refused to send the cases back to the communities for reconsideration (the usual course of action), instead directing the communities to issue permits immediately.

> The aesthetic concerns associated with satellite dishes are less worrisome, not only because the dishes themselves are being made smaller and thus much less obtrusive, but also because new, competing technologies, such as digital cable television, have reduced the overall market demand for dishes.

ernment regulation and also private rules and covenants (if the property in question is owned or controlled by the antenna user). "Impairment" includes any action that:

- unreasonably delays or prevents installation, maintenance, or use;

- unreasonably increases the cost of installation, maintenance, or use; or

- precludes reception of an acceptable signal quality.

The FCC has defined unreasonable delay in this context to include any review procedure that would delay a viewer's access to video programming. Thus, any local government review procedure, such as a conditional use permit review process or any private review by a homeowners' association, would be prohibited under these rules.

The unreasonable cost provision is interpreted by the FCC to require a multifactored balancing test to assess the reasonableness of costs imposed, based upon the relative costs of the device and the required improvements. The FCC's language is helpful:

> While we decline to adopt a formula based on a specific percentage of the costs of equipment or services, we do require that the costs of complying with governmental and nongovernmental restrictions on the installation, maintenance, and use of devices . . . not be unreasonable in light of the cost of the equipment or services and the visual impact of the antenna. Under this approach, restrictions cannot require that relatively unobtrusive . . . antennas be screened by expensive landscaping. On the other hand, a requirement to paint an antenna in a fashion that will not interfere with reception so that it blends into the background against which it is mounted would likely be acceptable. In determining the reasonableness of any additional cost, we will also consider the treatment of comparable devices. For example, if costs are imposed to screen other similar devices in the neighborhood, such as air conditioning units, trash receptacles, etc., similar requirements imposed on antennas may be reasonable under our rule even though they might increase the cost of installation, maintenance, or use, if such measures are justified by visual impact.[12]

Finally, public or private regulation may not impair reception of an acceptable quality signal. Thus, a requirement that a satellite dish be placed in the rear yard and not be visible from the public right-of-way, regardless of the impact on signal quality, would be prohibited under the rules. But a requirement with these same restrictions, and also a waiver provision if signal quality is impaired, likely would be acceptable (Ziegler 1998).

There are two exemptions to the rules for small satellite dishes. A restriction is permitted, even if it impairs or prevents reception, or imposes unreasonable cost or delay, if it is: (1) necessary to accomplish a defined safety objective,[13] or (2) is necessary to preserve an historic district listed or eligible for listing in the National Register of Historic Places.[14] In both instances, the regulation must be no more burdensome to affected antenna users than is necessary to achieve the desired objective and may impose restrictions no greater than otherwise imposed on the installation, maintenance, or use of other modern, comparable devices.

Large satellite dishes in commercial or industrial areas. The FCC has issued different, broader rules for satellite dishes of between one and two meters in diameter that are located in commercial or industrial areas (47 C.F.R. Section 25.104(b)). Rather than merely refraining from impairing reception or raising costs associated with these dishes, local governments may not adopt any regulation that "affects" these dishes. There are no exemptions for safety measures or protection of historic sites. The rules ensure that most dishes of this class will find a "safe haven" in nonresidential areas.

Local governments may nevertheless impose reasonable restrictions on dishes in this class if they apply for and obtain a waiver from the FCC. Waiver applications go through a public notice and hearing process prior to approval, and the burden of proof is on the government to demonstrate that the proposed restriction is reasonable. A reasonable regulation is one that is necessary to accomplish a clearly defined health or safety objective that is stated in the text of the regulation, is no more burdensome to satellite users than is necessary to achieve the health or safety objective, and is specifically applicable on its face to this class of satellite dish.

All large satellite dishes. Finally, a third set of rules applies to all satellite dishes more than one meter in diameter (47 C.F.R. Section 25.104(a)). Local governments may not adopt unreasonable regulations of this class of dishes that materially limit transmission or reception or that impose more than minimal costs on users. Reasonable regulations are allowed, however. In this context, reasonable regulations are those with a clearly defined health, safety, *or aesthetic* objective that is stated in the text of the regulation and that further such an objective without unnecessarily burdening access to services or fair competition. Waivers may be sought from the FCC for local concerns of a highly specialized or unusual nature.

Note that aesthetic objectives are considered a legitimate basis for regulation only under this largest class of dishes. Thus, controls on materials, color, size, height, setbacks, and other physical considerations clearly are acceptable tools for this largest class of dishes but are subject to much more scrutiny under the first class and are prohibited altogether for the second class.

AMATEUR RADIO ANTENNAS

Finally, a brief note on amateur radio antennas, the tall metal towers usually placed in the rear yards of private residences in order to allow residents to send and receive long-distance radio transmissions, is offered here. As with satellite dishes and television antennas, the aesthetic impacts of amateur radio antennas generally are limited more to surrounding residential properties and streets rather than entire communities. The antennas certainly can be more physically intrusive than satellite dishes, however, and heights of 50 feet are not uncommon.

Unlike personal wireless service facilities and satellite dishes, amateur radio antennas are not regulated by the 1996 TCA, and therefore local governments are much freer to regulate such devices based upon aesthetic and other impacts (Ziegler 1998, Section 55A.04). In general, courts uphold reasonable local zoning controls on the placement, installation, height, and screening of such antennas, despite potential freedom of speech issues under the First Amendment.[15]

In 1985, the FCC adopted rules providing for limited federal preemption of these antennas (FCC PRB-1, 101 FCC 2d 952 (Sept. 16, 1985)). Generally, under these rules, states and local governments may not regulate amateur radio antenna structures in such a way as to preclude amateur service communications. Rather, regulation—including aesthetic measures, such as controls on placement, screening, or height—must reasonably accommodate such communications and must constitute the minimum practicable regulation to accomplish the stated purpose.

Thus, in 1993, a federal appeals court upheld a Boulder County, Colorado, decision limiting the height of a ham radio antenna tower to 35 feet. The court ruled that the county's action served legitimate goals of protecting views of the Rocky Mountains and maintaining local property values, and screening of the tower and other mitigation measures proposed by the applicant would have been inadequate (*D.R. Evans v. Board of County Commr's*, 994 F.2d 755 (10th Cir. 1993)). Bans of amateur radio antennae are not acceptable in residential areas (*Thernes v. Lakeside Park*, 779 F.2d 1187, 1188 (6th Cir. 1986)). Antennas often are treated as accessory uses for purposes of zoning.

OTHER GENERAL LEGAL REQUIREMENTS FOR TELECOMMUNICATIONS FACILITIES

Other general requirements may apply to various types of telecommunications technologies. For instance, Congress gave the FCC the authority to require the painting or illumination of facilities when it determines that they may otherwise constitute a menace to air navigation.[16] The FCC website (www.fcc.gov) is an excellent source of up-to-date information on this and other policies and rules that may apply, in addition to the statutes and regulations discussed above.

Also note that, for all types of telecommunications facilities, state laws may preempt local regulatory authority in a variety of important ways not mentioned above. Some states have adopted procedures preempting local regulation. For instance, the Connecticut legislature has established a special siting council that has exclusive authority to regulate the siting of new communication towers in the state (Conn. Gen. Stat. Ann. Section 16.50k). Local governments are consulted, but their authority to regulate is specifically preempted. In other states, towers or other telecommunications facilities owned by governmental entities may be exempted from local land-use regulations, or they may qualify as "public utilities," thus meriting special treatment or possible exemption from local regulation. In New York, for example, cellular phone companies are considered utilities and thus are entitled to a reduced burden when seeking variances to establish cellular service (*Cellular Telephone Co. v. Rosenberg*, 82 N.Y.2d 364 (1993)).

LOCAL REGULATORY ISSUES

Given this somewhat exhausting array of legal requirements, what options are available for local governments that want to regulate the aesthetic impacts of telecommunications towers and antennas? This section outlines four essential tools local governments may use to regulate such facilities. First, a moratorium on new development will give the community time to evaluate and revise existing ordinances. Second, communities may plan in advance where such facilities should be located in a way that both complies with legal requirements and minimizes aesthetic and other impacts. Third, a range of zoning tools may be used to regulate spacing and placement of facilities in sensitive areas. And, finally, development standards may be applied to regulate specific physical features of such facilities.

Enacting Moratoria on New Development

Given the complexity of the legal and technical issues in this area, it is not surprising that many communities have attempted to suspend the siting and construction of new telecommunications facilities by enacting moratoria in order to give the community time to review its ordinances and procedures for compliance with federal and state requirements, and also to articulate local policy goals and objectives. Providers have challenged these moratoria under the TCA, alleging that moratoria constitute unreasonable discrimination among providers (by favoring those providers with facilities in place prior to the moratorium, at the expense of later applicants), and violate the TCA's requirement that applications be decided within a reasonable time. The moratoria that have been tested in court have met with mixed results.

> Given the complexity of the legal and technical issues in this area, it is not surprising that many communities have attempted to suspend the siting and construction of new telecommunications facilities by enacting moratoria in order to give the community time to review its ordinances and procedures for compliance with federal and state requirements, and also to articulate local policy goals and objectives.

Transmission towers for electrical service may provide suitable sites for mounting telecommunications antennas. Communities must work closely with telecommunications carriers, however, to make certain that there are no technical drawbacks to such sitings.

Valmont Microflect

Those moratoria enacted through proper procedures by local governments looking specifically to reconcile their ordinances with TCA requirements are most likely to withstand challenge. For instance, a six-month moratorium enacted by the City of Medina, Washington, was upheld by a federal district court in 1996 (*Sprint Spectrum v. City of Medina*, 924 F.Supp. 1036 (D. Wash. 1996)). A small community of 3,000 residents located on the eastern shore of Lake Washington, Medina consists almost entirely of residential development. Because of its proximity to a state highway, the city is a prime area for telecommunications providers. In 1996, just five days after the TCA became law, Medina enacted a six-month moratorium on the issuance of new special use permits for wireless communications facilities. Anticipating a substantial increase in the number of applications, the city was concerned it would become an "antenna farm" and sought time to revise its zoning.[17] A wireless provider sued, alleging the moratorium was illegal under the TCA.

A federal district court upheld the moratorium as a valid zoning tool. The court found that the moratorium did not constitute unreasonable discrimination in favor of existing providers since any new applications submitted by those providers would be subject to the "same rules governing newcomers' applications." Nor did it have a prohibitory effect on the provision of wireless services since the moratorium would not prevent any application from being approved. Noted the court: The moratorium is ". . . a short-term suspension of permit-issuing while the City gathers information and processes applications. Nothing in the record suggests that this is other than a necessary and *bona fide* effort to act carefully in a field with rapidly evolving technology" (at 1040).

The court also found that the moratorium did not violate the TCA's provision that applications be processed within a reasonable period of time. The TCA merely requires that applications be processed under the time frames generally applicable for all zoning decisions. And, since moratoria are a valid zoning tool under Washington state law, generally applicable time frames include any delays occurring under legally enacted moratoria. Noted the court: "There is nothing to suggest that Congress, by requiring action 'within a reasonable period of time,' intended to force local government procedures onto a rigid timetable where the circumstances call for study, deliberation, and decision-making among competing applicants" (at 1040).

Despite the *Medina* ruling, however, courts have not approved all moratoria and are particularly suspicious of communities that seem to be using moratoria as covers for application denials, rather than for providing opportunities for legitimate review and study. In 1997, for instance, a federal district court overturned a moratorium enacted by Jefferson County, Alabama, that was intended to suspend new rezoning applications as well as the processing of pending applications submitted under existing regulations (*Sprint Spectrum , L.P., v. Jefferson County*, 968 F.Supp. 1457 (N.D. Ala. 1997)). Although the moratorium was adopted with a set expiration date, it could be "extended by further action" of the county. Given that this was the third moratorium the county had enacted in less than two years, and that the county already had adopted a comprehensive regulatory scheme for regulating personal wireless facilities (based upon the TCA) over a year earlier, the court found this third moratorium to constitute unreasonable delay under the TCA. It also found the moratorium invalid as unreasonable discrimination among providers of functionally equivalent services and an effective prohibition of the provision of personal wireless services (since the moratorium's principal effect was to limit the introduction of digital service into the community).[18]

In August 1998, the FCC weighed in on the issue of the validity of moratoria under the TCA by entering into a formal agreement with the wireless industry (Federal Communications Commission, August 5, 1998). In response to a petition filed by the industry seeking to prohibit all local zoning moratoria affecting the siting of wireless telecommunications facilities, the FCC affirmed the use of moratoria as a valid zoning tool that does not conflict with the TCA, and presented appropriate moratoria guidelines for local governments. Briefly, the FCC and the industry agreed to these guidelines:

> Moratoria "may be utilized when a local government needs time to review and possibly amend its land use regulations to adequately address issues relating to the siting of wireless telecommunications facilities in a manner that addresses local concerns, provides the public with access to wireless services for its safety, convenience, and productivity, and complies with the Telecommunications Act of 1996."

> Local governments and affected wireless providers should "work together to expeditiously and effectively address issues" that led to the moratorium. Moratoria should be for a fixed period of time (180 days is a suggested, though not mandatory, period).

In response to a petition filed by the industry seeking to prohibit all local zoning moratoria affecting the siting of wireless telecommunications facilities, the FCC affirmed the use of moratoria as a valid zoning tool that does not conflict with the TCA, and presented appropriate moratoria guidelines for local governments.

During the duration of the moratorium, the local government should, "within the framework of the organization's many other responsibilities, continue to process and accept applications," and review its land-use regulations for TCA compliance.

"Local governments are encouraged to include both the community and the industry in the development of local plans concerning tower and antenna siting."

In an effort to head off further legal challenges created by moratoria, the FCC and the industry also created an informal dispute resolution process to be used when moratoria "may seem to be adversely affecting the siting of wireless telecommunications facilities." The process involves the appointment of two volunteers to a dispute, one representing the local government and one representing the industry, who work with their respective clients and each other to come to a mutually agreeable solution within 60 days. Neither party is bound by the volunteers' recommendation, and the parties may bring legal action if they are dissatisfied with the result.

Note that moratoria must comply not only with TCA requirements, but also must be recognized as valid land-use planning tools under applicable state law. In the *Medina* case, for example, the court noted that Washington law expressly allows communities to adopt moratoria or interim zoning ordinances, subject to certain criteria and procedural requirements, with which Medina had complied (at 1039).

Only 10 states (California, Colorado, Kentucky, Michigan, Minnesota, Montana, New Jersey, Oregon, Washington, and Wisconsin) have given local governments express authority to adopt interim zoning ordinances and moratoria (Ziegler 1998, Section 11.03). Eighteen additional states have found such authority inherent in the general authority granted to local governments to protect the public health, safety, and welfare—the so-called "police power." In the remaining states, local governments have no recognized authority to adopt such controls. Alabama is one such state, and the Jefferson County moratorium discussed above could have been overturned simply for lack of state enabling authority. Instead, the court noted that it would have been willing to find implied authority for the moratorium in the state's general zoning authority so long as the county followed the procedural (i.e., notice and hearing) requirements generally applicable to other forms of zoning. Yet, since the county had imposed the moratorium without following the proper procedures (it passed the moratorium without public comment or notice that the moratorium was being considered), the court struck down the measure.

Advance Planning

Communities should use the time gained through a moratorium to examine local aesthetic concerns, to consider how best to revise their land-use regulations to address those concerns, and to comply with federal and state legal requirements. This advance planning stage is crucial—local governments that quickly revise their zoning to impose harsh development standards and prohibit facilities in all sensitive areas, without undertaking advance planning, may very well effectively prohibit the provision of some services in the community and thereby violate the TCA. Instead, communities should plan carefully how they can comply with the law while still accomplishing local objectives. (For a good overview of planning for telecommunications facilities, see Campanelli 1997.)

Planning for telecommunications facilities is on the rise. A 1997 survey found that 16 percent of the jurisdictions surveyed had begun either to develop stand-alone telecommunications plans or to add telecommunications elements to their comprehensive plans. Almost half of the communi-

This advance planning stage is crucial—local governments that quickly revise their zoning to impose harsh development standards and prohibit facilities in all sensitive areas, without undertaking advance planning, may very well effectively prohibit the provision of some services in the community and thereby violate the TCA.

Clarion Associates

Jefferson County, Colorado, has concentrated its towers on one site. Lookout Mountain houses 23 towers ranging from 100 to 800 feet in height; only 10 are visible from public areas because of topography.

ties surveyed had developed a new telecommunications facilities ordinance since passage of the TCA in 1996, with another 15 percent in the process of doing so (Gregory 1997).

The best advance planning efforts should produce a comprehensive map detailing where and how telecommunications facilities should be sited in a community in order both to provide effective service and to minimize visual clutter ("Sticks in the Air, Stakes in the Sand" 1997). Such efforts should begin with a study of important background data. In order to identify more appropriate and less appropriate areas for location of facilities, the study should consider topography, population distribution, major transportation corridors, and existing and proposed land uses. As part of this review, the community should prepare an inventory of all sites within the jurisdiction that are structurally suitable for use as antenna support towers, including existing buildings over a certain height, existing tall facilities (e.g., water tanks), and any other tall structures.

Next, the community should identify those broad geographic areas that are well-suited and not well-suited for telecommunications facilities. More appropriate areas generally may include: land zoned for commercial and industrial uses; large, publicly owned properties, such as parking structures and maintenance yards; lands far removed from residential areas; and lands where visual impacts may be minimized. Less appropriate areas may include: residentially zoned areas; areas with important viewsheds or view corridors; agricultural areas; areas with sensitive environmental features; and areas with high visibility. These determinations of appropriateness should be made in cooperation with wireless industry representatives because their existing service networks are a crucial factor influencing the desirability of certain sites.

Within generally acceptable areas, the community should identify specific sites for locating telecommunications facilities, with the most preferable sites being those with the least impact on surrounding properties and community aesthetics, and the least preferable being those with relatively more impact. The most preferable sites will be existing towers that can support additional antennas or existing tall buildings or structures to which antennas may be mounted. A less attractive option would be construction of new towers in areas where natural topographical and vegetative features would make screening of the tower possible, thus minimizing the aesthetic impact of the towers. The least desirable option would be construction of new towers in areas where lack of such natural features would make screening difficult. Again, planners should interact with service providers in making these determinations to ensure the industry's perspective is reflected in local decision making.

Ideally, communities should plan for telecommunications facilities in cooperation with surrounding jurisdictions. As one consultant has noted, "Given that cellular providers plan their networks from a regional (and broader) perspective, it makes sense for the public to plan for the siting of telecommunications facilities at the same scale—instead of each locality seeking to plan for tower siting independently of neighboring communities" (Campanelli 1997, 5).

The end result of the advance planning efforts should be a master plan for all telecommunications facilities, functioning either as a stand-alone document or as an element of the local comprehensive plan. Such a plan should provide, in one place (and, ideally, for all the various types of facilities discussed in this chapter), a summary of the types of facilities that may (or must) be approved and a guide as to where they should be located.

> The end result of the advance planning efforts should be a master plan for all telecommunications facilities, functioning either as a stand-alone document or as an element of the local comprehensive plan.

One example of this approval is the Liberty, Missouri, "Wireless Communication Facilities Plan," which provides guidance to telecommunications providers about Liberty's preferences for facilities siting, educates readers on telecommunications technology and TCA Section 704 requirements, and lays the foundation for the city's wireless facilities ordinance (the ordinance does not, however, identify individual preferred sites). Another example is "Siting Criteria for Personal Wireless Service Facilities," prepared for the Cape Cod Commission in Barnstable, Massachusetts, which provides similar information for Cape Code towns, and is "intended to be a primer for the towns to help them understand industry needs and identify locations for those facilities that are suitable and consistent with community values."

Zoning Controls

Based on the results of advance planning efforts, communities should review their zoning ordinance and other land-use regulations to ensure compliance with federal and state laws, and compatibility with local aesthetic concerns. A multitude of techniques should be considered when conducting such a review, with the general goal being to limit telecommunications facilities to those areas where they will have the least adverse impact on surrounding properties and the community as a whole.

Restrict facilities in certain zoning districts. The most basic and widely used tool to achieving siting goals is the restriction of telecommunications facilities to certain zoning districts. Traditionally, this has been done by allowing facilities by right in preferred areas (typically commercial and industrial zoning districts) and restricting them in less preferred areas. Restriction may be accomplished by imposition of tough development standards, enactment of additional review procedures, or outright prohibition. Silver City, New

> The most basic and widely used tool to achieving siting goals is the restriction of telecommunications facilities to certain zoning districts. Traditionally, this has been done by allowing facilities by right in preferred areas (typically commercial and industrial zoning districts) and restricting them in less preferred areas.

Mexico, for example, allows all telecommunications facilities by right in its commercial and industrial zoning districts but requires a conditional use permit to locate such a facility in any of its three residential zones. Bloomington, Minnesota, permits towers as conditional uses in all zoning districts except the Conservation and High Intensity Mixed Use districts.

Conditional use permit processes, which typically involve review by a decision-making body and a public hearing, are a common means for restricting facilities in less preferred areas. Telecommunications facilities frequently are made conditional uses in sensitive areas, such as residential or agricultural zoning districts, transitional areas, or historic districts. In such instances, it is important that communities develop standard review and approval criteria to ensure that all applications are treated similarly, and also to provide a basis for the written record of denials required under Section 704 of the TCA. Such criteria also should reference the community's priorities for site selection, so that towers proposed for more appropriate sites are more likely to win approval than those proposed for less desirable sites.

Communities may enact outright bans on facilities in some zoning districts, thus requiring proposed facilities for those areas to obtain rezonings. Again, criteria are important to ensure consistency across applications, to provide a basis for a written record of decision, and to indicate an order of preference for site selection. An important note of caution, however: Local governments should consult with legal counsel and carefully consider the implications of denying facilities in some or all districts since they may inadvertently run afoul of Section 704 of the TCA by prohibiting the provision of wireless services in all or part of the community. Recall, also, that any procedural hoops—even a conditional use permit process—are forbidden for some types of satellite dishes in certain locations.

The community may or may not want to consider restricting the total number of facilities on a single site. The benefit of such a restriction is that no one area becomes an unsightly antenna or dish "farm." On the other hand, the community may wish to concentrate a number of facilities in one place to minimize visual obstructions in other parts of the area. Jefferson County, Colorado, for instance, just west of Denver, designated a specific area on Lookout Mountain for most of its towers. The site currently has 23 towers ranging from 100 to 800 feet in height (although only about 10 are visible from public areas because of the topography) (Gregory 1997).

Impose use standards. Increasingly, many communities are recognizing that they can save time and prevent bureaucratic headaches by not requiring telecommunications facilities to go through conditional use or rezoning procedures. Instead, recognizing that such facilities often have minor land-use impacts (since they generate little traffic, noise, odor, or other such concerns), communities permit the facilities as matters of right, subject to specific use standards. If the facilities fail to comply with the use standards, they cease to comply with the zoning ordinance, and appropriate enforcement measures may be taken. Common use standards include requirements that telecommunications facilities meet all applicable TCA requirements, be screened and/or painted to minimize visibility from residential areas, and be no higher than necessary to ensure effective service for the relevant market area.

Cuyahoga County, Ohio, has developed a model ordinance for municipalities within its boundaries that suggests a number of use regulations.

> When the proposed wirelesss telecommunications facility is to include a new tower, a plot plan at a scale of not less than one inch equal to 100 feet shall be submitted. This plot plan shall indicate all building uses within 300 feet of the proposed facility. Aerial photos and/or renderings may augment the plot plan.

Telecommunications facilities frequently are made conditional uses in sensitive areas, such as residential or agricultural zoning districts, transitional areas, or historic districts. In such instances, it is important that communities develop standard review and approval criteria to ensure that all applications are treated similarly, and also to provide a basis for the written record of denials required under Section 704 of the TCA.

Increasingly, many communities are recognizing that they can save time and prevent bureaucratic headaches by not requiring telecommunications facilities to go through conditional use or rezoning procedures. Instead, recognizing that such facilities often have minor land-use impacts (since they generate little traffic, noise, odor, or other such concerns), communities permit the facilities as matters of right, subject to specific use standards.

- The location of the tower and equipment shelter shall comply with all natural resource protection standards established in the Zoning Code, including those for floodplain, wetlands, and steep slopes.

- Security fencing eight feet in height shall surround the tower, equipment shelter, and any guy wires, either completely or individually as determined by the Planning Commission.

- Existing vegetation (trees and shrubs) shall be preserved to the maximum extent possible.

- The tower shall be painted a noncontrasting gray or similar color, minimizing its visibility, unless otherwise required by the FCC or the FAA.

- No advertising is permitted anywhere on the facility, with the exception of identification signage. (Cuyahoga County Planning Commission, "Wireless Telecommunications Facilities," November 1996)

Because the FCC prohibits any special procedural requirements for certain types of satellite dishes, as noted above, many communities permit satellite dishes by right in all zones and impose use standards to achieve certain aesthetic goals. Cary, North Carolina, for instance, permits satellite dishes in any zoning district provided they meet certain criteria, including:

> Dishes shall not be located within 10 feet of any side or rear property line or in any required buffer, whichever is greater; and Dishes shall be screened so that no more than 30 percent of the area of the dish is visible from any public street or private street open to the public (the screen may consist of fences, buildings, plantings, or any other opaque vegetation or structure permanently affixed to real property). (Town of Cary, North Carolina, Unified Development Ordinance, Section 13.1.3)[19]

Waiver and exemption provisions ensure that such requirements do not impair signal quality or impose unreasonable cost burdens.

Consider overlay zones and floating zones. Special, flexible zoning districts also may be used to apply specific standards to telecommunications facilities. Overlay zone districts layer additional regulations atop the requirements of the underlying zoning classification and do not necessarily follow the geographic boundaries of the base zoning districts. Floating zone districts also attach specific requirements to a particular use but are not limited to any set geographic area. Either overlay or floating zoning districts may be used to attach specific requirements to telecommunications facilities. Both approaches require some initial data gathering and mapping in order to identify preferred areas for towers and sensitive resources to be protected.

Prohibit facilities in environmentally sensitive areas. Despite the TCA's limitations, communities generally should be able to prohibit or severely limit telecommunications facilities in environmentally sensitive areas. Pursuant to the federal National Environmental Policy Act (NEPA), the FCC requires applicants for towers in certain areas to prepare "environmental assessments," which evaluate the potential environmental effects of a proposed action (47 C.F.R. Section 1.1301-1.1319). The specific areas for which such assessments must be prepared include:

- officially designated wilderness areas or wildlife preserves;

- situations that may affect listed threatened or endangered species or critical habitats;

> Despite the TCA's limitations, communities generally should be able to prohibit or severely limit telecommunications facilities in environmentally sensitive areas.

- situations that may affect historical sites listed or eligible for listing in the National Register of Historic Places;

- Native-American religious sites;

- 100-year floodplains;

- situations that may cause significant change in surface features, such as wetland fills, deforestation, or water diversion; and

- proposed use of high-intensity white lights in residential neighborhoods.

NEPA merely requires public notice and a comment period before construction in such an area can begin. If the FCC and the local governing body approve, the project may still go forward despite public opposition. Nevertheless, in practice, the public hearing process provides an opportunity for citizen concerns to be vocalized and incorporated into the record of decision, thereby providing a handy opportunity for a governing body to deny an unwanted tower application.

To further ensure scrutiny of applications in environmentally sensitive areas, communities should consider requiring proof of compliance with the NEPA procedures prior to local approval, or else, assuming they have adequate enabling authority, adopting their own provisions similar to the federal requirement.

Impose time limits. Given the rapidly evolving technology in this field, many communities are justly concerned that a telecommunications facility approved today may be abandoned in a few years if it becomes obsolete or too costly for its owner to maintain. In response, communities should consider imposing a continuous-use requirement, such that, if the facility is not used for a set period, it is considered abandoned and must be removed at the owner's expense. Or a bond might be required, so that the community may itself remove the structure if the provider goes out of business or otherwise abandons the structure.

In its communications towers and facilities ordinance, Overland Park, Kansas, requires that "any antenna or tower that is not operated for a continuous period of 12 months shall be considered abandoned, and the owner of such antenna or tower shall remove the same within 90 days of a receipt of notice. . . ." Or a community might limit permits to a fixed duration (e.g., five years), making them renewable only if certain conditions have been met, including continuous use and compliance with development standards.

Note that the community can use the fixed-duration requirement to accomplish a variety of policy goals, such as encouraging co-location. (Generally, co-location means that multiple antennas, often broadcasting at different frequencies and operated by different providers, share space upon a single tower. This concept is discussed in more detail in a subsection below.) The Overland Park ordinance limits initial special use permits for telecommunications towers to five years. At the time of renewal, the applicant must demonstrate that "a good-faith effort has been made to cooperate with other providers to establish co-location at the tower site. Good-faith effort shall include, but is not limited to, timely response to co-location inquiries from other providers and sharing of technical information to evaluate the feasibility of establishing co-location. Failure to demonstrate that a good-faith effort has been made may result in the denial of the request for a renewal."

Rely on expert advice. One especially helpful innovation in the planning and zoning office can be the addition of a consultant or an advisory committee of experts to assist with the technical aspect of application review. A tech-

Given the rapidly evolving technology in this field, many communities are justly concerned that a telecommunications facility approved today may be abandoned in a few years if it becomes obsolete or too costly for its owner to maintain. In response, communities should consider imposing a continuous-use requirement, such that, if the facility is not used for a set period, it is considered abandoned and must be removed at the owner's expense.

nical review committee or an independent engineering consultant can provide technical advice to governing bodies on questions such as the height proposed for a tower, the feasibility of a proposed co-location, or the potential impacts of a permit denial on existing service networks. A technical committee or consultant also could help the community establish an inventory of existing facilities in the jurisdiction, which could be used both to help providers and staff determine appropriate sites for co-location, and also to determine where service gaps exist and new facilities are required. Furthermore, the findings of a committee or expert would help provide the substantial evidence needed to support a decision under Section 704 of the TCA. Communities can require applicants to deposit money into an escrow account to pay for the services of such a committee or consultant.

Require visual simulations. Planning departments are increasingly requesting that applicants provide visual simulations of how proposed telecommunications facilities, especially wireless towers, will look once constructed. Overland Park, Kansas, for instance, requires special use permit applicants for towers to provide "a photo simulation of the proposed facility from [affected] residential properties and public rights-of-way as coordinated with the Planning staff."

In the past, these simulations have involved floating balloons to the approximate height of a proposed tower and photographing it from numerous vantage points. Today, computer technology has taken such simulations to a much more sophisticated level. Image-processing software can take a photograph of an existing scenic vista, for instance, and illustrate a proposed tower, both at varying heights and painted various colors (Ervin 1998). As this technology becomes even more widely available and less expensive, computerized simulations may become mandatory for proposed facilities in some communities. Even low-tech perspective drawings can help tremendously as planners and elected officials weigh the visual impact of a facility. The new, sophisticated, computerized simulations should prove invaluable.

Development Standards

Beyond modifying zoning ordinance district and use provisions, communities may adopt development standards to control those specific physical features of telecommunications facilities that most dramatically affect community character. For towers, communities should consider enacting controls on height, location, setbacks, screening, color, and materials in order to minimize visibility. For antennas and satellite dishes, communities should regulate those same features, albeit on a smaller scale, as is discussed below.

As long as they are carefully drafted to apply to specific types of structures, further a legitimate public purpose, and do not run afoul of any TCA or FCC limitations discussed above, these aesthetic development standards generally will be upheld by the courts. Note, however, that whether or not some of these controls violate federal law—for example, whether they impair signal quality or have the effect of prohibiting the provision of wireless service—will not be apparent until their effects in a particular set of circumstances are understood.

Height. Since the taller of the telecommunications towers can be highly visible for many miles, it is not surprising that most communities that regulate such facilities impose height restrictions. Many ordinances set maximum height limits on towers and antennae, and, to obtain an exemption, a provider must demonstrate why the prescribed height is insufficient to provide adequate service.

Haywood County, North Carolina, adopted detailed height restrictions in its 1998 ordinance regulating telecommunications facilities. Towers that are visible from any public road or publicly owned property within a half- mile radius of a proposed tower site shall not exceed 60 feet in height. Several exceptions allow for higher towers if, among other things, there is a dense vegetative canopy surrounding the site or if the towers are to be used by the state transportation department for cameras, sensors, or monitors for governmental use. Towers that are not visible from any public road or publicly owned property within a half-mile radius of the proposed tower site may be up to 199 feet high. Furthermore, properties located on protected mountain ridges, which are defined in the ordinance, shall not exceed 100 feet; they may extend slightly higher if surrounded by a dense vegetative canopy exceeding that height but may not exceed 60 feet if no vegetative canopy exists within 100 feet of the site. The ordinance also requires many towers that will not be shielded by existing foliage to be "disguised" as trees.

Location, setbacks, and screening. Many localities also impose controls on location. For towers, commercial and industrial areas are preferred over residential areas. Setbacks are imposed to provide a comfortable distance between towers and public spaces and residential properties; Cuyahoga County's model ordinance, for instance, requires a minimum distance of 300 feet between a tower and any single-family or two-family residential use or district. Setbacks are also imposed for safety reasons, because they provide a "fall area" into which ice or other debris may fall off the tower without harming passersby. For satellite dishes and other private antennae, front yards usually are prohibited. Screening controls, such as fencing or landscaping, are common for both types of facilities.

Color and materials. Because restrictions on height, location, and screening may interfere with reception, they are subject to special scrutiny under the TCA and FCC regulations. However, color and material are not especially important components of reception and thus generally may be controlled more strictly by localities. Localities may require freestanding towers and attached antennas to be camouflaged, as discussed below. For satellite dishes, communities may require that dishes be painted subdued or natural colors to minimize visibility.

Stealth towers. Increasingly, local ordinances are encouraging or requiring that telecommunications facilities be made as inconspicuous as possible through camouflaging, concealment in existing vegetation, or some similar technique. This has become an especially common practice with personal wireless service facilities. Wireless antennas attached to existing structures often are required to be painted to blend in with the color and materials of the surface to which they are attached, while freestanding towers must be disguised as some natural feature, like a palm or pine tree.

Liberty, Missouri, in its 1997 Wireless Communications Facilities Plan, encourages the use of such "stealth" technology to make towers resemble common structures, such as church steeples, light poles, bell towers, clock towers, grain silos, gateway elements, and monuments. The city requires that, when the stealth structure is part of an existing building, the tower's construction and equipment should complement that of the existing structure. When the stealth structure is freestanding, it should "fit the context of its surroundings and look as though it could serve the purpose of the real structure." As an incentive to use "stealth" technology and to locate in preferred areas, the town allows quick, administrative approvals for stealth antennas placed on existing buildings ("A Wireless Miscellany" 1997).

Co-location. In an attempt to restrict the total number of telecommunications towers within their borders, many communities either encourage or require "co-location" of facilities. Generally, co-location means that multiple antennas, often broadcasting at different frequencies and operated by different providers, share space upon a single tower. Because some types of antennas, such as television antennas, serve ranges of 30 miles or more,

Increasingly, local ordinances are encouraging or requiring that telecommunications facilities be made as inconspicuous as possible through camouflaging, concealment in existing vegetation, or some similar technique. This has become an especially common practice with personal wireless service facilities.

Ray Foote

Valmont Microflect

Valmont Microflect

Valmont Microflect

As is evident from these photos, there are a number of ways to disguise telecommunications facilities. From a fancy light pole to a "cactus" to a "tree" with an unusual trunk, some telecommunications companies are becoming adept at using "stealth" technology to hide their equipment and respond to the complaints of citizens.

CO-LOCATION: COVENANT OF GOOD FAITH
(Bothell, Washington)

A. All new monopole towers, and any pre-existing monopole or lattice towers, owned by a licensed carrier, upon which this Chapter permits co-location of additional PWS facilities, shall be made available for use by the owner or initial user thereof, together with as many other licensed carriers as can be technically co-located thereon. However, nothing in this Chapter shall prevent such licensed carrier from charging a reasonable fee for the co-location of additional PWS facilities upon said tower which does not exceed the fair-market value for the space occupied.

B. All licensed carriers shall cooperate with each other in co-locating additional PWS facilities upon such towers. All licensed carriers shall exercise good faith in co-locating with other licensed carriers and in the sharing of towers, including the sharing of technical information to evaluate the feasibility of co-location. *In the event that a dispute arises as to whether a licensed carrier has exercised good faith in allowing other licensed carriers to co-locate upon its tower, the City may require a third party technical study to evaluate the feasibility of co-location at the expense of either or both licensed carriers. This covenant of good faith and fair dealing shall be a condition of any permit issued pursuant to this Chapter for a new monopole tower.*

C. Any licensed carrier which allows co-location upon a tower permitted pursuant to this Chapter may condition said co-location to assure that the co-located PWS facility does not cause electronic or radio-frequency interference with its existing PWS facility. In the event that the co-located licensed carrier is unable to remedy the interference, the owner of the tower shall be relieved of its obligation to allow co-location of the interering PWS facility upon its structure. (Bothell, Washington, Telecommunications Ordinance, Section 12.11.080, emphasis added)

towers that support co-location can be very tall—750 to 1,000 feet is not uncommon—and thus can be quite visually obtrusive. Yet, co-location can also be a good tool for reducing aesthetic blight since it reduces the overall number of towers that must be constructed.

Incentives, such as expedited processing times or administrative approvals, that encourage co-location are common. In addition, if a provider chooses not to co-locate, a number of ordinances require applicants to explain why—for instance, because no tower exists in an area needing service or because existing towers are not equipped to handle additional antennas. The Daly City, California, ordinance is typical: Applicants for a permit "shall specifically state the reasons for not co-locating on any of the existing monopoles and lattice towers within a 3,000 foot radius. . . . [T]he applicant may also be asked to provide a letter from the telecommunications carrier owning or operating the existing facility, stating reasons for not permitting co-location." Operators of all new freestanding monopoles must submit a written pledge that they "shall allow other wireless carriers to co-locate antennas on the monopoles where technically and economically feasible" ("A Wireless Miscellany" 1997).

While the aesthetic benefit of co-location is clear, a number of commentators have pointed out disadvantages associated with the technique, especially when it is mandatory. For instance, technological concerns may arise if certain types of antennas are required to co-locate that will potentially interfere with each other's signals. Bothell, Washington, has a co-location requirement with a "good faith" provision in its permitting process that attempts to address the problem of one carrier insisting that technological concerns mandate that a new monopole be erected to serve its antennas. (See sidebar.)

From a business standpoint, providers will be reluctant to share information about their customer base or existing service networks with competitors. For these reasons and others, the wisest course of action may be for communities to encourage co-location rather than require it.

In an effort to reduce the overall number of new wireless towers constructed, and also to capitalize on a growing and highly lucrative business, some utility companies have begun aggressively marketing their existing electric transmission towers as prime sites for wireless antennas. In North and South Carolina, for example, Duke Energy is offering to lease antenna space on any of its 32,000 towers, ranging from 70 feet to 200 feet. While some of the towers may not be appropriate due to location or geographic constraints, many do provide excellent opportunities for wireless providers to save costs and forego negotiating with a local government for the right to erect a new tower and antenna structure on their own. The company has a software program that provides potential customers with an up-to-date list of all the suitable sites in both states.

CONCLUSION

The field of telecommunications law and planning continues to evolve at a dizzying pace, as new industries are formed, new technologies are invented, and new techniques are developed to minimize aesthetic impacts. The ultimate effects on local community character remain unclear. What will be the effects of digital television (DTV), for example; will new towers be required to make the technology work? or will existing towers be sufficient? It is likely that, in at least some communities, entirely new towers will be required. Because the FCC has mandated accelerated development of DTV (in the top 10 markets in the country), providers will have to work quickly with local governments to determine where these new towers should be located and to gain the necessary approvals.[20]

The legal framework continues to evolve at a rapid pace, also, as the courts issue decisions and the FCC issues new rules clarifying the vague provisions of the TCA. No doubt many important new lessons will be learned in the months and years following publication of this report. More so than for any other topic covered here, it is essential that local governments stay abreast of new legal and technological developments in the field. Of course, there is no substitute for regular consultation with informed legal counsel. One other excellent way to keep informed is, not surprisingly, the Internet, and especially the FCC's website (www.fcc.gov).

Regardless of which direction the technology and law take, however, communities simply cannot wait until the dust settles and all the rules are clear. Planners and local officials must work now to establish and adopt sound, legally defensible controls before they are faced with a barrage of applications over which they have no control. Federal and state laws make regulation in this area challenging, but there still is much room for local action that, if drafted and implemented carefully, can reduce many of the more serious aesthetic impacts of telecommunications facilities.

In general, local governments should remember the following general guidelines in regulating telecommunications facilities.

- Ensure that community ordinances and policies—both formal and informal—are in compliance with both the general TCA directive to encourage competition, as well as the specific limitations discussed above. Again, one usually cannot simply look at a zoning ordinance and tell if a community is in compliance with the TCA. More often, specific information will be necessary (including the topography of the area, the population distribution, the road network, and, most importantly, what telecommunications services are already available to area residents) to determine TCA compliance.

- Develop criteria for determining preferred sites for telecommunications facilities. For example, encourage placement on existing buildings and structures rather than construction of new towers, and encourage placement in industrial and commercial areas as opposed to residential and agricultural areas.

- If discretionary reviews are required, make sure they are authorized by law for that type of facility. Have written, objective criteria in place to ensure consistency across applications, to ensure community aesthetic goals are considered, and to provide an adequate foundation for judicial review.

Regardless of which direction the technology and law take, however, communities simply cannot wait until the dust settles and all the rules are clear. Planners and local officials must work now to establish and adopt sound, legally defensible controls before they are faced with a barrage of applications over which they have no control.

Notes

1. For the complete, authoritative discussion of the legal aspects of the regulation of telecommunications facilities, see Ziegler (1998).

2. A number of useful overview reports and articles have been written on the legal requirements of the TCA. Some of the best include: Abrams (1998); Heverley (1996); Miller, Canfield, Paddock, and Stone (1996); and the *Planning Commissioners Journal*, Fall 1997, which was a special edition devoted to wireless towers.

3. Note that the complex, technical distinctions between various types of telecommunications facilities are beyond the scope of this report. Nevertheless, some brief technical background information describing the key operating characteristics of these facilities is provided, since such features in part determine how specifically the facilities may be regulated by local governments.

4. Note there are various ways in which a community might run afoul of this provision. It might prohibit service by expressly banning a certain type of facility, thus denying residents access to that particular type of technology. Such a direct prohibition might apply either to the entire community, or else to specific areas, such as residential neighborhoods. Or, it might indirectly prohibit the provision of service by limiting the overall number of sites and towers approved, thereby making it impossible for the provider to deliver service to all areas because of geographic or other constraints.

5. Also see the Virginia Beach case, mentioned at the beginning of this chapter, in which the court refused to find.that an individual permit denial by the city council amounted to a general policy to deny such applications, in the absence of any evidence to support such a claim (979 F.Supp. 416, at 426-27).

6. For a similar result, see *BellSouth Mobility, Inc. v. Parish of Plaquemines*, 40 F. Supp. 2d 372).

7. Also see the Santa Fe case discussed above, in which the court concluded that the "generalized concerns" expressed by neighbors who testified and wrote letters to the local zoning authority did not constitute "substantial evidence" to support a permit denial (957 F.Supp.1230, 1236). For another example, see *Illinois RSA No. 3, Inc. v. County of Peoria*, 963 F.Supp.732 (C.D.Ill.1997)).

8. In addition to the Ferrysburg case discussed in the text, see *Sprint Spectrum v. Board of County Commissioners of Jefferson County*, 59 F. Supp. 2d 1101 (D. Colo. 1999) for a similar result. A federal district court upheld a local government's decision to deny a special use permit for a new tower, in part because the decision was based on substantial evidence that the tower would have violated local view protection regulations.

9. See also *Sprint Spectrum v. Willoth*, 996 F.Supp. 253 (1998), in which a local government denied a permit for a complex of three towers based on substantial evidence—offered by the provider itself—showing that the same level of service could be achieved with just one, taller tower.

10. For an example of a community failing to meet the standard, see *Sprint Spectrum L.P. d/b/a Sprint PCS v. Town of West Seneca*, 659 N.Y.S.2d 687 (1997), in which the court held that a town failed to act within a reasonable time since the town never took action on any of plaintiff's nine applications, effectively constituting a denial not supported by substantial evidence.

11. Specifically, Section 207 prohibits "restrictions that impair a viewer's ability to receive video programming services through devices designed for over-the-air reception of television broadcast signals, multichannel multi-point distribution service [MMDS], or direct broadcast satellite services" *(Telecommunications Act of 1996*, Sec. 207, Pub. L. No. 104-104, 119 Stat. 56 (1996)).

12. FCC Order No. 96-328, par. 19. Ziegler (1998) notes that this issue of relative costs under similar, previous FCC rules was discussed in *Abbott v. City of Cape Canaveral*, 840 F.Supp. 880 (M.D.Fla. 1994), in which purchase and installation costs of $1,254, compliance costs of $400 relating to location, installation, and height restrictions were not found to be excessive.

13. Safety restrictions must be clearly defined and stated and applied equally to other comparable modern devices. Examples of safety restrictions that the FCC has indicated it would consider acceptable include restrictions on proximity to power lines and prohibitions for blocking fire exits.

14. Note that the exemption applies only to *federally* designated historic districts or places, not properties subject only to state or local designation. To enforce a restriction in a state or local historic district or area not on the National Register, the local government would have to obtain a waiver from the FCC.

15. See, for example, *Schroeder v. Municipal Court*, 7 Cal.App. 3d 841 (1977), in which the California court upheld a zoning ordinance that prohibited antenna over 40 feet in height in any single-family residential district, based in part on the fact that the proposed antenna, to be encased in concrete, would be out of character with the neighborhood's aesthetic character.

16. A fact sheet on the requirements is available from the Federal Communications Commission, Mass Media Bureau, Policy and Rules Division: "Antenna Tower Lighting and Marking Requirements." The regulations are located at 47 U.S.C. Section 303(q).

17. The findings of fact adopted by the Medina City Council included the following: "The citizens of Medina have expressed significant concern relating to the location of wireless communication facilities within the City. The primary concerns relate to potential health hazards and the aesthetic effects of such facilities on neighboring properties and the community as a whole. . . . Processing applications for wireless communications facilities at the present time without the information to determine the need for or the ability to design such facilities to allow for co-location or nearby siting of additional facilities may result in the inability to allow adequate sites for competing providers. . . . The City Council . . . does declare that an emergency exists in that the issuance of special use permits for communication facilities . . . without study of the ability of wireless providers to eliminate or minimize health esthetics [sic] concerns is likely to result in adverse effects on the health and safety of the citizens of Medina . . ." (924 F.Supp. 1036, 1038-1039).

18. See also *Sprint Spectrum L.P. d/b/a Sprint PCS v. Town of Farmington*, 1997 WL 631104 (D.Conn. 1997), in which a federal district court overturned a nine-month moratorium adopted by the Town of Farmington, Connecticut. The court found the action constituted unreasonable delay under the TCA. The court distinguished the *Medina* decision, noting that Farmington had not only suspended the issuance of new permits, but had also forbade providers from even applying for permits in the first place, which was impermissible.

19. Again, note that, under FCC regulations, legal requirements vary for different types of satellite dishes, and communities should tread carefully in attempting to impose any cumbersome restrictions on such facilities.

20. See the fact sheet on DTV available from the FCC's Mass Media Bureau, available at the FCC web site (www.fcc.gov).

Chapter 7

Emerging Issues

A place designated by Congress where natural, cultural, historic, and recreational resources combine to form a cohesive, nationally distinctive landscape arising from patterns of human activity shaped by geography.

CONGRESSIONAL DEFINITION OF
NATIONALLY DESIGNATED HERITAGE AREAS (H.R. 2532)

WHILE THE PRINCIPAL CHAPTERS OF THIS REPORT COVER THE MAJOR HOT-BUTTON AESTHETIC ISSUES FACING COMMUNITIES TODAY, SEVERAL NEW TOPICS ON THE HORIZON ARE WORTH MENTIONING. This chapter provides a brief glimpse into some of these emerging issues, including efforts by local governments to control public infrastructure development for aesthetic reasons and initiatives to regulate wind turbines. The chapter concludes with a quick overview of "heritage areas," which may provide an excellent opportunity to implement many of the tools discussed in this report on a regional basis.

THE AESTHETICS OF PUBLIC INFRASTRUCTURE

Any comprehensive scheme to protect community character must rely heavily on controls that regulate private conduct and private property, such as design review, sign controls, tree protection, and the like. Yet such restrictions cannot do the job by themselves. Publically controlled areas and facilities, including everything from highways to parks to telephone poles, also have tremendous potential to affect community character. Local governments increasingly are realizing that they must control the aesthetic impacts of such facilities. Two rapidly evolving public infrastructure issues include efforts to design roads and highways in ways that are more sensitive to community character and to bury utility lines underground to remove unsightly poles and overhead wiring.

Innovative Road and Highway Design

Road and highway design in this country traditionally has emphasized safety, resulting in roads that are wide, flat, and straight, but often unattractive and disconnected from their surroundings. In response, some communities and states are investigating ways to venture from traditional design and construct roads that are functional and safe but also aesthetically pleasing and respectful of local character.

This new trend in road construction, part of a broader movement, colorfully termed the "Asphalt Rebellion" by some planners and engineers, is actually an attempt to move away from the sterile requirements of road design proscribed for more than 45 years in the official roadway standards: the *Policy on Geometric Design of Highways and Streets,* or the so-called "Green Book," published by the American Association of State Highway and Transportation Officials (AASHTO). The Green Book's standards for road construction are the result of transportation studies conducted by engineers whose overriding concern is to make roads safe for persons traveling at speeds considerably in excess of posted limits. To accommodate high speeds, the standards often require greater widths. The results often include: two-lane country highways expanded to four lanes; streets that are wider than necessary platted in new urban neighborhoods; and historic, narrow bridges torn down in favor of new, wider steel structures. According to the Green Book, safety is the primary objective of road design; other concerns, including historic preservation and protection of aesthetic character, are secondary.

The Green Book has, until recently, enjoyed tremendous influence in road construction; indeed, until 1991, any road built with federal funding had to be built in accordance with Green Book standards. Today, although the book's standards are rarely legally mandatory, they nevertheless still constitute the unofficial "bible" of road design, and deviations are uncommon. For years, state departments of transportation have required local governments to comply with Green Book standards in order to receive funding assistance, often forcing communities to choose among fighting congestion, breaking the bank, or losing irreplaceable local treasures.

A 1995 situation in a rural Connecticut county just outside Redding illustrates the typical conflict. County officials sought funding from the state Department of Transportation (DOT) to repair an attractive, historic, stone arch bridge on an infrequently traveled county road at Poverty Hollow. The state offered $350,000 in funding support, but only if the 17-foot bridge was torn down and a 28-foot steel and concrete bridge was erected in its place. Torn between accepting the money and saving an important part of its cultural and historic landscape, the county decided to decline state and federal assistance and repair the stone bridge itself using money from the local coffers. Noted a local official, "It's a sad commentary on our system when historic preservation, neighborhood aesthetics, and common sense are displaced by cookie-cutter design requirements" ("The Asphalt Rebellion" 1997)

Similar incidents have occurred in other New England states where many communities are fighting to end the reign of the Green Book. Legislators in Vermont, for instance, have for years been proposing legislation to loosen the state's transportation design standards to allow more flexibility. In response, the state's Agency of Transportation recently drafted its own road standards and codified them. An overriding principal in the reform law is that roads be designed for the safety of cars traveling *at* the posted speed limit, not 20 miles over. Vermont's newly adopted legislation is considered one of the strongest highway design reform laws in the country so far.

According to the Green Book, safety is the primary objective of road design; other concerns, including historic preservation and protection of aesthetic character, are secondary.

Legislators in Vermont, for instance, have for years been proposing legislation to loosen the state's transportation design standards to allow more flexibility. In response, the state's Agency of Transportation recently drafted its own road standards and codified them. An overriding principal in the reform law is that roads be designed for the safety of cars traveling at the posted speed limit, not 20 miles over.

The incident at Poverty Hollow, along with other road design issues, persuaded the Connecticut legislature to pass a law to draft new design guidelines. The state now has a new Highway Design Manual that encourages "context-sensitive highway design." Importantly, the manual specifically instructs highway designers to develop solutions that meet operational and safety requirements, "while preserving the aesthetic, historic or cultural resources of an area."

In addition to highway and bridge standards, road design has become an issue in many urban neighborhoods. The Green Book's emphasis on wide streets runs counter to the trend in many communities that encourages neotraditional forms of development. In response, these communities are passing ordinances allowing more flexibility in road widths. Phoenix, for example, used to require all new residential streets be at least 32 feet wide; in 1997, however, the city passed an ordinance offering developers the option of building narrower streets (minimum 28 feet) in residential developments. Similarly, Eugene, Oregon, has reduced its minimum street width requirement from 28 to 20 feet.

The Federal Highway Administration (FHWA) has recognized that, sometimes, exceptions to the standards of the Green Book may be acceptable, especially in the design and maintenance of secondary roads. Indeed, Congress included language in two federal laws making clear that good highway design *should* take into account the surrounding natural and built environment. The Intermodal Surface Transportation Efficiency Act (ISTEA), passed in 1991, notes that:

> If a proposed [roadway] project . . . involves a historic facility or is located in an area of historic or scenic value, the Secretary may approve such project . . . if such project is designed to standards that allow for the preservation of such historic or scenic value and such project is designed with mitigation measures to allow preservation of such value and ensure safe use of the facility. (Intermodal Surface Transportation Efficiency Act of 1991, Section 1016(a))

The National Highway System Designation Act of 1995 (NHS) went further, permitting context-sensitive design (also known as place-sensitive design) on federal highways more generally:

> A design for new construction, reconstruction, resurfacing . . . restoration, or rehabilitation of a highway on the National Highway System (other than a highway also on the Interstate System) may take into account . . . [in addition to safety, durability, and economy of maintenance] . . .
>
> [a] the constructed and natural environment of the area;
>
> [b] the environmental, scenic, historic, community, and preservation impacts of the activity; and
>
> [c] access for other modes of transportation. (National Highway System Designation Act of 1995, Section 304)

In a recent publication, *Flexibility in Highway Design*, FHWA discusses how to design highways that ensure safety and efficiency while preserving and protecting environmental and cultural values. While the book does not establish new design standards or criteria, it does promote innovative thinking by highway designers and encourages consideration of the "aesthetic, scenic, historic, and cultural resources" that "help give a community its identity and sense of place" (Federal Highway Authority 1997). The book highlights projects that demonstrate the flexibility of the Green Book and shows how road designers can work within designated parameters to obtain safety and mobility, while also preserving environmental and cultural resources.

The Federal Highway Administration (FHWA) has recognized that, sometimes, deviations from the sterile standards of the Green Book may be acceptable, especially in the design and maintenance of secondary roads. Indeed, Congress included language in two federal laws making clear that good highway design should take into account the surrounding natural and built environment.

In sum, while the Green Book is still the nation's principle reference book of road design, it increasingly is serving as recommended parameters and guidelines, rather than being steadfast, inflexible "rules of the road."

Underground Utility Lines

Many communities are also focusing on removing another major aesthetic headache, utility poles and overhead utility lines, by working to bury such lines underground. The thinking is that burying (or "converting," as the process is often called) the unsightly wires will help protect parks, scenic views, and other significant aesthetic amenities, and reduce overall visual clutter.

One of the most widely publicized programs for underground utility conversions is in San Antonio, Texas, where more than 25 such projects have been completed or are underway. San Antonio's program is unusual in that the city has identified a dedicated funding source for utility conversion projects. Because San Antonio owns its utility company, the city has the authority to designate a portion of the revenues from sales of electricity for various municipal projects, such as utility conversions. Through the City Public Service (CPS) program, San Antonio sets aside one percent of annual revenues from electricity to fund the utility conversions. Since the set-aside generates only about $6 million per year, and it would take about $17 billion to convert the entire citywide electric system, the city has established a multi-step process for selecting and implementing projects. The selection criteria include potential impacts on scenic views or corridors, among other considerations. CPS funds may be used to convert overhead electric lines to underground wiring, to relocate overhead routes to different overhead locations, or to improve utility pole design. Revisions to the San Antonio zoning ordinance set forth criteria for overlay districts where utility conversion may occur. (For a useful summary of the San Antonio program, see Pasley 1997.)

Most of the projects completed thus far have been located in public areas, including the new Alamodome basketball arena and the downtown campus of the University of Texas at San Antonio, site of some noteworthy architecture. In 1998, the city buried the utility lines in San Pedro Park, the second oldest city park in the country, in an attempt to restore some of the park's original aesthetic integrity. Another major conversion effort begun in 1997 is the mission trails project, a $10 million endeavor that will link together several historic missions throughout the city. The conversion to underground utility lines is part of a comprehensive package of aesthetic upgrades to the missions. Because utility conversion projects can be quite expensive, they often combine CPS funds with money from other sources; the mission trails project, for instance, is relying on money from the CPS program, ISTEA funds, and other city funds.

California is another hotbed for underground utility conversions, and two cities, Palo Alto and Laguna Beach, have especially active programs. In Palo Alto, the city has been converting utility lines since the 1960s, with the ultimate objective of converting the entire electric system to underground lines. Local officials estimate that 40 percent of the city has been converted, and the remaining 60 percent will take another 60 years to complete. The city funds the conversion through a program similar to the one used in San Antonio; namely, by setting aside revenues from sales of electricity by the city-owned utility company. The program generates enough income to complete one project (about 150 homes) every other year ($2 million per project). Projects are selected based on degree of dilapidated overhead lines, tree obstructions, and the volume of unsightly poles.

In a wealthy community like Laguna Beach, California, private citizens can afford to take on the cost of removing overhead lines themselves to protect valuable views of the Pacific Ocean. The city has been converting overhead lines at the request of residents for more than a decade. Generally, the city helps citizens establish assessment districts to fund the conversion and facilitate the process, and the residents foot the bill through annual assessments added to their property tax bill. The average cost of a utility conversion is $8,000 to $16,000 per single-family residence. The city rarely contributes any funding to the projects, unless a citizen applies for a hardship assistance grant. The only requirements to establish an assessment district are that owners of at least five parcels must be willing to participate, at least 600 feet of line must be placed underground, and a petition to have the work completed must be circulated to all the affected parcel owners. If 70 percent of the residents in a district sign the petition, the district may be formed and the conversion can occur. The typical time frame for a conversion is four to five years.

Interestingly, although aesthetic concerns have been the primary motivation for conversions in Laguna Beach, city officials also cite safety as a factor. Several years ago, a brush fire destroyed several expensive homes in the city. The fire allegedly started when a bird flew into overhead utility lines, caught on fire, and fell into the dry brush below. Residents realize that such incidents are uncommon, but many are willing, and can afford, to invest in underground utility line conversions to prevent similar occurrences in the future.

As the move to convert overhead lines becomes an emerging issue in land-use development, it is worth noting that most new construction today is being built with underground lines. Many communities require undergrounding as part of the subdivision approval process. In Colorado, the major public utility company rarely installs overhead electrical lines in new construction projects. A recent informal national survey conducted by that company revealed that, in almost all cases, utility companies are installing underground lines for new construction. Although burying lines during construction is more costly than erecting overhead lines, it is still drastically less expensive than converting to underground lines once construction is complete.

WIND TURBINES

Another area in which communities are becoming increasingly concerned about impacts on community character and local aesthetics is the use of so-called "green energy"—energy derived from clean sources, such as the sun and wind, as opposed to fossil fuels. As the trend toward using green energies becomes increasingly accepted worldwide, communities must learn to deal with the aesthetic impacts caused by the facilities used to gather and store such energies. Thus far, most aesthetic concerns in this area have dealt with "wind farms," the term for large arrays of wind turbines.

Modern wind turbine towers are far different than their farm/country counterparts of a century ago. They typically reach heights of 80 to 120 feet, and the 2,000-pound rotor blades on each tower can extend 52 feet each, for a total diameter of greater than 100 feet. The principal aesthetic concern associated with wind farms is how a broad array of such giant machines will affect scenic resources. To try to alleviate such impacts, wind farm operators typically work with local governments to design projects that meet the standards and objectives of the community. Key design factors considered include: location (most communities prefer to keep the facilities confined to industrial, semi-rural, or rural locations); size (communities may choose to regulate base circumference, height, and blade length); spacing; setback requirements; and color/finish.

FOR MORE INFORMATION:

The American Wind Energy Association is a good resource for all matters related to wind energy. AWEA can be contacted at:

122 C St., N.W.4th Floor
Washington, DC 20001
(202) 383–2500
(202) 383–2505 (fax)
www.awea.org

National Renewable Energy Laboratory

Clarion Associates

National Renewable Energy Laboratory

It's not your great grandparents' windmill anymore. Contrast the quaint windmill with these high-tech wind mill "farms." As the cost of wind power decreases, communities may find themselves dealing with issues of aesthetics related to these facilities. Citizens are understandably attracted to this source of "clean," renewable energy.

National Renewable Energy Laboratory

In seeking to accommodate wind farms, developers and local officials must balance the competing goals of efficiency and aesthetics. The taller the turbine, the more energy it will generate, yet local communities may want to restrict the height of the turbines to protect scenic views. Sometimes the need for efficiency wins out over aesthetic concerns. In colder climates, local governments have had to make concessions regarding color because black blades are necessary to conduct heat and melt any ice that forms on the blades, which would reduce the efficiency of the turbine. Two additional design factors that make turbine farms more pleasing to the eye are spacing and rotational direction of the blades. Turbines typically are placed in straight lines or in grid patterns. A haphazard layout or blades rotating in different directions not only reduces the efficiency of each turbine, but also creates an illusion of chaos.

Riverside County and Palm Springs are two California communities that have adopted stringent design standards to minimize the aesthetic impact of wind farms on the landscape. With more than 13,000 wind turbines, California has been a prime location for wind power facilities for several decades; indeed, in 1995, the state produced 30 percent of the world's wind-generated electricity. Riverside County and Palm Springs have adopted standards regulating a number of windmill characteristics, including height, noise, and color. Advertising and logos are prohibited, and electrical distribution lines must be buried underground. In addition to these requirements, a series of setbacks must be observed. Palm Springs, for example, imposes a three-part system of setbacks on "wind energy conversion systems":

> General setbacks require the facilities to be located no more than 50 feet from any lot line and no closer than 1,200 feet from any residence (unless the noise, aesthetic, or other environmental impacts of the project on adjacent properties will not be any more significant than if the 1,200-foot setback were applied).

> Safety setbacks must be met (for example, no facility may be located where the center of the tower is within a distance of 1.25 times its total height from any above-ground electrical transmission line).

> Scenic setbacks restrict the facilities from interfering with mapped viewsheds and view corridors.

The use of wind energy is being promoted at all levels of government. At the federal level, the Department of Energy (DOE) spearheads the nation's Wind Energy Program, whose function is to implement programs to educate state and local officials and utility providers on the benefits of wind energy and to encourage its development and use. Many state agencies are also involved in promoting the use of wind power, adopting statewide policies designed to make acquisition of land for wind farms more attractive and monitoring the effectiveness of established wind power projects. Local communities become involved in the process by adopting policies and ordinances to regulate the operation and appearance of wind farms and by encouraging (or restricting) wind farm operation in certain zone districts.

As the cost of wind power becomes more competitive with other forms of energy, demand will continue to rise. Currently, wind power is less costly than nuclear energy and is only slightly more expensive than fossil fuels, and the gap is narrowing. In addition, customers have demonstrated a willingness to pay extra for electricity generated through renewable resources; in Colorado, the major public utility company has had more than 14,500 customers (including 250 businesses) agree to pay extra for their electricity each month to receive energy generated by the company's 29

Sidebar (margin):

In seeking to accommodate wind farms, developers and local officials must balance the competing goals of efficiency and aesthetics.

As the cost of wind power becomes more competitive with other forms of energy, demand will continue to rise. Currently, wind power is less costly than nuclear energy and is only slightly more expensive than fossil fuels, and the gap is narrowing.

turbines located in northern Colorado. As wind power becomes an increasingly attractive option for consumers, both for economic and environmental reasons, local governments should expect to see an increase in applications for wind farm developments.

REGIONAL PARTNERSHIPS AND HERITAGE AREAS

Heritage-area protection efforts often involve a number of interrelated issues, including landscape protection, historic preservation, economic development, environmental protection, and preservation of community character. Common elements of such projects include an attempt at reconciling these numerous issues, which often work at cross-purposes, and also an overarching, cooperative management framework involving multiple jurisdictions.

As communities become more sophisticated at using techniques to protect aesthetics and community character at the local level, many are broadening their focus to apply similar techniques on a larger scale. Indeed, one of the more encouraging new trends in aesthetic regulation is an increased emphasis on strategies that seek to preserve and protect the distinct character of entire regions.

The best example of this trend toward regionalism is the movement to protect so-called "heritage areas," which are broad geographic areas with a distinctive sense of place, often unified by large-scale resources, such as rivers, canals, railroads, or highways. Heritage-area protection efforts often involve a number of interrelated issues, including landscape protection, historic preservation, economic development, environmental protection, and preservation of community character. Common elements of such projects include an attempt at reconciling these numerous issues, which often work at cross-purposes, and also an overarching, cooperative management framework involving multiple jurisdictions. Protecting aesthetic resources, while not the singular focus of such projects, nevertheless is usually a primary objective, since heritage areas often seek to transform dilapidated or depressed areas into destinations attractive enough to encourage increased use by tourists and nearby residents.

State Programs

New Jersey has one of the best-known examples of a protection program for an entire, unique region. In 1981, the state authorized a system of transferable development rights (TDR) to protect the Pinelands, which is an agriculturally and environmentally sensitive region extending over almost 1 million acres in the south-central part of the state. About 13,000 acres have been protected by the TDR program since its inception. A primary goal is the protection of farmland, although the area also has a number of strict aesthetically oriented laws, including a prohibition against new billboards.

Pennsylvania also has a successful regional heritage program. During the late 1970s and early 1980s, many areas in the state experienced severe economic declines, with unemployment rates in some areas reaching as high as 20 percent. Searching for new industries to stimulate economic growth, the state in 1989 formed the Pennsylvania Heritage Parks program in an attempt to draw tourists to some of these economically depressed areas by capitalizing on the state's rich industrial history, as well as significant scenic, recreational, and educational resources. Today, the state has eight formally designated State Heritage Parks, such as the National Road Heritage Park Corridor in Somerset, Fayette, and Washington counties, which celebrates the history, culture, and scenery of one of the country's oldest byways.

The Pennsylvania statewide program encourages development of public-private partnerships to help revitalize heritage areas. The state provides grants to organizations and agencies on a competitive basis for feasibility studies, management plans, and implementation projects. Municipalities may apply for the grants, provided they are acting in conjunction with other municipalities in their region. Since the program's establishment, more than $70 million has been invested in infrastructure, historic preservation, and parks. Barren landscapes have been reforested, and streams previously contaminated with acid by mining have been cleaned. Where the landscape was previously marked by deteriorating or abandoned mills, mines, and rail yards, it now boasts parks, museums, and historic landmarks.

Federal Programs

The movement to create regional heritage areas received a major boost at the national level in November 1996, when Congress created the National Heritage Areas Partnership Program, which provides national recognition and federal funding for such efforts. The program authorizes the creation of nationally designated heritage areas, defined by law as:

> A place designated by Congress where natural, cultural, historic, and recreational resources combine to form a cohesive, nationally distinctive landscape arising from patterns of human activity shaped by geography. These patterns make National Heritage Areas representative of the national experience through the physical features that remain and the traditions that have evolved in the areas. Continued use of National Heritage Areas by people whose traditions helped to shape the landscape enhances their significance.

Nine such areas were designated initially, including the "Rivers of Steel" region in southwestern Pennsylvania, the Erie Canal in Ohio, the Hudson River Valley in New York, Essex County in Massachusetts, and silos and smokestacks in Iowa. Annual funding support for each heritage area is capped at $150,000, with an overall maximum limit of $1 million per heritage area.

The goals of the national effort are:

* to protect scenic, natural, and cultural resources;

* to promote tourism and other forms of economic development; and

* to provide recreational and public educational opportunities.

The program authorizes the Secretary of the Interior to evaluate proposed heritage areas using uniform criteria set forth in the enabling legislation, to advise state and local governments on suitable methods for recognizing and conserving regional heritage areas, and to make grants to governments and nonprofit groups for planning efforts and management. The program does not authorize federal acquisition of heritage areas; rather, the idea is to maintain as much local control and ownership as possible, with the federal government providing technical assistance and funding support for planning efforts. Indeed, many efforts are regional in nature, bringing together local governments in economic development/cultural development partnerships (Means 1999).

Augusta, Georgia, is using the federal National Heritage Area designation to help stimulate and revitalize the entire surrounding region. The Augusta Canal, which runs along the Savannah River through the city, was originally constructed in 1845 to provide hydropower and a water supply to the city of Augusta. It survives today as one of the most intact canal systems in the country and continues to serve its original purposes, while also helping to educate area residents and tourists about the history of the region.

Designation of the canal region as a National Heritage Area in 1996 led to implementation of the ambitious Augusta Canal Master Plan, adopted in 1994. In brief, this plan seeks to revitalize the three sections of the canal

FOR MORE INFORMATION:

There are a number of National Heritage Areas. The National Park Service web pages (www.nps.org) provides contact information for regional NPS offices, which can further explain the program

The program does not authorize federal acquisition of heritage areas; rather, the idea is to maintain as much local control and ownership as possible, with the federal government providing technical assistance and funding support for planning efforts. Indeed, many efforts are regional in nature, bringing together local governments in economic development/ cultural development partnerships.

FOR MORE INFORMATION

The American Heritage Rivers website (www.epa.gov/rivers) contains contact information for 14 designated rivers, the federal working group state contacts, and local groups working to protect rivers, lakes, and streams. Regional EPA offices should also be helpful in providing information about the program.

FOR MORE INFORMATION

The National Scenic Byways website (www.byways.org) contains information on grants, nominations, and technical assistance.

in different ways: the upper portion will be preserved in its natural state for hiking, bicycling, canoeing, kayaking, and fishing; the midsection will be an active recreational area with picnic areas, foot bridges, and a board-walk-type setting; and the lower (urban) section of the canal that runs through central Augusta will include historic restoration projects, neighborhood revitalization, the rehabilitation of a mill, and clean-up of a deteriorated manufacturing plant. The physical improvements are accompanied by an educational effort drawing attention to the role the canal has played in the growth and development of Augusta.

A second federal program aimed at protecting regional heritage areas is the American Heritage Rivers Initiative, announced by President Clinton in 1997. Briefly, the program is intended to recognize and support local efforts to enhance the nation's rivers and river fronts by bringing targeted, active federal assistance, but imposing no new regulatory requirements or rules. A specially identified "River Navigator" assists local and regional governments and organizations in identifying programs and resources to implement their plans. The president invited local communities to nominate their rivers for designation as American Heritage Rivers. The first 14 rivers designated are scattered across the country and include the New River (North Carolina, Virginia, and West Virginia), St. John's River (Florida), the Willamette River (Oregon), the Rio Grande River (Texas), and the Hanalei River (Hawaii).

Already, the initiative has helped match community needs with available resources in a variety of ways. For the Upper Susquehanna-Lackawanna Watershed in Pennsylvania, for instance, the initiative led to development of an $800,000 project to create a comprehensive ecosystem restoration master plan using GIS technology. The project will assist communities to identify various environmental, historical, cultural, and economic problems and issues that are key to addressing the overall restoration and revitalization of the regional watershed area.

The National Scenic Byways program, discussed in Chapter 3, View Protection, is a third example of a federally supported effort to protect resources that are aesthetically and environmentally significant at a regional level. Recall that the program, created by federal legislation in 1991, provides technical, administrative, and funding support for the protection of scenic roadways nationwide. In part because of this federal program, about 40 states now have their own scenic byway programs.

The national program requires preparation of a corridor management plan for any road nominated to the National Scenic Byways system. As part of this planning process, the Mountains to Sound Greenway in Washington is engaged in land conservation and scenic preservation on a grand scale along a 100-mile stretch of Interstate 90. The highway, which is the state's main east/west thoroughfare, runs through beautifully scenic areas from Puget Sound, over mountains and through forests, to the valleys of eastern Washington. A regional nonprofit organization, composed of environmentalists, highway engineers, historians, and foresters, has built an impressive coalition to plan for the Greenway. As a result, in 1998, the Greenway became the only interstate highway in the nation to be designated a National Scenic Byway.

In sum, two features appear to distinguish all heritage areas, whether designated under national or state programs. First, heritage areas are *multifaceted*, involving a wide array of issues that are important to preserving a region's sense of place. They therefore provide an ideal means of integrating and reconciling the protection and preservation of aesthetic resources with other important policy goals, including environmental protection, economic development, education, and recreational development.

Second, and perhaps more importantly, heritage areas emphasize *regional, multijurisdictional* cooperation. To be successful, regional management teams must be formed, with both public- and private-sector involvement, to oversee heritage areas and to generate grassroots enthusiasm for promoting and preserving community assets. The efforts should bring together industrial developers, downtown interests, small business groups, economic development corporations, tourism promoters, banks, utilities, telecommunications providers, and environmental and historic preservation advocates, all of whom are concerned with the preservation of the unique resources.

As heritage areas become more widely implemented, these regional partnerships may provide a standardized framework for implementing many of the initiatives discussed in this report at a broader level. A heritage area might be an ideal vehicle for implementing, for example, a regional tree protection program that focuses on protecting large stands of woodlands. Or, a heritage area program might be used to implement a system of regional design review along an entire highway corridor.

Abrams, Stanley D. 1998. "Update on the 1996 Telecommunications Act: Personal Wireless Services." *Land Use Law and Zoning Digest* (April): 3-8.

Akbari, Hashem, et al. 1992. *Cooling Our Communities: A Guidebook on Tree Planting and Light-Colored Surfaces*. Prepared for the U.S. Environmental Protection Agency. Washington, D.C.: USGPO.

American Farmland Trust. 1977. *Saving American Farmland: What Works*. Washington, D.C.: American Farmland Trust.

Arendt, Randall. 1994. *Rural by Design: Maintaining Small Town Character*. Chicago: Planners Press.

Arnold, Henry. 1980. *Trees in Urban Design*. New York: Van Nostrand Reinhold.

"The Asphalt Rebellion." 1997. *Governing*, October 20.

Beaumont, Constance. 1994. *How Superstore Sprawl Can Harm Communities and What Citizens Can Do About It*. Washington, D.C.: National Trust for Historic Preservation.

Bishop, Kirk R. 1989. *Designing Urban Corridors*. Planning Advisory Service Report No. 418. Chicago: APA.

Bobrowski, Mark. 1995. "Scenic Landscape Protection Under the Police Power." *Boston College Environmental Affairs Law Review* 22: 697.

Bonderman, David. 1983. "Federal Constitutional Issues." In *A Handbook of Historic Preservation Law*, edited by C. J. Duerksen. Washington, D.C.: The Conservation Foundation, 350-68.

Bosselman, Fred P., D. Callies, and J. Banta. 1973. *The Takings Issue*. Prepared for the Council on Environmental Quality. Washington, D.C.: Government Printing Office.

Campanelli, Ben. 1997. "Planning for Cellular Towers." *Planning Commissioners Journal*, no. 28 (Fall): 4-6.

Charlotte Observer. 1997, "Carolinas' Billboard Clutter Ranks Among Worst." April 26.

Clarion Associates, RNZ Design, et al. 1998. Chaffee County Comprehensive Plan. Public Hearing Draft. July. Appendix B.

Clark, Edwin, III, Jennifer A. Haverkamp, and William Chapman. 1985. *Eroding Soils: The Off-Farm Impact*. Washington, D.C. : Conservation Foundation.

Clark, Paul. 1996. "Businesses Can Blend with Beauty." *Asheville Citizen-Times*, December 10.

Constantine, James. 1992. "Design by Democracy." *Land Development* (Spring-Summer): 11.

Coughlin, Robert E., D. C. Mendes, and A. L. Strong. 1984. *Private Trees and Public Interest: Programs for Protecting and Planting Trees in Metropolitan Areas*. Research Report Series No. 10. University of Pennsylvania, Department of City and Regional Planning.

Cranes & Cranes, Inc., in cooperation with the Cape Cod Commission. 1997. "Siting Criteria for Personal Wireless Service Facilities." Barnstable, Mass., June.

Cuyahoga County Planning Commission. 1996. "Wireless Telecommunications Facilities." (November).

Duerksen, Christopher J. ed. 1983. *A Handbook of Historic Preservation Law*. Washington, D.C.: The Conservation Foundation.

Duerksen, Christopher J. 1986. *Aesthetics and Land-Use Controls: Beyond Ecology and Economics*. Planning Advisory Service Report No. 399. Chicago: APA.

_____. 1993. *Tree Conservation Ordinances: Land-Use Regulations Go Green*. Planning Advisory Service Report No. 446. Chicago: APA/Scenic America.

_____. 1996. "Site Planning for Large-Scale Retail Stores." *PAS Memo* (April).

_____. 1997. "Historic Preservation Law." In *The Law of Zoning and Planning*, edited by Arden Rathkopf. 4th edition. New York: Clark Boardman, Co.

Duerksen, Christopher J., and Richard J. Roddewig. 1994. *Takings Law in Plain English*. Washington, D.C.: American Resources Information Network.

Ebenreck, Sara. 1989. "The Value of Trees." In *Shading Our Cities*, edited by Gary Moll and Sara Ebenreck. Washington, D.C.: Washington, D.C.: Island Press, 50.

Erickson, Donald. 1986. "Legislating Urban Design." *The Western Planner* 7, no. 2 (March/April).

Ervin, Stephen. 1998. "Answering the 'What Ifs'." *Landscape Architecture* (October): 64.

Federal Highway Administration. U.S. Department of Transportation. 1997a. *Community Guide to Planning and Managing a Scenic Byway*. Washington, D.C.

_____. 1997b. *Flexibility in Highway Design*. Washington, D.C.

Fenneman, N. M. 1931. *Physiography of the Western United States*. New York: McGraw-Hill.

_____. 1938. *Physiography of the Eastern United States*. New York: McGraw-Hill.

Fleming, Ronald Lee. 1994. *Saving Face: How Corporate Franchise Design Can Respect Community Identity*. Planning Advisory Service Report No. 452. Chicago: APA.

Fletcher, June. 1991. "Selling Green." *Builder*, July, 62.

Fletemeyer, Heidi. C. 1997. "The First Amendment and Newspaper Vending Machine Regulation." *University of Colorado Law Review* 69: 223.

Floyd, Charles F., and O. Lee Reed. 1997. "Controlling Newsbox Clutter." *Land Use Law and Zoning Digest* (September): 3-8.

Gregory, Michelle. 1997. "Cell-Mania." *Planning*, July, 16-17.

Grey, Gene and F. Deneke. 1978. *Urban Forestry*. New York : Wiley.

Heverley, Robert A. 1996. "Dealing with Towers, Antennas, and Satellite Dishes." *Land Use Law and Zoning Digest* (November): 3-9.

Heyer, Fred. 1990. *Preserving Rural Character*. Planning Advisory Service Report No. 429. Chicago: APA.

Hinshaw, Mark L. 1995. *Design Review*. Planning Advisory Service Report No. 454. Chicago: APA.

Hiss, Tony. 1990. *The Experience of Place*. New York : Knopf.

Howe, Jim, Ed McMahon, and Luther Propst. 1997. *Balancing Nature and Commerce in Gateway Communities*. Covelo, Calif.: Island Press.

Kelly, Eric, and Gary Raso. 1989. *Sign Regulation for Small and Midsize Communities*. Planning Advisory Service Report No. 419. Chicago: APA.

Lu, Weiming. 1980. "Preservation Criteria: Defining and Protecting Design Relationships." *Old and New Architecture: Design Relationships*. Washington, D.C.: Preservation Press, 180.

Macie, Ed. 1989. "Characteristics of a Model Tree Protection and Landscaping Ordinance." In *Proceedings of the Fourth Urban Forestry Conference*. Washington, D.C.: American Forestry Association.

Mallett, William J. 1998. "Homeowner Associations: Characteristics, Problems, and Prospects." *PAS Memo* (January).

Marriott, Paul Daniel. 1998. *Saving Historic Roads: Design & Policy Guidelines*. New York: Preservation Press and John Wiley & Sons, Inc.

Means, Mary. 1999. "Happy Trails." *Planning*, August, 4-9.

Miller, Canfield, Paddock and Stone, P.L.C.. 1996. *Implementing the New Telecommunications Law: A County and Local Officials Guide to the Telecommunications Act of 1996*. Prepared for the National Association of Counties, et al. Washington, D.C.

Olshansky, Robert B. 1996. *Planning for Hillside Development*. Planning Advisory Service Report No. 466. Chicago: APA.

Pasley, Dave. 1997. "Pole to Pole in San Antonio." *Planning*, December, 18.

Phillips, Don. 1997. "A Bumpy Ride for Highway Cleanup." *Washington Post*, April 25, A4.

"Process for Scenic Quality Analysis Along the Blue Ridge Parkway." 1997. Available from the Community Planner of the Blue Ridge Parkway, Asheville, North Carolina.

Raisz, Erwin. 1957. *Landforms of the United States: To Accompany Atwood's Physiographic Provinces of North America*. 6th edition. Cambridge, Mass.: Raisz Landform Maps.

Rathkopf, Arden. 1975. *The Law of Zoning and Planning*. 4th edition. New York: Clark Boardman, Co., Ltd., Sec. 15.01, p. 15-4.

Rodbell, Phillip D., ed. 1990. "The Role of Trees in Human Well-Being and Health." In *Proceedings of the Fourth Urban Forestry Conference*. Washington, D.C.: American Forestry Association.

_____. 1991. "Planting the Urban Desert." *Urban Forests* 11 (July): 8.

Roddewig, Richard J. 1983. *Preparing a Historic Preservation Ordinance*. Planning Advisory Service Report No. 374. Chicago: APA.

Scenic America. 1992a. *Trees Make Sense*. Technical Information Series Vol. 1, no. 1. Washington, D.C.

_____. 1992b. *On the Value of Open Spaces*. Technical Information Series Vol. 1, no. 2. Washington, D.C.

_____. 1992c. *The Value of Nature and Scenery*. Technical Information Series Vol. 1, no. 3. Washington, D.C.

_____. 1992d. *Signs, Signs: The Economic and Environmental Benefits of Community Sign Control*. Videotape. Washington, D.C.

_____. 1993a. *Aesthetics and Commercial Districts*. Technical Information Series Vol. 1, no. 6. Washington, D.C.

_____. 1993b. *Does Preservation Pay?* Technical Information Series Vol. 1, no. 4. Washington, D.C.

_____. 1993c. *Looking at Change Before It Occurs*. Videotape. Washington, D.C.

_____. 1993d. *Trees Are Treasure: Sustaining the Community Forest*. Videotape. Washington, D.C.

_____. 1993e. *Wetlands NOT Wastelands*. Technical Information Series Vol. 1, no. 5. Washington, D.C.

_____. 1995. *Economic and Community Benefits of Scenic Byways*. Technical Information Series Vol. 2, no. 1. Washington, D.C.

_____. 1996. *Evaluating Scenic Resources*. Technical Information Series Vol. 3, no.1.

_____. 1997. *Getting It Right In the Right-of-Way*. Technical Information Series Vol. 4, n. 1.

_____. 1997. *The Highway Beautification Act: A Broken Law*. Washington, D.C.

_____. 1999. *Fighting Billboard Blight: An Action Guide for Citizens and Local Officials*. Washington, D.C.

Scenic America; Rivers, Trails and Conservation Assistance Program, National Park Service; and Department of Landscape Architecture, College of Environmental Science and Forestry, State University of New York. 1999. *O, Say Can You See: A Visual Awareness Tool Kit for Communities.* Washington, D.C.

Scenic North Carolina News. 1998. Spring.

Schwab, James. 1992. "Urban Trees, Air Quality, and Energy Conservation." *Environment and Development* (March).

Shirvani, Hamid. 1981. *Urban Design Review: A Guide for Planners.* Chicago: Planners Press.

Southern Environmental Law Center. 1987. *Visual Pollution and Sign Control: A Legal Handbook on Billboard Control.* Charlottesville, VA.

Spirn, Anne. 1984. *The Granite Garden: Urban Nature and Human Design.* New York : Basic Books.

"Sticks in the Air, Stakes in the Sand." 1997. *Planning Commissioners Journal* (Fall): 7.

Stokes, Sam; A. Elizabeth Watson, and Shelley Mastran. 1997. *Saving America's Countryside: A Guide to Rural Conservation, 2nd ed.* Baltimore: Johns Hopkins University Press.

"'Sunny' Mall Plan Generating Heat." *Denver Post,* January 13, C1.

Telecommunications Act of 1996. Sec. 207, Pub. L. No. 104-104, 119 Stat. 56 (1996).

Tylka, David. "Critters in the City." In *Shading Our Cities,* edited by Gary Moll and Sara Ebenreck. Washington, D.C.: Washington, D.C.: Island Press, 112-18.

Ulrich, Roger S. 1986. "Human Responses to Vegetation and Landscapes." *Landscape and Urban Planning* 13: 29-44.

_____. 1991. "Stress Recovery During Exposure to Natural and Urban Environments." *Journal of Environmental Psychology* 11: 201-30.

_____. 1992. "How Design Impacts Wellness." *Healthcare Forum Journal* (September/October): 20-25.

Whyte, William H. 1980. *The Social Life of Small Urban Spaces.* Washington, D.C. : Conservation Foundation.

Williams, Norman. 1974. *American Land Planning Law,* 3.31 Sec. A.07.

"A Wireless Miscellany." 1997. *Planning Commissioners Journal* (Fall): 11.

Ziegler, E. H. 1995. "Regulation of Signs and Billboards." In *The Law of Zoning and Planning,* edited by Arden Rathkopf. 4th edition. New York: Clark Boardman, Co., Limited, Sec. 14A.08.

_____. 1998. "Zoning for Broadcasting Towers, Cellular and Personal Wireless Facilities, Amateur Antennae, and Satellite Dishes." In *The Law of Zoning and Planning,* edited by Arden Rathkoph. 4th edition. New York: Clark Boardman, Co., Limited, Release 65.